CH00674132

THE CAMBRIDGE COMPA
ANTHONY TROLLC

Anthony Trollope was among the most prolific, popular, and richly diverse writers of the mid-Victorian period, with forty-seven novels and a variety of other writings to his name. Both a serial and a series writer whose novels traversed Ireland, England, Australia, and New Zealand, and genres from realism to science fiction, Trollope also published criticism, short fiction, travel writing, and biography.

The Cambridge Companion to Anthony Trollope provides a state-of-the-field review of critical perspectives on his work, with the volume's essays addressing Trollope's biography, autobiography, canonical fiction, short stories, and travel writing, as well as surveying diverse topics including gender, sexuality, vulgarity, and the law.

A complete list of the books in the series is at the back of this book.

THE CAMBRIDGE
COMPANION TO
ANTHONY TROLLOPE

EDITED BY
CAROLYN DEVER
AND
LISA NILES

CAMBRIDGE
UNIVERSITY PRESS

CAMBRIDGE UNIVERSITY PRESS

Cambridge, New York, Melbourne, Madrid, Cape Town, Singapore,
São Paulo, Delhi, Dubai, Tokyo, Mexico City

Cambridge University Press
The Edinburgh Building, Cambridge CB2 8RU, UK

Published in the United States of America by Cambridge University Press, New York

www.cambridge.org
Information on this title: www.cambridge.org/9780521713955

First published 2011

Printed in the United Kingdom at the University Press, Cambridge

A catalogue record for this publication is available from the British Library

Library of Congress Cataloging-in-Publication Data

The Cambridge companion to Anthony Trollope / [edited by] Carolyn Dever, Lisa Niles.
p. cm. – (Cambridge companions to literature)
ISBN 978-0-521-88636-9 (Hardback) – ISBN 978-0-521-71395-5 (pbk.)
1. Trollope, Anthony, 1815–1882–Handbooks, manuals, etc. 2. Trollope, Anthony,
1815–1882–Criticism and interpretation. I. Dever, Carolyn. II. Niles, Lisa.
III. Title. IV. Series.
PR5687.C36 2010
823'.8–dc22

2010028668

ISBN 978-0-521-88636-9 Hardback
ISBN 978-0-521-71395-5 Paperback

CONTENTS

CONTENTS

ILLUSTRATIONS

CONTRIBUTORS

AYELET BEN-YISHAI, University of Haifa

GORDON BIGELOW, Rhodes College

NICHOLAS BIRNS, Eugene Lang College, The New School

JAMES BUZARD, Massachusetts Institute of Technology

AMANDA CLAYBAUGH, Harvard University

WILLIAM A. COHEN, University of Maryland

CAROLYN DEVER, Vanderbilt University

KATE FLINT, Rutgers University

VICTORIA GLENDINNING

LAURIE LANGBAUER, University of North Carolina at Chapel Hill

ELSIE B. MICHIE, Louisiana State University

LISA NILES, Spelman College

MARY POOVEY, New York University

DAVID SKILTON, Cardiff University

JENNY BOURNE TAYLOR, University of Sussex

ROBERT TRACY, University of California at Berkeley

MARK W. TURNER, King's College London

ACKNOWLEDGMENTS

Our warmest thanks go to the contributors to this volume, to Linda Bree and her colleagues at the Cambridge University Press, and to Elizabeth Meadows for her timely and thorough research assistance. We wish to thank Vanderbilt University and Spelman College for providing resources for the book. Stephen Knadler, Karissa McCoy, Noah Dever Young, and Paul Young have been of invaluable support and we thank Diane R. Hampton and Melissa Wocher for their help at critical points.

CHRONOLOGY

1815	Born on April 24 at 16 Keppel Street, Bloomsbury, London.
1823–34	Schooling at Harrow, Winchester, and Arthur Drury's school at Sunbury.
1834	Leaves Harrow; family flees to Bruges to escape creditors; begins service with General Post Office in London as a junior clerk.
1841	Accepts surveyor's clerk appointment to Central Ireland; begins keeping official accounts of his travels.
1843	Begins first novel, *The Macdermots of Ballycloran*.
1844	Marriage to Rose Heseltine; transferred to Southern District of Ireland as an assistant surveyor.
1846	Birth of first son, Henry Merivale Trollope.
1847	Publishes first novel, *The Macdermots of Ballycloran*; birth of second son, Frederic James Anthony Trollope.
1851	Sent on postal mission to Western England and Channel Islands; recommends the use of pillar boxes for postal pick-up.
1852	Continues official postal travel to England and Wales; conceives the idea for *The Warden* while at Salisbury.
1853	Begins *The Warden*.
1854	Appointed surveyor of Northern District of Ireland.
1855	*The Warden* published by Longman; writes *The New Zealander*; begins *Barchester Towers*.

1857	Publishes *Barchester Towers* and *The Three Clerks*.
1858	Publishes *Doctor Thorne*; travels to Egypt, the Holy Land, Malta, Gilbraltar, Spain, the West Indies, and Central America.
1859	Returns home from West Indies after visiting New York and Niagara Falls; *The West Indies and the Spanish Main* published by Chapman & Hall; offers collection of short stories to W. M. Thackeray's *Cornhill Magazine* and is engaged to write a novel for *Cornhill* instead; accepts General Post Office transfer to the Eastern District of England and moves to Waltham House, Waltham Cross, Hertfordshire.
1860	*Framley Parsonage* begins appearing in *Cornhill*; meets Kate Field while on vacation in Florence.
1861	*Orley Farm* published; *Tales of All Countries* short story collection published; agrees to write book on North America for Chapman & Hall.
1862	*The Small House at Allington* begins appearing in *Cornhill*; *The Struggles of Brown, Jones, and Robinson* appears in *Cornhill*; finishes *North America*; elected to the Garrick Club.
1863	*Tales of All Countries Second Series* published; travels to Switzerland, the Rhine, and Cologne; Frances, Trollope's mother, dies.
1864	*Can You Forgive Her?* begins appearing in monthly numbers; elected to general committee of the Royal Literary Club; becomes member of the Athenaeum Club.
1865	Begins writing for *Pall Mall Gazette* with first "Travelling Sketch"; first number of *Fortnightly Review* appears, with *The Belton Estate* in serial parts.
1866	*The Last Chronicle of Barset* issued in weekly numbers from 1 December 1866 through 6 July 1867; invited to edit new monthly magazine, *St. Paul's*.
1867	*Phineas Finn* begins appearing in first issue of *St. Paul's Magazine*; retires from Post Office.

1868	Travels to United States; loses election as Liberal candidate for Beverley, Yorkshire.
1870	*The Commentaries of Caesar* published; gives up editorship of *St. Paul's*.
1871–72	*The Eustace Diamonds* begins appearing in *Fortnightly Review*; visits son Fred in Australia; travels to New Zealand, Honolulu, and the Western United States; moves to new home at 39 Montagu Square.
1873	*Australia and New Zealand* published; *Phineas Redux* begins appearing in *Graphic*.
1874	*The Way We Live Now* issued in monthly numbers by Chapman & Hall.
1875	*The Prime Minister* issued in monthly numbers by Chapman & Hall; travels to son Fred's sheep farm in New South Wales, stopping at Rome, Naples, and Ceylon en route; begins *An Autobiography* during return trip from New York to Liverpool.
1876	Completes *An Autobiography* and locks the manuscript in a safe, with instructions for his son Henry to see it printed upon his death.
1877	Travels to South Africa.
1878	*South Africa* published by Chapman & Hall.
1879	*Cousin Henry* serialized simultaneously in *Manchester Weekly Times* and *North British Weekly Mail*; *The Duke's Children* begins appearing in *All The Year Round*.
1880	*The Life of Cicero* published; moves from 39 Montagu Square to North End, South Harting.
1881	*The Fixed Period* begins appearing in *Blackwood's*; last holiday in Europe.
1882	Travels to Dublin to research Irish novel; begins *An Old Man's Love* and *The Landleaguers*; dies on December 6 in London nursing home after suffering a stroke.
1883	*An Autobiography* published by Blackwood.

NOTE ON THE TEXTS AND ABBREVIATIONS

Although much of Trollope's work has remained in print since its initial publication, no authoritative edition exists. With *An Autobiography*, for example, there have been numerous editions and reissues, but the Oxford University Press edition of 1950 in the Oxford Trollope series, edited by Michael Sadleir and Frederick Page, with a preface by Frederick Page, was the first to go back to the text of the MS in the British Museum (now in the British Library) and to note the many discrepancies in the version prepared and seen through the press in 1883 by Henry Trollope, who also deleted a couple of passages. The best modern edition is the Penguin Classics edition (1996), for which David Skilton prepared a new text from the British Library MS. Skilton's text was also the basis for the Trollope Society's edition, with an introduction by John Sutherland (1999). Oxford World's Classics, Penguin, and the Trollope Society have issued many of the novels, but to provide ease of reference, quotations from all Trollope's works will be cited by chapter number (e.g., ch. 3) unless otherwise attributed. The edition of the short stories used is *Anthony Trollope: The Complete Shorter Fiction*, edited by Julian Thompson, and is cited by page. The editors have retained Trollope's original punctuation throughout.

What follows is a list of abbreviations for Trollope's texts (based on abbreviations cited in the *Oxford Reader's Companion to Anthony Trollope*, edited by R. C. Terry) and frequently cited reference materials.

WORKS BY ANTHONY TROLLOPE

A	*An Autobiography*
AA	*Ayala's Angel*
ANZ	*Australia and New Zealand*
AS	*The American Senator*
B	*The Bertrams*
BT	*Barchester Towers*
C	*The Claverings*

CC	*The Commentaries of Caesar*
CH	*Cousin Henry*
CR	*Castle Richmond*
CYFH	*Can You Forgive Her?*
DC	*The Duke's Children*
DT	*Doctor Thorne*
ED	*The Eustace Diamonds*
FixP	*The Fixed Period*
FP	*Framley Parsonage*
HHG	*Harry Heathcoate of Gangoil*
HKWR	*He Knew He Was Right*
JC	*John Caldigate*
KD	*Kept in the Dark*
KOK	*The Kellys and the O'Kellys*
L	*The Landleaguers*
LA	*Lady Anna*
LC	*The Life of Cicero*
LCB	*The Last Chronicle of Barset*
LP	*Lord Palmerston*
MM	*Miss Mackenzie*
NA	*North America*
NB	*Nina Balatka*
OF	*Orley Farm*
PF	*Phineas Finn*
PM	*The Prime Minister*
PR	*Phineas Redux*
RH	*Ralph the Heir*
SA	*South Africa*
SBJR	*The Struggles of Brown, Jones, and Robinson*
SHA	*The Small House at Allington*
T	*Thackeray*
TC	*The Three Clerks*
VB	*The Vicar of Bullhampton*
W	*The Warden*
WISM	*The West Indies and the Spanish Main*
WWLN	*The Way We Live Now*

REFERENCE MATERIALS

Crit. Her.	*Trollope: The Critical Heritage*, ed. Donald Smalley (London: Routledge, 1969)
Letters	*The Letters of Anthony Trollope*, ed. N. John Hall. 2 vols. (Stanford: Stanford University Press, 1983)

Oxford   *Oxford Reader's Companion to Anthony Trollope*, ed. R. C. Terry (Oxford: Oxford University Press, 1999)

Sadleir   Michael Sadleir, *Trollope: A Commentary* (1927. Repr. London: Oxford University Press, 1961)

Thompson   *Anthony Trollope: The Complete Shorter Fiction*, ed. Julian Thompson (New York: Carroll & Graf, 1992)

CAROLYN DEVER AND LISA NILES

Introduction

Anthony Trollope was one of the most prolific, popular, and richly diverse Victorian writers. In a literary career that extended from the 1840s to the 1880s, Trollope published forty-seven novels, including the monumental Barsetshire and Palliser series and such major stand-alone works as *Orley Farm* (1862) and *The Way We Live Now* (1875). A serial and series writer whose novels traverse Ireland, England, Australia, and New Zealand and genres from realism to science fiction, Trollope also published criticism, short fiction, travel writing, and biography; his *Autobiography*, published posthumously, codified – in terms best described as notorious – the labor practices of the professional Victorian writer. At the peak of his career Trollope's standing was well established among both literary and popular readers. His reputation declined rather precipitously after his death, however, when his *Autobiography* pulled the curtain from a writing process that included a firm commitment to the production of a certain number of words each day, and a muse who kept an unblinking eye trained on the sales figures. Yet, even in the midst of what appeared to be an irrevocable critical decline, Trollope remained in print. He was always read. This unbroken continuity has something to tell scholars about the cultural relevance of Trollope's work.

Anthony Trollope means many different things to many different people. For some readers, Trollope epitomizes the most conservative, and most Conservative, aspects of Victorian fiction in novels in which the Home Counties and the thrill of the hunt feature prominently. The sword cuts both ways for readers of the conservative Trollope: for some his vulgarity smacks of self-satisfaction, an investment in the status quo; for others, Trollope is the mythmaker of an England long lost to modernity, in which honor and industry carry the day. Another Trollope has emerged more recently, however, among readers who find in those same novels plots of class mobility in all directions, queer desire, a uniquely cosmopolitan world view, the subversion of the formal and social imperatives of mid-Victorian realism.

It is both the great challenge and the great opportunity of the *Cambridge Companion to Anthony Trollope* to speak to, and of, the insights enabled by Trollope's persistently bimodal reception. Indeed, it is the cumulative argument of this volume that Trollope's very bimodality is at the heart of his readers' passionate, diverse responses to his work. Exploring that bimodality, essays in this volume contend that Britain's greatest domestic novelist is gloriously cosmopolitan; that the author behind some of the Victorian period's most memorable, and conventionally realistic, marriage plots is drawn to their queer, polymorphous, and sensationalized undertones; that this most familiar and even cozy of novelists is experimental in form and in theme; that the biographer of the Home Counties is acutely aware of modernity's creeping advent. Trollope, we contend, is an artist of the dialectic. His writing stages encounters between the polarities of the day. It drives toward a synthetic vision that holds opposing terms continuously in frame, thereby ensuring that what's old looks new, and that what's new remains familiar.

The contributors to this volume present a Trollope who is both known and unsettling. Situating Trollope in his contemporary literary milieu, for example, Mark W. Turner makes a claim for a "global Trollope," an author keenly aware of the global marketing potential of the Trollope "brand," as well as fully alive to the opportunities his globe-hopping provided for new material. Turner reveals a Trollope who worked hungrily in all genres of the Victorian literary marketplace, as a novelist, non-fiction and short-fiction writer, and editor, and a Trollope keenly attuned to the export potential of domestic fictions. Further defamiliarizing the question of what we know of the familiar Trollope, Victoria Glendinning turns the focus from Trollope's much-discussed role as an autobiographer to his four less-known works of biography. Glendinning declares *An Autobiography* indispensable to any study of Trollope, as it not only reveals an aging Trollope's values but outlines his theory of novel-writing. Through this lens, Glendinning further examines Trollope's biographies as works that provide more insight into Trollope himself than into his various subjects.

In three essays on Trollope's series fiction, the Barset and Palliser novels emerge as sites in which old and young, heritage and innovation, struggle for dominance. Mary Poovey takes up the concept of seriality in the Barset novels in order to identify a shift in critical consensus about novelistic practices in the 1860s, and about the artistic merits of Trollope's novels in particular. Poovey argues that rather than emerging as a coherent whole, the Barset series was conceived as such only through the publication of *The Last Chronicle* in 1867. Poovey argues that *The Last Chronicle* deploys narrative strategies that make the sprawling panorama of the other Barset texts cohere, creating order from chaos. In his chapter on the Palliser series, William A. Cohen examines the reciprocity of the political and the psychological, of public and private lives. Taking Trollope's own paradoxical political stance – the self-described "advanced conservative Liberal" – as his starting point, Cohen proposes a systematic tension between the liberal and conservative that, ironically, comes to look very much like modernity. Robert Tracy further identifies the Palliser series as Trollope's most successful late fiction, in large part because these novels retain their English settings and characters, providing a familiar formula with which to experiment. Tracy identifies Plantagenet and Glencora Palliser's marriage as a template of the sacrificial marriage plot – one that is rewritten, repeatedly, throughout the series, to offer a glimpse into the problems of time and social change on character. Tracy suggests that through multiple iterations of the same plot and its resolution throughout the series, the Palliser novels offer a stability of character in an unpredictable world.

In a further examination of Trollope's experimental impulse, Lisa Niles addresses Trollope's short fiction, a genre that provided Trollope with a freedom in subject matter that is rarely seen elsewhere. Niles claims that the generic constraints of the short story – singularity of focus and spatial limitations – paradoxically offered Trollope an unrestrained hand in authorship. The short stories offer Trollope a formal template for thematic experimentation, an opportunity he pursues vigorously in his full-length fictions as well. Jenny Bourne Taylor, for example, explores the provocative tension between form and theme in her chapter on Trollope and sensationalism. Bourne Taylor reads Trollope's novels alongside those of sensation novelists such as Wilkie Collins, and argues that rather than functioning as the "other" of realism, sensationalism is embedded within Trollope's novels. Their synthetic relationship offers a more nuanced view of two forms too often conceived as oppositional. Moving to a broader claim about thematic experimentation and social worlds, Kate Flint reads much of Trollope's fiction as queer. Flint establishes queerness itself as contingent – "queer" simultaneously invokes same-sex desire and signals an aberrant form of self-presentation in the socially codified world of the mid-nineteenth century. Flint returns to Trollope's short fiction, arguing that the short story is itself a "queer narrative," a form that can imagine the absorption of the extraordinary into the quotidian.

As Niles, Bourne Taylor, and Flint suggest, Trollope's exploration of gender roles, sexuality, and erotic and romantic relations occurs on the level of form as well as theme. In "The hobbledehoy in Trollope," Laurie Langbauer further identifies Trollope's remarkable construction, the "hobbledehoy," as just such a juncture of form and theme. The hobbledehoy is embodied in Johnny Eames of the Barsetshire novels, but he is found throughout Trollope's fiction and is perhaps a surrogate for the young Trollope himself. Langbauer argues that the hobbledehoy's intractable awkwardness counters conventional paradigms of development in favor of a reiterative, circular logic akin to serial fiction itself: gawky male adolescence illuminates Trollope's formal investment in recurrence and reiteration.

Expanding outward from the hobbledehoy to masculinity more broadly conceived, David Skilton argues that masculinity exposes Trollope's strategic layering of ethical choices within an imperfect world. Trollopian masculinity, Skilton suggests, maps the development of a middle-class, secular conscience that is so normalized by its male author as to be invisible within the masculine critical establishment. Skilton notes that for this reason, Trollope's women characters have historically attracted much more critical interest than his men. In the chapter "Vulgarity and money," Elsie B. Michie turns the lens on a number of Trollope's women who are conspicuous precisely because of their extravagant vulgarity. Michie argues that Trollope's vulgar women highlight the British ambivalence – characterized by pride on one hand and revulsion on the other – toward new wealth. In identifying with and also satirizing crass, material vulgarity, Michie suggests that Trollope demonstrates the strategies by which new commercial wealth is both claimed and set apart in mid-Victorian culture.

The law is another means by which Trollope interjects moral puzzles into his fiction, and Ayelet Ben-Yishai contends that Trollope's legal fictions index his interest in the social power of community during a time of massive social upheaval. Ben-Yishai demonstrates that Trollope presents common law and positive law as opposites, as signs of the tensions between tradition and modernity. In the negotiation of this tension, the codes of a new civil society find their expression. Trollope's novels tested relations between the old and the new, and also between the local and the global. As James Buzard makes clear in "Trollope and travel," the contours of Trollopian civil society were expanding not only conceptually in the domestic milieu, but globally: Trollope, Buzard notes, was a perpetual world traveler, with the travel books and articles to show for it. The confrontations with alterity recorded in Trollope's travel writings permeate even the domestic fictions, Buzard argues, within a common ideal of divinely ordained Englishness.

In "Trollope and the Antipodes," Nicholas Birns considers the effect of the opening of the Suez Canal on Trollope's conception of Australia and New Zealand, and particularly the tightness of their connections to the imperial center. Post Suez, the Antipodes were much closer to "home," and for Trollope they posit a vision for futurity, expanding his conception of the social body to include the consideration of indigenous people. Closer to home, Gordon Bigelow argues that Ireland, where Trollope lived for two decades both before and after the famine, allowed Trollope to begin life as a fiction writer, and catalyzed a favorite fictional scene, the hunt. Ireland turned Trollope from hobbledehoy to man; and the Irish Land War provided the scene of his last published novel, *The Landleaguers*. If Ireland gave rise and fall to Trollope's authorial career, the United States provided his prehistory. Amanda Claybaugh investigates Trollope's revisiting of the notorious work of his mother, Frances Trollope, in her *Domestic Manners of the Americans* (1832). Trollope's American characters, Claybaugh suggests, maintain a difference sustained over commonalities of language and history, and they function in Trollope's fiction to propose the potential for new alliances constructed against the history of colonial domination.

Today's Trollope is at once global and local, conservative and liberal, experimental and conventional, and even queer and straight. Trollope's unique literary contribution, we contend, inhabits the heart of the paradox. In a modern world of Ponzi schemes and financial bubbles, of a globe that is ever shrinking and yet prolifically diverse, of human identities that flex in response to unprecedented social pressures, and writing technologies that reveal the entanglements of creativity and automation, the Victorians' Anthony Trollope has never been more valuable in our efforts to explain ourselves to ourselves.

I

Trollope's literary life and times

Anthony Trollope is well known as one of the most prolific and energetic of Victorian novelists. Forty-seven novels, four lengthy travel books, four biographical studies, five collections of short stories, three collections of non-fiction sketches, a range of journalism – this would be an impressive output for any writer over a lifetime, but it is perhaps more striking because Trollope did not publish his first book until 1847 at the age of thirty-two. By this time he had already established himself as a rising civil servant in the General Post Office, having gradually worked his way up from a junior clerk in London, to surveyor's clerk in Ireland, and finally to a surveyor and inspector himself; he remained devoted to the civil service job until 1867, when he resigned, with a view to entering Parliament. But Trollope's professional life was not always so smooth; according to *An Autobiography*, it was the move to Ireland at the age of twenty-four that was the making of the man and which saved him from an aimless, unambitious London life. As a studious inspector of postal routes in Ireland, he would follow in the footsteps of postal deliverers, seeking to find ways to improve speed of delivery and generally improve service. Among his notable achievements in the Post Office was his role in developing the first pillar box for the collection of post. So, Trollope had a double professional life – as career civil servant and then as popular writer – and these professions ran parallel for nearly twenty years and mutually informed each other. As a local and global traveler often engaged in government and colonial business, and as a writer whose works were widely disseminated and reprinted, Trollope is a particularly interesting figure who sheds light on the shifting and complex literary marketplace in the middle of the nineteenth century.

Writing was as serious a profession as his work for the Post Office, and he approached both with the same industrious professionalism. There is no greater evidence of this than his writing diaries, which reveal a focused and disciplined man, quite different from the hobbledehoy he describes himself as in the early chapters of *An Autobiography*. The method documented in the diaries suggests a workmanlike approach to writing, with an underlying belief that a few hours each day would allow a man to write as much as he ought:

> When I have commenced a new book, I have always prepared a diary, divided into weeks, and carried on for the period which I have allowed myself for the completion of the work. In this I have entered, day by day, the number of pages I have written, so that if at any time I have slipped into idleness for a day or two, the record of that idleness has been there, staring me in the face, and demanding of me increased labour, so that the deficiency might be supplied. (*A* ch. 7)

> It had at this time become my custom,– and it is still my custom, though of late I have become a little lenient to myself,– to write with my watch before me, and to require from myself 250 words every quarter of an hour. I have found that the 250 words have been forthcoming as regularly as my watch went. But my three hours were not devoted entirely to writing. I always began my task by reading the work of the day before. . . This division of time allowed me to produce over ten pages of an ordinary novel volume a day, and if kept up through ten months, would have given as its results three novels of three volumes each in the year. (*A* ch. 15)

Such a determined method of writing enabled him "to have always on hand,– for some time back now,– one or two or even three unpublished novels in my desk beside me" (*A* ch. 15). He was nothing if not reliable, always at the ready with a novel for a publisher or editor. But the writing diaries were more important to Trollope than a mere record of output, and in her study of them, Mary Hamer suggests that "the novels are evidence of a very strong need for self-approval, an approval which had to be won by proof of meritorious achievement."[1] By treating writing as a serious form of labor, Trollope was able to accept it as a suitable profession, a real career.

Such honesty about his writing met with little praise when it was revealed posthumously in the *Autobiography*, at least not by other writers, and whether Trollope's methods detract from his art has been a matter of much critical discussion. Henry James, for example, commenting on Trollope's writing method in a lengthy essay in the New York-based *Century Magazine* in 1883 believed that Trollope

> abused his gift, overworked it, rode his horse too hard. As an artist he never took himself seriously; many people will say this was why he was so delightful. The people who take themselves seriously are prigs and bores; and Trollope, with his perpetual "story," which was the only thing he cared about, his strong good sense, hearty good nature, generous appreciation of life in all its varieties, responds in perfection to a certain English ideal. According to that ideal

it is rather dangerous to be explicitly or consciously an artist – to have a system, a doctrine, a form. Trollope, from the first, went in, as they say, for having as little form as possible; it is probably safe to affirm that he had no "views" whatever on the subject of novel-writing. His whole manner is that of a man who regards the practice as one of the more delicate industries, but has never troubled his head nor clogged his pen with theories about the nature of his business. (*Crit. Her.* 527)

The view that Trollope was more a craftsman than an artist cast a long shadow and shaped critical, though not popular, opinion of Trollope for generations thereafter, probably until the 1970s to 80s. James is expressing a particular but not uncommon set of cultural values, which is uneasy about the coupling of art and the marketplace and which sees "industry" and "industriousness" as more suited to the commercial world than to the world of letters. The mid to late nineteenth century was precisely a period of transition in the literature industry, as copyright laws were hotly debated and authorship became increasingly professionalized. Trollope was one of those writers who unapologetically kept one eye on the market, and he proudly lists in the *Autobiography* the sums he received for each of his books, totaling over £68,000 by the end of the 1870s – a staggering amount for the time. For Trollope, his industrious writing life, meticulously, even compulsively, documented in the diaries, offered proof that writing could not only provide a worthwhile career, but also ensure a comfortable life as a middle-class gentleman. Alongside his exhaustive literary output, he tells us, "I hunted always at least twice a week. I was frequent in the whist-room at the Garrick. I lived much in society in London, and was made happy by the presence of many friends at Waltham Cross. In addition to this we always spent six weeks at least out of England" (*A* ch. 15). His genteel life was made possible through the rich rewards offered by his literary career.

Unlike contemporaries such as Charles Dickens, or, to a lesser degree George Eliot, Trollope's literary success was gradual rather than immediate. His first two novels, *The Macdermots of Ballycloran* (1847) and *The Kellys and the O'Kellys* (1848), were both Irish tales, mostly ignored at the time but read with great interest by critics and readers today for the insight they give into an English novelist writing about the Irish during one of the most troubled periods of Ireland's history. His third novel, a historical romance about Revolutionary France, *La Vendée* (1850), fared no better and failed to make a mark with the public. It was not until Trollope began to write about the fictional county of Barsetshire that he captured at least some of the reading public's imagination. With the publication of *The Warden* (1855) and then *Barchester Towers* (1857), Trollope became more confident, and he found one of his natural subjects – the daily dramas of middle-class gentlemen and gentlewomen.

Trollope's literary ascent

Trollope found his natural medium in 1860, when William Makepeace Thackeray, editor of the new shilling monthly *Cornhill Magazine*, invited him to serialize a novel in his periodical. This, you might say, was Trollope's big break; that the offer came from his literary idol and perhaps the most eminent novelist of the day was all the more flattering for Trollope, who craved the acceptance of literary men. The *Cornhill* was launched as a handsome new magazine aimed at the middle-class reading market, with two serial novels in each issue, alongside a range of well-written miscellaneous articles and poetry, accompanied by lavish full-page illustrations. Trollope's *Framley Parsonage* was the lead serial in the first issue, and the success was immediate and extraordinary. While reviews of the volume form of the novel were mixed – "trivial and purposeless," according to the *Westminster Review*, but "a beautiful novel," for the *London Review* – none could refute that the serialization of *Framley Parsonage* in *Cornhill* found its popular readership and led to his being one of the most sought-after serial novelists of the next decade (*Crit. Her.* 133, 126).

The success of the *Cornhill*, with over 120,000 copies sold of the early monthly issues, points to at least two things. First, there was a huge market of middle-class readers of serial fiction, willing to pay a shilling each month for a variety of contents. Second, it demonstrated Trollope's talent for the series novel, and for writing serial fiction, both of which allow for the slow development of plot and character over an extended period of time, which suits Trollope's subjects. After the great success of *Framley Parsonage*, Trollope conceived of each novel he wrote as a serial; that is, he composed his fiction with the idea of publishing and reading in parts in mind, and, from that point on, he never abandoned this way of organizing and conceptualizing his novels. While not all of his novels published thereafter were published as serials, many did appear in either magazines or newspapers or as part-issues. Furthermore, Trollope became particularly noted for his series fiction, since *Framley Parsonage* and *The Small House at Allington*, serialized in the *Cornhill* between 1862 and 1864, both returned to Barsetshire, with characters and locations from *The Warden* and *Barchester Towers* reappearing and overlapping. Later in life, as Trollope had long hoped, all these novels, along with *Doctor Thorne* (1858) and *The Last Chronicle of Barset* (1867) were published together as a coherent set, acknowledging that part of their power and appeal was in reading them in relation to one another, rather than as self-standing texts. He turned to the idea of the series a second time with the Palliser novels, which focus largely on political life in London, but that series, altogether darker in its view of society, never replaced the Barsetshire novels in the hearts of his readers. While other Victorian novelists also wrote series fiction – Margaret Oliphant in her "Chronicles of Carlingford," for example – none exploited the series as successfully as Trollope.

The 1860s was the period of Trollope's greatest popularity – popular with magazine readers and circulating library subscribers who had a healthy appetite for his fiction – and he began earning large sums: £3,200 per novel at his peak. By the middle of the 1860s, "Trollope" was a reliable and hard-working brand, one that was trumpeted loudly and frequently in advertise-ments for his works. A review of Trollope's collection of essays, *Hunting Sketches* (1865), first published in the evening newspaper the *Pall Mall Gazette*, speaks precisely to the power of the Trollope brand:

> [The essays] are just light, pleasant, easy reading, lively enough, and appar-ently written by one who understands his subject. Had an ordinary man contributed them to any newspaper, they would have probably been applauded at the time and consigned to oblivion; but they had appended to them the name of Mr. Anthony Trollope.[2]

Partly as a way of testing whether readers were simply buying a "Trollope" or whether it was some intrinsic literary value that his public responded to, he experimented with anonymous publication – *Nina Balatka* (1866–67) and *Linda Tressel* (1867–68) in *Blackwood's Magazine*, for which he received a greatly reduced fee without his name attached. Neither novel was particularly popular or well received.

Like so many of his contemporaries, Trollope was not only a writer of fiction but also an editor of others'. At the same time that he had been contributing fiction to a range of periodicals – *Once a Week, Good Words*, the *Fortnightly Review*, and *Blackwood's Magazine* among others – Trollope became editor of his own shilling monthly magazine. Following the lead of novelist-editors throughout the 1860s, including popular nov-elists such as Mary Braddon, who edited *Belgravia*, and of course Dickens, who was editing *All the Year Round* at this time, Trollope launched *St. Paul's Magazine* in 1867, the year in which he resigned from the Post Office, with his own *Phineas Finn* as the inaugural serial. The publisher of the new venture, James Virtue, approached Trollope with the idea of launching "Anthony Trollope's Magazine," a title clearly designed to make the most of the writer's literary celebrity. By this time, Trollope had published nineteen novels, two travel books, collections of short stories, and a range of non-fiction journalism. However, he was modest enough to balk at Virtue's suggestion and settled on the more common use of a London location for the title instead. *St. Paul's* entered a particularly competitive periodicals marketplace, during a short-lived boom period when a number of new monthly magazines were launched in the wake of *Cornhill's* success: *Temple Bar* (1860), *The Argosy* (1865), *Belgravia* (1866), and *Tinsley's Magazine* (1867), among others. While Trollope excelled as a popular novelist, he was less successful as a popular editor, and, never having managed to make his magazine distinct in the market-place, he parted company with *St. Paul's* in 1870, only three years after its launch. Trollope never missed an opportunity to turn his life experiences into literary product, and his period as editor was no exception. In add-ition to serializing a novel and writing some journalism, he published a series of short stories about the trials and tribulations of a jobbing maga-zine editor in *St. Paul's*, which were published in volume form as *An Editor's Tales* (1870), for which he received £378, separate from his editor's salary.

Trollope was as promiscuous across print as he was prolific. He published material in a number of forms (periodical serials, part-issues, volumes) and genres (novels, short stories, non-fiction sketches, journalism) and in differ-ent types of publication (daily, weekly, and monthly, conservative and liberal, religious and secular). Frequently, novels by Trollope were published simultaneously, competing in an already crowded marketplace – *The Last Chronicle* overlapped with *The Claverings*, and *Phineas Finn* with *He Knew He Was Right*, for example – which proved too much for the reading public. "Such fertility is not in nature," wrote the *Saturday Review* in 1866, though they had the reputation for being especially harsh, earning them the nick-name the "Saturday Reviler."[3] Still, even less hostile reviewers felt that too much Trollope might be too much of a good thing. Compared to, for example, his friend George Eliot, who published seven novels during her lifetime and who was not nearly as widely published across forms of print culture, or even compared to Dickens, who wrote a lot, but who published in relatively regular and consistent ways, Trollope was hardly ever out of the public eye. While we know how extensively Trollope's work appeared in magazines, we know far less about the publication of his work in newspapers, though, as Graham Law has shown, between 1881 and 1882, *Ayala's Angel* was published in no fewer than three regional newspapers – the Dundee *People's Friend*, the Plymouth *Western Weekly*, and the *Wake-field & West Riding Herald* – and that was after it had already appeared in America in the *Cincinnati Commerical*.[4] Furthermore, he was always keen to try new ways of expanding his audience. He was willing to experiment with weekly part-issue publication, seemingly well after that form of publication had had its heyday:

> In 1866 and 1867 *The Last Chronicle of Barset* was brought out by George Smith in sixpenny monthly numbers. I do not know that this mode of publication had been tried before, or that it answered very well on this occasion. Indeed the shilling magazines had interfered greatly with the success of novels published in numbers without other accompanying matter. The public finding that so much might be had for a shilling, in which a portion of one or more novels was always included, were unwilling to spend their money on the novel alone. (*A* ch. 15)

It was not a particularly successful experiment for Smith, though it was attempted again when James Virtue published *He Knew He Was Right* in weekly parts in 1868. The risk was all the publishers', since Trollope, who was canny in selling his goods in the literary market, received £3,200 for *The Last Chronicle* and the same for *He Knew He Was Right*. The *Publishers' Circular*, a fortnightly trade journal which commented on new developments in the industry, watched the progress of this "bold innovation," but the sixpenny weekly experiment was not repeated a third time.[5]

Global Trollope

Although I have been emphasizing the rise and consolidation of Trollope's place in the literary marketplace of 1860s Britain, it is also important to realize that he was a prominent figure publishing in and for a global market, as James Buzard, Nicholas Birns, Gordon Bigelow, and Amanda Claybaugh emphasize elsewhere in this volume. Trollope was among the most well traveled of Victorian novelists, visiting four continents (Europe, North America, Africa, and Australia) and writing about them all in stories, travel books, or novels. He lived in a period of increasing and striking globalization, in which developments in transport (especially the railway) and new media technologies (such as the telegraph) began to reshape notions of distance and proximity. Countries were "in touch" with other countries in ways they hadn't been before, whether through colonial, Anglo-American, or other international networks of exchange and communication. Trollope – so often thought of in connection with the genteel landscape of rural England or the social politics of the drawing room – also embraced modernity and explored and wrote about the changing world open to him.

It is worth emphasizing that Trollope's work as a civil servant for the Post Office is what first enabled him to travel abroad. In his first travel book,

The West Indies and the Spanish Main (1859), he tells us that he takes the trip in order to attend to "certain affairs of State," but says no more about his official duties (*WISM* ch. 1). Moving through the West Indies in 1858–59 – with visits to Jamaica, Cuba, Barbados, Trinidad, Panama, Costa Rica, and Bermuda – he was on a delicate mission to restructure the way the postal system in the colonies was administered, to renegotiate contracts, and, generally, to inspect and improve the speed and quality of the service (*Letters* 1:172 ff). Given this brief, it is perhaps not surprising that he devotes a whole chapter in *The West Indies* to "Central America – Railways, Canals, Transit," discussing new transport proposals for the Panama and Suez Canals among other things (*WISM* ch. 21). He puts these questions about local movement and access in the context of global movement more generally, comparing railway lines across America and Europe and demonstrating a conscious understanding of international trade routes and a desire for the free and easy movement of people across countries and cultures.

Characteristically, Trollope tended to multi-task on his trips; though he almost always kept to his strict writing schedule – writing on steamers and trains as he crossed exotic locations – he was simultaneously doing the business of the British government, so that his twin professions were closely enmeshed. In addition to the travel book about the West Indies, for which he was paid £250, he wrote five short stories based on the trip. The link between his global travel and literary output continued whenever he took an extended trip. His two visits to Australia and New Zealand (1871–72 and 1875), largely to see his sheep-farming son who had emigrated to Australia, were financed partly by contracts for writing secured in advance. In addition to the travel book on Australia published after his first trip (which he had nearly completed by the time of his return to Britain), he published a series of letters signed "Antipodean" in London's *Daily Telegraph* (December 23, 1871–December 28, 1871); and, during his second trip to Australia, twenty letters were published in the *Liverpool Mercury*, which were, in turn, syndicated to several other provincial newspapers. His two series of short stories, *Tales of All Countries* (1861 and 1863) were the direct result of his travels, as were his other travel books, *North America* (1862) and *South Africa* (1878), and a number of novels and stories were informed directly through his international travels. In short, Trollope made the most of his travels.

While Anthony Trollope traveled widely himself, "Trollope" traveled across British colonial and other international networks of print culture in other ways, too. North America, which Trollope visited on several occasions, was one of the largest literary markets by the 1860s, and there was already an established transatlantic literary culture, with virtually all of the bestselling British writers widely available in America, and vice versa. "The poem that is popular in London," Trollope writes, "will certainly be popular in New York. The novel that is effective among American ladies will be equally so with those of England" (*NA* ch. 30).

Trollope was keen for his fiction to tap into this potentially vast readership. In the second volume of *North America* he devotes a full chapter to the broad subject "Literature," focusing initially on the huge market of American readers. "As consumers of literature," he says, "they are certainly the most conspicuous people on earth" (*NA* ch. 30). According to Trollope, "English books are preferred," and the market in the United States for English reprints even larger:

> Almost everything is reprinted; certainly everything which can be said to attain any home popularity. I do not know how far English authors may be aware of the fact; but it is undoubtedly a fact that their influence as authors is greater on the other side of the Atlantic than on this. It is there that they are recognized as teachers by hundreds of thousands. It is of those thirty millions that they should think, at any rate in part, when they discuss within their own hearts that question which all authors do discuss, whether that which they write shall in itself be good or bad,– be true or false. (*NA* ch. 30)

This is a significant claim to make because it acknowledges that British writers like Trollope are always already embedded in a larger, transatlantic literary culture, whether they like it or not. This is welcome for Trollope, for whom millions of readers are certainly preferable to mere hundreds of thousands. What vexed Trollope, and many of his contemporaries, notably Dickens, was that there was no copyright agreement between the United States and Britain. American firms could reprint as many titles by British authors as they chose, and as soon after the first publication as they could manage, without any direct recompense to the author. Trollope, who tended to be conservative in arranging contracts for his work, usually selling rights to his novels outright to a publisher in advance of publication, recognized the injustice of the system and laid responsibility for it with the Americans: "At present there is no international copyright between England and the United States, and there is none because the States have declined to sanction any such law" (*NA* ch. 30). He blamed the large publishing houses, however, rather than the American people or American authors. He continued to campaign for international copyright, being commissioned by the Foreign Office to lobby for change while on a trip to Washington in 1868 and serving on the Royal Commission on International Copyright in 1876.

If Trollope was keenly aware of the transatlantic literary market, he was no less aware of the even larger global market linked to the colonies:

> The English author should feel that he writes for the widest circle of readers ever yet obtained by the literature of any country. He provides not only for his own country and for the States, but for the readers who are rising by millions in the British colonies. Canada is supplied chiefly from the presses of Boston, New York, and Philadelphia, but she is supplied with the works of the mother country. India, I believe, gets all her books direct from London, as do the West Indies. Whether or no the Australian colonies have as yet learned to reprint our books I have never heard; but I presume that they cannot do so as cheaply as they can import them. London with us, and the three cities which I have named on the other side of the Atlantic, are the places at which this literature is manufactured; but the demand in the western hemisphere is becoming more brisk than that which the old world creates. (*NA* ch. 30)

Trollope's world traveling, engaged in colonial business, would have made him more acutely aware than some of his contemporaries of the various nodes on the international publishing network, and this network could interestingly be mapped by other kinds of media and communications routes at the time – by looking closely at postal, shipping, and communications routes that were spreading across the globe more quickly than ever before.[6] Though relatively little scholarship has explored in depth Trollope's publications abroad, we know that his work was obviously embedded in colonial print culture. The *Australasian*, the *Illustrated Sydney News*, and the *Sydney Mail* all published imported serial work by Trollope, sometimes simultaneously with publication in British periodicals, sometimes years later.[7] His "Australian novel," *Harry Heathcote of Gangoil* was serialized in 1882, nearly a decade after its first publication in the British *Age*; his travel book on Australia, published in two volumes in Britain in 1873, was serialized weekly in the *Australasian*, was also published in six parts subsequently bound, and then finally published in volume form by a Melbourne publisher. These two texts in particular raise interesting questions about whom Trollope is addressing in his Australian subjects. Is he "writing back" to the metropole, or does he have his international and specifically Australian readership in mind? What it might mean to read Trollope serially in Australia, one of the other colonies, or in North America, has been relatively little considered so far, but it raises significant questions about the global movement of literature at the time. As several chapters of this volume suggest, Trollope's travel writing, fiction and non-fiction alike, opens such questions for rich examination.

Trollope's literary life and times help us to see the complexity of a popular writer at mid-century. In order to understand this complexity, however, we need to understand that there were at least three Trollopes: Trollope the boisterous but conventional middle-class gentleman, fond of such genteel pursuits and pleasures as hunting and club-life; Trollope the civil servant, interested in the development and spread of communications networks across the globe; and Trollope the writer, whose range of work and whose forms of publication are, at least in part, informed by the other two. Trollope is often read for the light he sheds on contemporary Britain, for the way topical subjects, whether in relation to single women and marriage, or to the Second Reform Bill and the machinations of Parliament, become part of the content of his novels. But by looking closely at Trollope as a figure in the marketplace, at home and abroad, we perhaps begin to see his work afresh. The different aspects of "Trollope" are not contradictory; on the contrary, they may make him a quintessential writer of his times.

NOTES

1 Mary Hamer, *Writing by Numbers: Trollope's Serial Fiction* (Cambridge: Cambridge University Press, 1987), p. 42.
2 "Current Literature," *Illustrated London News* 46 (May 20, 1865), 491.
3 *The Saturday Review* (February 3), 1866, 140–42.
4 See Graham Law, "Trollope and the Newspapers," *Media History* 9:1 (2003), 47–62.
5 *Publishers' Circular* (October 1, 1868), 564.
6 For more on the establishment of media and communications networks at the time, see Dwayne R. Winseck and Robert M. Pike, *Communication and Empire: Media, Markets, and Globalization, 1860–1930* (Durham, NC: Duke University Press, 2007).
7 See Toni Johnson-Woods, *Index to Serials in Australian Periodicals and Newspapers: Nineteenth Century* (Canberra, Australia: Mulini Press, 2001), pp. 134–35.

2

VICTORIA GLENDINNING

Trollope as autobiographer and biographer

Trollope began writing his autobiography towards the end of 1875 and finished it at the end of April 1876. It was not until summer 1878 that he told his son Henry. There was a letter with the manuscript, both to be read only after his death. In the letter he wrote that he wanted Henry to edit and publish it as soon as possible, and *An Autobiography* came out in two volumes from Blackwood in autumn 1883. Henry suppressed two passages critical of men still living and, in his preface, filled in the main events between the completion of the autobiography and his father's death in December 1882, and listed the further books which his father had written.

As Trollope writes on the first page, his intention was not to reveal "the little details of my private life," but to discuss what he and some of his contemporaries had achieved in literature, "and the opening which a literary career offers to men and women for the earning of their bread" (*A* ch. 1). He was always thinking of his influence on the young. He tells how he determined never to have any personal dealings with critics, neither to court or thank for praise, nor to argue over adverse criticism, "and this rule I would recommend to all young authors" (*A* ch. 4). He stresses that there is no shame in writing to make money, and that his example may show how "a man devoting himself to literature with industry, perseverance, certain necessary aptitudes, and fair average talents, may succeed in gaining a livelihood" (*A* ch. 6). This was his stated reason for setting out, in the final chapter, a list of his books and the sums of money derived from each. He is contemptuous of authors who sit around waiting for inspiration, "and therefore advise[s] young men who look forward to authorship as the business of their lives, even when they propose that the authorship be of the highest class known ... to seat themselves at their desks day by day as though they were lawyers' clerks – and so let them sit till the allotted task shall be accomplished" (*A* ch. 7). If he himself had merit, it should be accorded "for persevering diligence in my profession"; he makes this claim "for the benefit of those who may read these pages when young and who may intend to follow the same career. *Nulla dies sine linea.*[1] Let that be their motto" (A ch. 20). These exhortations, based on his own experience and conviction, are scattered throughout his narrative and elaborated with increasing vehemence, leading to some repetition.

Trollope presents the story of his life as a progress from an unutterably wretched boyhood to a fulfilled and successful maturity. "My boyhood was, I think, as unhappy as that of a young gentleman could well be," owing to his difficult, depressive father's professional failure at the Bar and subsequent abject poverty, and to young Anthony's own humiliations – resulting from his ill-made clothes, dirtiness, lack of funds, and total friendlessness (A ch. 1). He longed to have friends, and to be popular. (The friendlessness was exaggerated. At least one school-mate, John Merivale, was a life-long friend.) He assuaged his loneliness by daydreaming, telling himself stories, building those "castle[s] in the air" without which he believed he might never have written a novel (A ch. 3).

He paints a picture of squalor and loneliness at home, and total alienation and misery at both Harrow and Winchester, where he "learned nothing" (ch. 1). His eldest brother Thomas Adolphus in *What I Remember* (3 vols. 1887–89) presented their young days as less bleak. But then Thomas Adolphus was their mother's darling. Lacking a fully functioning husband, she made Tom her chief support and ally. When she went to America in an attempt to make money with a "Bazaar" selling fancy goods in Cincinnati, all of the children accompanied her at different times – except Anthony, always left behind. At nineteen, he felt himself to be "an idle, desolate hanger-on," a "hobbledehoy," with no prospects (A ch. 2).

Nowhere does he reproach his parents for his unhappiness, but he did not forget it. In later years, as he writes, he would look back, "meditating for hours together" on his father's ill-luck: "The touch of his hand seemed to create failure" (A ch. 2). In a chapter devoted to "My Mother," he describes her character as a mixture of "joviality and industry." When he describes how she would be "at her table" at four in the morning, writing the books which kept the family afloat, finishing her work before anyone else was up, it seems clear whence Trollope derived his own energy and his working routine, though he does not make the connection. Though he admires her for her industry, and for her courage as two of her children – and later a third – die of tuberculosis, he does not idealize her, summing her up thus: "She was an unselfish, affectionate, and most industrious woman ... but she was neither clear-sighted nor accurate; and in her attempts [in her books] to describe morals, manners, and even facts, she was unable to avoid the pitfalls of exaggeration" (A ch. 2). Again there is an unacknowledged link; later, in discussing his own books of travel, he claims he never took notes or did any research, and as a result was frequently "very inaccurate," while writing "the exact truth as I saw it" (A ch. 7). This echoes his critical comment on his mother as "judging everything from her own standing-point" (A ch. 2). A close reading of An Autobiography would suggest that Trollope is very much his mother's son, but that constant brooding on his father's failure and intractable nature gave him access to the underlying darkness and despair of some of his most memorable creations.

When writing about his time (1834–41) as a clerk in the General Post Office, he refers the reader to his novel The Three Clerks (1858) for the detail of his rackety life in London, and takes the opportunity to voice his strong disapproval of the new system of competitive examinations, as opposed to private recommendation and patronage, for entry to the Civil Service. Though one may not learn "the little details of my private life" from An Autobiography, one learns almost everything about Trollope's values and attitudes. One reason he was against competitive examinations was that there was no examination which he himself could have come out of "other than disgracefully"; luckily he had the patronage of a family friend (A ch. 3). The other reason concerned social class. Knowing that his view "already subjects one to ignominy," he asserts that "there are places in life which can hardly be well filled except by 'Gentlemen,'" and that competitive examinations sought to deny barriers which were real and meaningful (A ch. 3).

His most extreme remark about social and economic differences is that they are "of divine origin" (A ch. 16). This comes in the chapter "Beverley," about his unsuccessful attempt to become a Member of Parliament, some-thing which should be "the highest object of ambition to every educated Englishman," and for which he had an "almost insane desire" – though emerging disgusted by the corruption and bribery which successful election-eering involved (A ch. 16). Debarred, as he puts it, from expressing his opinions in the House of Commons, he began his sequence of political novels as "a method of declaring myself" (A ch. 17). No one, he writes, could possibly know how much Plantagenet Palliser and Lady Glencora meant to him, "or how frequently I have used them for my political and social convictions" (A ch. 10).

"I consider myself to be an advanced, but still a conservative Liberal." What the "conscientious Liberal" had in mind was – "I will not say equality, for the word is offensive, and presents to the imagination of men ideas of communism, of ruin, and insane democracy, – but a tendency towards equality" (A ch. 16). The concept of the English gentleman was central to Trollope's view of the world. "I think that Plantagenet Palliser, Duke of

Omnium, is a perfect gentleman. If he be not, then I am unable to describe a gentleman" (*A* ch. 20). Trollope enjoyed, in the years of his success, the acquaintanceship of the privileged and, though there is no social name-dropping in *An Autobiography*, he is comfortable in saying that he prefers "the society of distinguished people, and that even the distinction of wealth confers many advantages." The society of the well-born and wealthy "will as a rule be worth seeking" (*A* ch. 9). The never-forgotten misery of his youth made the sweets of society all the sweeter.

Trollope identifies his first stepping-stone to a happier life as his move to Ireland as a Surveyor's Clerk for the Post Office in 1841. He re-invented himself, and "led a very jolly life there" (*A* ch. 4). He married Rose Heseltine, whom he met holidaying there with her family. He duly reports that her father was the manager of a bank in Rotherham, but not that her father cooked the bank's books and was disgraced. His reticence about Rose, and about his marriage, was lapidary: "My marriage was like the marriage of other people, and of no special interest to any one except my wife and me" (*A* ch. 4). That is all, or almost all. Until he became engaged to her, he had never attempted novel-writing. His first novel, *The Macdermots of Ballycloran*, was completed a year after his marriage.

Not until *Barchester Towers* (1857) did he begin to make money, and the second major stepping-stone came when he was flatteringly invited by Thackeray to write a serial novel for the *Cornhill*, and gave him *Framley Parsonage*. It was illustrated by Millais, one of the three people of whom Trollope writes in *An Autobiography* with open affection: "To see him has always been a pleasure. His voice has been a sweet sound in my ears ... These words, should he ever see them, will come to him from the grave, and will tell him of my regard, – as one living man never tells another" (*A* ch. 8). Thackeray is the second, no longer living when Trollope wrote that he was "one of the most tender-hearted human beings I ever knew," and *The History of Henry Esmond* (Trollope always abbreviated the novel's title to *Esmond*) "the greatest novel in the English language" (*A* ch. 10). The third, and the most striking given Trollope's habitual reticence, is Kate Field, who is not named: "There is an American woman of whom not to speak in a work purporting to [be] a memoir of my own life would be to omit an allusion to one of the chief pleasures which has graced my later years." She was, outside his family, "my most chosen friend," and a "ray of light to me." He allows himself a sentimental flourish, hoping she would live "to read the words I have now written, and to wipe away a tear as she thinks of my feelings while I write them" (*A* ch. 17). Rose, though undoubtedly "bone of his bone" as he often called a loved spouse in his fiction, receives no such public tribute.

He writes with ingenuous pride and satisfaction about his life after he moved back to England, especially his delight in being a member of the Garrick Club and the Athenaeum, a period when he was hugely prolific, comfortably off and, above all, "I think I became popular among those with whom I associated" (*A* ch. 9). He describes the twelve years (1859–71) when he and Rose lived just outside London at Waltham Cross: "I am confident that in amount no other writer contributed so much during that time to English literature." (It is always the quantity, rather than the quality, of his literary work that he permits himself to praise.) "I did the work of a surveyor of the Post Office ... I hunted always at least twice a week. I was frequent in the whist-room at the Garrick. I lived much in society in London ... In addition to this we always spent six weeks at least out of England. Few men I think ever lived a fuller life, and I attribute the power of doing this altogether to the virtue of early hours" (*A* ch. 15). There follows the account of rising before dawn to write, of his 250 words per quarter-hour, his ten pages a day. His only bitter disappointment, frankly conceded, comes when he is passed over for the post of Under-Secretary to the Post Office, which led to his resignation.

Apart from and allied to his advice to aspiring authors, a running theme in *An Autobiography* is Trollope's theory of novel-writing. The highest merit for him lies in "delineation of character, rather than in plot, or humour, or pathos" (*A* ch. 9). He thinks his best work was done fast; and he rushed at the work "as a rider rushes at a fence he does not see," with little idea of the denouement of the plot. But his intimate absorption in his characters, including in his non-writing hours, was all-consuming: "I have been impregnated with my own creations till it has been my only excitement to sit with the pen in my hand, and drive my team before me at as quick a pace as I can make them travel" (*A* ch. 10). He knew, he says, the tone of their voices, the color of their hair, the clothes they wore, and how, in the Barchester and political sequences, they changed as time passed.

Equally important, he justifies his novel-writing as a moral undertaking. "I have ever thought of myself as a preacher of sermons, and my pulpit as one which I could make both salutary and agreeable to my audience. I do believe that no girl has risen from the reading of my pages less modest than before ... I think that no youth has been taught that in falseness and flashness is to be found the road to manliness" (*A* ch. 8). It is from novels that young people learn about life and love, and for himself as a novelist "it is a matter of deep conscience" how he handles these matters (*A* ch. 12), in which he is wholly conventional – apart from a spirited defense of Carrie Brattle, the fallen woman in *The Vicar of Bullhampton* (1870), in which he raised a matter of "fearful importance" (*A* ch. 18). "In regard to a sin common to the two sexes, almost all the punishment and all the disgrace is heaped upon the one who in nine cases out of ten has been the least sinful." He writes with passion about the circumstances that may lead a girl into "sin" and the degradation and ostracism to which she is condemned. "How is the woman to return to decency to whom no decent door is opened?" (*A* ch. 18). It is an eloquent burst of feminism from one who was normally no feminist as we understand the word.

In assessing his literary contemporaries, most of whom he knew, he is quite brusque. He names Thackeray as the first and best. George Eliot – whom he consistently mis-spells as George Elliot – is more of a philosopher than a novelist. "She lacks ease." Dickens was enormously popular but created "puppets," not human beings, investing them with a charm that has "enabled him to dispense with human nature." He runs through Bulwer Lytton, Charlotte Brontë, Charles Reade ("endowed almost with genius"), and Wilkie Collins, whose novels were plotted in advance to the last detail: "Such work gives me no pleasure." Annie Thackeray, his friend's daughter, "writes like a lazy writer who dislikes her work." Disraeli's most recent novel *Lothair* (1870) is condemned for "that flavour of hair-oil, that feeling of false jewels, that remembrance of tailors ... It is the very bathos of story-telling" (*A* ch. 13). So Trollope shows his teeth, and his prejudices.

His assessment of his own novels is chiefly surprising when it comes to those which he considers failures. Elements of the plot of *Castle Richmond* (1860) resemble Thackeray's *The History of Henry Esmond* (1852), in that a young girl's rival in love was her own mother, but Trollope felt that Thackeray's Lady Castlewood was "admirably depicted," while his own Countess of Desmond was "almost revolting" (*A* ch. 9). He writes of *He Knew He Was Right* (1869) that "I do not know that in any literary effort I ever fell more completely short of my own intention." He had intended to evoke sympathy for Louis Trevelyan: he was "made to be unfortunate enough, and the evil he does is apparent." But the sympathy for him did not come through, "had not been created" (*A* ch. 17). Readers may feel that, on the contrary, both the Countess of Desmond and Mr. Trevelyan are, in their different ways, highly successful as perceptive and piteous examples of inappropriate obsession.

The lucidity of his writing is widely acknowledged. What have perhaps been insufficiently considered are his thoughtful remarks, in the chapter "On Novels and the Art of Writing Them," about the musicality of sentences and the necessary "harmony" of language. "The harmony which is required must come from the practice of the ear"; the novelist "must so train his ear that he shall be able to weigh the rhythm of every word as it falls from his pen." This should come so naturally "that he will have appreciated the metrical duration of every syllable before it shall have dared to show itself upon paper." The readers will be charmed even though "they will probably not know how they have been charmed" (*A* ch. 12). Trollope was right that his subtle harmoniousness may pass unnoticed, though one has only to read the unforgettable last sentence of *An Autobiography* to imagine its author "weigh[ing] the rhythm of every word," and to good effect.

An Autobiography has received much comment over the years, both positive and negative. But most critics would agree with Hugh Walpole's assertion that, for any study of Trollope, *An Autobiography* is "the corner-stone of the building."[2]

With his autobiography locked up in his desk, Trollope wrote and published at his usual headlong rate until he took seven weeks off in spring 1879 to write *Thackeray*, which came out later the same year in the "English Men of Letters" series, edited by John Morley and published by Macmillan. Thackeray had died in 1863. Trollope's ambition to be his first biographer was somewhat foiled by Thackeray's surviving daughter Annie who, as Trollope explains at the outset, respected her father's wish to have no biography, and released no papers or letters. "Such being the case, it certainly is not my purpose now to write what may be called a life of Thackeray." The most that Annie would do was to answer a factual questionnaire submitted by Trollope. All the reader is "entitled to ask" about the life, apart from a few personal anecdotes scattered elsewhere, is concentrated in a preliminary chapter. Trollope also obtained the brief reminiscences of an old school-friend of Thackeray. The bulk of the book, however, consists of a commentary on Thackeray's literary career, on each of the novels, and on his work for the periodicals, with hefty passages of quotation and general remarks about novel-writing.

"Something of his manner, something of his appearance I can say, perhaps of his condition of mind"; for Trollope knew him well, if only for the last four years of his life. He deals briefly but tenderly with the tragedy of Thackeray's wife's mental collapse, which left him "as it were a widower till the end of his days." He tells how he himself came to write for the *Cornhill* under Thackeray's editorship; but he does not recount his first meeting with the great man at the first and only *Cornhill* dinner, when Thackeray was curt towards him – suffering at that moment a painful spasm of the gut, a chronic condition which Trollope takes into account elsewhere in his book. "His face and figure, his six feet four in height, with his flowing hair, already nearly gray, and his broken nose, his broad forehead and ample chest, encountered everywhere either love or respect." Thackeray was "one of the most soft-hearted of human beings, sweet as Charity itself, who went about the world dropping pearls, doing good, and never wilfully doing harm" (*T* ch. 1). Trollope loved and revered Thackeray. There is no doubt about that.

Yet Trollope's tone is that of a man watching his best friend play tennis and agonizing as he sees him constantly knocking the ball into the net. Thackeray studied drawing as a young man in Paris, but he "never learned to draw, – perhaps never could have learned. That he was idle, and did not do his best, we may take for granted. He was always idle ..." and, having lost what money he had, took up writing, a career which requires no special training or apprenticeship. "Unsteadfast, idle, changeable of purpose, aware of his own intellect but not trusting it, no man ever failed more generally than he to put his best foot forward." Even his best works "seem to lack something that might have been there. There is a touch of vagueness which indicates that his pen was not firm while he was using it." As for his poetry, "he seems to have tumbled into versification by accident; writing it as amateurs do, a little now and again" (*T* ch. 1).

Trollope cannot enter fully into Thackeray's playfulness; as he admitted in *An Autobiography*, humor was not his forte. He cannot come to terms with Thackeray's desultory approach to his work or with Thackeray's throwaway natural talents, though he describes the drawings as "of the Hogarth kind" – than which there can be no higher compliment – and perceives "some lambent flame flickering over everything that he did, even the dinner-cards and the picture pantomimes. He did not in the least know what he put into those things." Thackeray was "always trifling, and yet always serious" (*T* ch. 1).

Not surprisingly, Trollope expresses exasperation at Thackeray's wish to be appointed Assistant-Secretary at the General Post Office via the patronage of Lord Clanricarde. Thackeray had no experience of administration, and his appointment would have involved passing over more deserving candidates. He could not have done the work, and it would have been "a disgraceful job." Trollope – not surprisingly again, given his own disappointed ambition – was equally dismissive of Thackeray's attempt to enter Parliament: he was "too desultory for regular work," and too quickly bored. As to the *Cornhill*, the magazine was a great success, "but justice compels me to say that Thackeray was not a good editor. As he would have been an indifferent civil servant, and an indifferent member of Parliament, so was he perfunctory as an editor" (*T* ch. 1).

Trollope gets to the root of the matter in the chapter "*Esmond* and *The Virginians*." "When we were young we used to be told, in our house at home, that 'elbow-grease' was the one essential necessary to getting a tough piece of work well done ... It is from the want of this special labour, more frequently than from intellectual deficiency, that tellers of stories so often fail to hit their nails on the head." He makes an exception of *Esmond*, which was "a whole from beginning to end ... its purpose developed, its moral brought home, – and its nail hit well on the head and driven in" (*T* ch. 5). What bothered Trollope about Thackeray was his customary failure to employ "elbow-grease" – industry, diligence, perseverance, regularity, all those qualities on which Trollope prided himself and which he believed to be essential for literary success.

Trollope is also disturbed by Thackeray's view of society and his "morbid horror" of snobbishness (*T* ch. 1). "The little courtesies of the world and the little discourtesies became snobbish to him ... Surely there is no greater mistake than to suppose that reverence is snobbishness" (*T* ch. 2). The endemic satire of Thackeray troubles him. "There can be no doubt that the heroic had appeared contemptible to him, as being untrue" (*T* ch. 3), but Thackeray goes too far: "A satirist by trade will learn to satirise everything, till the light of the moon and the sun's loveliness will become evil and mean to him. I think that he was mistaken in his view of things" (*T* ch. 8). Trollope struggles to prove that Thackeray was not a cynic, which he sees as a terrible thing to be, managing to persuade himself that he was not cynical "at heart," and that his amoral characters will not be taken by young readers as models, but as warnings.

Discussing the effects on young readers of Thackeray's satire, and his creation of "abnormally bad" characters, Trollope expands the argument for novelists' moral responsibilities that he made in *An Autobiography* (*T* ch. 1). The novelist "creeps in closer than the schoolmaster, closer than the father, closer almost than the mother. He is the chosen guide, the tutor whom the young pupil chooses for herself" (*T* ch. 9). He elaborates too on his astute observations about how to write dialogue, also sketched briefly in *An Autobiography*. "The realistic must not be true," since the conversation of even educated people, literarily transcribed, would consist of "ill-arranged words and fragments of speech," and seem ludicrous; while if they were made to speak grammatically, in complete sentences, it would seem "stilted and unreal." The novelist must "go between the two" (*T* ch. 9). Thackeray could do that; but he is drily mocked by Trollope for creating "a new language which may not improperly be called Hyberno-Thackerayan ... for in truth he was not familiar with the modes of pronunciation which make up Irish brogue" (*T* ch. 8). Trollope, having lived for many years in Ireland, felt at home with Irish idiom and pronunciation, which he rendered phonetically in his Irish novels.

Some have felt that *Thackeray* could as well have been written by an enemy than by a friend and admirer, and Annie Thackeray was not pleased with the book. Trollope, whose intuition gave him access to the hearts and minds of so many disparate kinds of men and women in his fiction, could not, however, encompass the "otherness" of Thackeray – an "otherness" which, had he not reaffirmed his own theory and practice at every turn, might have shaken his sense of himself. *Thackeray* is a double portrait, full of insights for the reader into not one great man, but two.

Trollope arrived at the writing of *The Life of Cicero*, which came out in two volumes from Chapman & Hall in 1880, over time and in stages. His interest in Latin literature and ancient history, and particularly in Cicero – advocate and master of rhetoric, statesman and man of letters – was inspired by reading and reviewing, back in 1851, the first installments of *A History of the Romans Under the Empire* (7 vols., 1850–68) by Charles Merivale, brother of his friend John. Subsequent hard study made Trollope familiar with Latin texts as he never had been as a schoolboy. In 1870 he produced a short book, *The Commentaries of Caesar*, for the series "Ancient Classics for English Readers," edited by the Rev. W. Lucas Collins and published by Blackwood. It took him three months, and was written "for the aid of those who do not read Latin," which meant most women, and men who did not attend a public school or grammar school (*CC* ch. 1). Occasionally he forgets whom he is writing for: "Is there a schoolboy in England ... who does not remember those memorable words, 'Tigna bina sesquipedalia'?" (*CC* ch. 5). He paraphrases, condenses, and adds his own commentaries to the *Commentaries*.

Greatly struck by the cruelty of the Romans, he catalogues with appalled gusto the massacres and murders, torturings, floggings, decapitations, drownings, and starvings. "I think we hate Caesar the more for his cruelty to those who were not Romans, because policy induced him to spare his countrymen" (*CC* ch. 12). Trollope being Trollope, it is not events but characters and personalities which chiefly interest him, particularly the despotic and devious character of the great Julius Caesar himself. It would become clear in *The Life of Cicero* that it is not just Caesar whom Trollope hates, but "Caesarism" – the demagogic mindset which makes a tyrannical dictator a law unto himself (*LC* vol. I, ch. 11; vol. II, ch. 5).

He concedes that, in crushing the Gauls, Caesar thought he was doing "a thoroughly good thing" (*CC* ch. 9). Colloquial phrases such as this, like his description of the Germans as "a horrid, hirsute, yellow-haired people" who inspired "blubbering awe" in the Italians, remind one, *avant la lettre*, of *1066 and All That* (*CC* ch. 2). He was satisfied with his "little work" (*CC* ch. 8), claiming in *An Autobiography* that "a well-educated girl who read it ... would perhaps know as much about Caesar and his writing as she need know." But one "old and very learned friend" – it was Charles Merivale – "to whom I sent it thanked me for 'my comic Caesar' but said no more. I do not suppose he intended to run a dagger into me." But it was not a book for eminent classical scholars. It was lightly written on purpose, as he asserted in *An Autobiography*, as "something that would carry the purposes of the school room into the leisure hours of adult life" (*A* ch. 18).

The Life of Cicero, ten years on, after more reading and re-reading, was a genuinely perilous undertaking for a non-specialist. Since Trollope first became fascinated by Cicero there had appeared the two-volume *Life of Marcus Tullius Cicero* by William Forsyth (1864) and J. A. Froude's *Caesar* (1879) – which might well, Trollope writes, have been entitled "Anti-Cicero" – just as his own *Cicero*, one could suggest, might well have been entitled "Anti-Caesar" (*LC* vol. 1, ch. 3). Confessing in his introduction to "a certain audacity," Trollope justifies his project by citing the wrongful denigration of Cicero by all previous writers. "His intellect they have admitted and his industry; but his patriotism they have doubted, his sincerity they have disputed, and his courage they have denied" (*LC* vol. 1, ch. 1). Cicero's patriotism, sincerity and courage are the planks on which Trollope builds his apologia. It was, as he writes, "an uphill task, – that of advocating the cause of a man who has failed. The Caesars of this world are those that make interesting stories" (*LC* vol. 1, ch. 3).

Trollope trudges through Cicero's career and the minefield of Roman conspiracies, betrayals, and political duplicities, sidling round matters he knows to be the subject of scholarly controversy, tying himself in knots in defense of his hero. Cicero's patriotism, he argues, consists in his clinging to the Republican idea, in the face of both the corruption of Roman governance and of Caesar's brutal militarism and personal ambition, and later Antony's. Cicero began as a democrat and joined the aristocracy as he climbed the ladder of official posts – quaestor, aedile, praetor, consul – guided in his insincerities "by the sincerity of his purpose" (*LC* vol. 1, ch. 3). If Cicero wanted power and influence, he had to conspire with other conspirators against the Republic. But he was "true to his country, and ever on the alert against tyranny and on behalf of pure patriotism" (*LC* vol. 11, ch. 1). So he pretended, he toadied, he flattered Caesar (but not Antony, hence his courage) – up to the time of his assassination. "Absence of sincerity there was not. Deficiency of sincerity there was" (*LC* vol. 1, ch. 1).

Cicero became rich, but never, Trollope insists, took bribes or illicit payment for his advocacy. Where Cicero got his money from, Trollope cannot say. "We are unable to produce in our own minds a Roman's estimation of Roman things" (*LC* vol. 11, ch. 4). That being so, Trollope takes another tack. Cicero was the "least Roman" of Romans (*LC* vol. 11, ch. 3). He was, habitual readers of Trollope will not be amazed to learn, a "gentleman," and a Christian one at that, even though Christ was not yet born. "I was not dealing with a pagan's mind" (*LC* vol. ii, ch. 14). Cicero believed in "the immortality of the soul, in virtue for the sake of its reward hereafter, in the omnipotence of God, the performance of his duty to his neighbors, in conscience, and in honesty" (*LC* vol. ii, ch. 14). Read all the works of this "greatest writer of prose that the world has produced" (*LC* vol. i, ch. 7), "and you shall feel that you are living with a man whom you might accompany across the village green to church, should he be kind enough to stay with you over the Sunday" (*LC* vol. ii, ch. 14). This is mawkish.

There is more in the vein. Cicero was guilty in his rhetoric of "mendaciuncula" – "little white lies" – but such fibs are "in the mouth of every diner-out in London and we may pity the dinner parties at which they are not used" (*LC* vol. i, ch. 7). Cicero was "modern."

> What a man he would have been for London life! How he would have enjoyed his club, picking up the news of the day... How popular he would have been at the Carlton, and how men would have listened to him while every great or little crisis was discussed! How supreme he would have sat on the Treasury bench, – or how unanswerable, how fatal, how joyous when attacking the Government from the opposite seats! How crowded would have been his rack with invitations to dinner! (*LC* vol. i, ch. 1)

The fantasy expands into Cicero holding intellectual flirtations with middle-aged countesses, and girls seeking his autograph, thrilling to the touch of his lips on theirs. "And what letters he would write! With the penny post instead of travelling messengers at his command ..." (*LC* vol. i, ch. 1). Thus Cicero is transformed into a Victorian gentleman, and a day-dream version of his biographer. If the savagery towards conquered peoples, the slave-ownership and corruption of the Romans do not quite fit this vision, it is because of advancing civilization. "The ages have gone their way, and the sufferings are lessened by increased humanity" (*LC* vol. ii, ch. 7). Though Trollope does draw a fleeting parallel between Caesar and Bismarck, the other possible parallel – between the Roman empire and the British empire, and the ambiguous "humanity" of the latter – is not touched upon.

Lord Palmerston was another short biographical book for a series, "English Political Leaders," published by William Isbister in June 1882, by which time Trollope had passed his sixty-seventh birthday. He was, naturally, still writing fiction but was feeling old, and beginning to be unwell.

He told his brother Thomas Adolphus in late 1881 that he did not intend to write a "Life of Palmerston," but "a small memoir, such as I did as to

Caesar for one series, and as to Thackeray for another, to inform those who wish to know a little by a little easy reading" (*Letters* II:935). In tracing Palmerston's complex career – Foreign Secretary, Home Secretary, twice Prime Minister – Trollope acknowledged taking as his guide the biographies by Evelyn Ashley (1879) and Sir Henry Bulmer, Lord Dalling (1870). He also used the existing volumes of A.W. Kinglake's *History of the Crimean War* (9 vols., 1863–87).

He disagreed with his brother's belief that Palmerston behaved badly to Queen Victoria. On the contrary, "I think that the Queen and Prince Albert, and Baron Stockmar behaved badly to Lord Palmerston" (*Letters* II:935). As with *Cicero*, he finds his justification in explicitly pitting himself against authority, in this case Sir Theodore Martin's *Life of the Prince Consort*, (5 vols., 1875–80) commissioned by the Queen. Trollope was not alone in understanding that Palmerston had "a tendency to lessen the power of the Crown rather than to increase it, and to think more of the House of Commons year by year as years ran on"; and that it was "only natural that with the Prince the tendencies should be on the other side" (*LP* ch. 1). Trollope's is a mild and politic assessment of Prince Albert's unconstitutional view that the monarch should be like a "permanent Premier," in Stockmar's phrase.[3]

Trollope criticizes Palmerston's arrogance but sums him up in now-familiar terms of approval: "Against his honesty, his industry and his courage we feel that no true word can be said." He injudiciously fictionalizes a little, imagining, between quotation marks, what Palmerston privately said to himself about his defense of Don Pacifico: "'Even this Pacifico, – the vile Portuguese Jew, this scum of the Mediterranean, – shall have such justice as he may deserve'" (*LP* ch. 8). He ploughs through the intricacies of the foreign politics central to Palmerston's career and, towards the end, concedes defeat: "Then came the affair of Schleswig-Holstein, which it would be very difficult to explain in the penultimate chapter of a book such as this; and which would be very uninteresting if explained" (*LP* ch. 13). This is a book by a tired man, though it will not be disregarded by those sufficiently interested in Trollope to want to read every book he wrote.

All Trollope's biographical writing, like his novels, reveals how accurate, in regard to himself, is his statement in *A Life of Cicero*: "The man of letters is, in truth, ever writing his own biography. What there is in his mind, is being declared to the world at large by himself." He goes on to say that if "the world at large" reads an author's works, "no other memoir will, perhaps, be necessary" (*LC* vol. 1, ch. 1). Even as he wrote those words, *An Autobiography* was safe in his desk. Furthermore, posterity has found it necessary to make Trollope the subject of biography, over and over again. That is another story.

NOTES

1 "No day without a line" – i.e., never let a day pass without writing something.
2 Hugh Walpole, *Trollope*, English Men of Letters series, (New York: Macmillan, 1928), p. 1.
3 Baron Stockmar to the Prince Consort 5 January 1854, quoted in Edgar Feuchtwanger, *Albert and Victoria: The Rise and Fall of the House of Saxe-Coburg-Gotha* (Hambledon: Continuum, 2006), p. 105.

3

MARY POOVEY

Trollope's Barsetshire series

At what point did the six novels set in or near Trollope's fictional county of Barset – *The Warden, Barchester Towers, Doctor Thorne, Framley Parsonage, The Small House at Allington*, and *The Last Chronicle of Barset* – become a *series*? Neither Trollope's own account, which appears in *An Autobiography*, nor the critical responses to the first five novels suggests that a series was a planned or an attractive option in the period between the 1855 publication of *The Warden* and December 1866, when the first episode of *The Last Chronicle* appeared. While Trollope and his readers viewed *Barchester Towers* as the "sequel" to *The Warden* (A ch. 5), Trollope admitted that he did not even invent the plot of *Doctor Thorne*, that he cast *Framley Parsonage* near Barset only because a publisher asked for a clerical drama, and that, when he did begin to imagine a series, he was not sure that *Doctor Thorne* or *The Small House at Allington* belonged in it. Those reviewers who commented on the repetitions within the novels did not typically welcome what they saw as Trollope's "habit" of "borrowing from himself"; most frequently, they viewed this as a "weakness" that betrayed "a great poverty of invention" on the part of the author (*Crit. Her.* 131, 123, 134).

If we credit his own account, Trollope first began to consider (at least some of) these novels to be a series in 1860, while he was composing *Framley Parsonage* for *Cornhill Magazine*. Still, seven years passed before reviewers could both see and appreciate the value of the "chain of novels" that Trollope could, by then, be said to have forged. Writing just after the last number of *The Last Chronicle* was published, in July 1867, a reviewer for the *Examiner* declared the group of novels of which this was undeniably the last "the best set of 'sequels' in our literature." This reviewer identified such series as a generic innovation, which was "essentially a birth of our own time."

Until of late, novelists hardly ventured beyond a second novel introducing persons of the first and carrying on the story of their lives. But in our day a new fashion has arisen, fostered in part by Mr. Thackeray's tendency to return to some of his old characters in a new story, and realize them more and more completely to himself and to his readers. Thus Sir Bulwer Lytton has dwelt also on his Caxton family, and we have more recent examples in Mr. Percy Fitzgerald's carrying on his Jenny Bell and some of her friends through three successive novels, and in the excellent series of the "Chronicles of Carlingford" [by Margaret Oliphant]. Mr. Trollope has yielded, in fact, to a tendency inherent in the best form of the realism of modern fiction.

In this reviewer's judgment, such series should be published in a format that would underscore the unity readers might otherwise overlook. "In justice to Mr. Trollope and to itself," he wrote, "the public should have these Barsetshire novels extant, not only as detached works, but duly bound, lettered, and bought as a connected series" (*Crit. Her.* 297). Over a decade was to pass before such a "duly bound" set was available: between 1878 and 1879, Chapman & Hall finally issued an eight-volume set, entitled *The Chronicles of Barset*, that indisputably fused these novels into a "connected series."

Even if these novels were not marketed as a series until 1878, the *Examiner* review makes it clear that something enabled readers to link them as early as 1867. Beyond their shared setting in or near the imaginary county of Barset, what features seemed to unite these six novels? Or, more to the point, what features did *The Last Chronicle* so emphasize that the discordant aspects of the first five novels seemed to disappear as the six coalesced into a single whole? The answers to these questions reveal much about the ways that Trollope's artistic practice changed between 1855 and 1867, but they tell us more about changing attitudes toward the British novel as a genre. For what we see in the history of responses to these novels is the emergence of a consensus, among reviewers and novelists alike, about the qualities that elevate a novel to the status of "art." The retrospective judgment that these six novels constituted a series articulated this consensus and helped some writers understand it in theoretical terms.

The reviewer for the *Examiner* clearly identifies what he considered the most important feature of these novels, in terms of both their value and their unity as a series: the reappearance of noteworthy characters. By 1867, in fact, most reviewers agreed that when an author carried a character over from one novel to another, he or she was not simply borrowing from earlier work but "realiz[ing these characters] more and more completely," so that "their shadowy forms," to quote another reviewer, seemed "to take equal substance with that of our living neighbours" (*Crit. Her.* 299). Such repetition helped make the characters seem real, in other words – so lifelike that they seemed to live outside the pages of the novels. "It tells of great gifts," echoed a third reviewer, "that Mr. Trollope should thus endow his characters with flesh and blood and individuality of interest; make their surroundings graphic and tangible, and yet make the men and women stand out from their background, and live and move like human beings" (*Crit. Her.* 302). "Like human beings," beloved characters like Archdeacon Grantly, Mr. Harding, Lily Dale, and the Reverend Crawley move in and out of these novels so convincingly that they prompted Margaret Oliphant (herself the author of a novel series) to proclaim these novels "the most perfect art." "The cunning of the craftsman here reaches to so high a point," she declared, "that it becomes a kind of inspiration" (*Crit. Her.* 304).

In (retrospectively) viewing the novels set in Barset as parts of a single whole, reviewers were tacitly agreeing to overlook some features of the earlier novels that undeniably worked against Trollope's lifelike characterization. Even though the first five Barsetshire novels earned much critical praise, in fact, Trollope was repeatedly criticized for shattering the illusion of life the novels created by intruding into the fictions. This criticism was expressed as early as 1855, in one of the first notices of *The Warden*. "The 'illusion of the scene' is invariably periled, or lost altogether," the reviewer for the *Leader* declared, "when the writer harangues in his own person on the behaviour of his characters, or gives us, with an intrusive 'I,' his own experiences of the houses in which he describes those characters as living. This is a fault in Art" (*Crit. Her.* 37). Three years later, *Barchester Towers* provoked the same complaint from the *National Review*: the novel would have been better, this reviewer decided, if Trollope had "refrained from frequently and somewhat offensively coming forward as author to remind us that we are reading a fiction" (*Crit. Her.* 83). In 1863, another reviewer even more roundly criticized such authorial intrusions – even though he exempted Trollope from the "affectation" that (for him) William Thackeray epitomized. "Mr. Thackeray's curious taste for careless, rambling, 'round-about writing' ... has set the fashion to a host of imitators, who do not scruple to stop at every convenient point of their narration to indulge in a few personal confidences, and enunciate their views about their story, themselves, or the world in general." Trollope might have avoided such egregious violations of "the wholesome rule of impersonality," according to this reviewer, but he did occasionally intrude into his fictions "to bustle about, to adjust the ropes, to hurry the scene-shifters, and to assure the beholders that no pains are being spared for their entertainment" (*Crit. Her.* 175, 176).

The shift from complaints about authorial intrusion to praise for Trollope's lifelike characters does not represent a change in aesthetic judgment, of course; both the complaints and the praise express these reviewers' opinion that the highest form of novelistic art effaces all signs of craft.

The point is that, for the reviewers of the first five Barset novels, Trollope's violations of "the wholesome rule of impersonality" were too blatant to ignore, whereas the reviewers who viewed these novels as a series after the publication of *The Last Chronicle* either forgot about these transgressions or decided to ignore them. This shift was undeniably a response to changes in Trollope's novelistic practice, as we are about to see, but it also marked a departure from an earlier critical consensus, which valued novelists precisely to the degree that they provided moral guidance by insisting that their fictions were just that. The preference for such explicit reminders of the crafted nature of novels was theorized by Henry Fielding in 1742, when he insisted that the novel was a new species of writing whose value derived from its ability to comment upon itself even as it offered readers a picture of the world. In practicing the self-conscious artistry he explicitly endorsed, Fielding was building on a philosophical rationale that John Locke had articulated in 1690. According to Locke, only "art" could elevate observation to a productive level of self-consciousness: "The understanding, like the eye, whilst it makes us see, and perceive all other things, takes no notice of itself: and it requires art and pains to set it at a distance and make it its own object."[1] In 1765, Samuel Johnson reiterated this point when he declared that "the consciousness of fiction" is the quality that makes art effective. "The delight of tragedy proceeds from our consciousness of fiction," Johnson explained in the "Preface" to *The Plays of William Shakespeare*. "Imitations produce pain or pleasure not because they are mistaken for realities, but because they bring realities to mind."[2]

The very fact that Johnson had to make the case for the superiority of a self-conscious aesthetic practice means, of course, that an alternative was also gaining ground. Among eighteenth-century British novelists, Samuel Richardson was the principal practitioner of a novelistic practice that rejected this self-conscious aesthetic, and instead seemed simply to convey real people's thoughts and actions. When Richardson claimed that the letters of his eponymous heroine Clarissa Harlowe contained "instantaneous descriptions and reflections" written as she fled the heartless Lovelace, he implied that no novelist stood between the frantic young lady and her readers.[3] Despite Richardson's undeniable popularity, however, his aesthetic of artistic self-effacement remained a minority practice until well into the nineteenth century. This was true in part because critics repeatedly insisted that a fiction that produced *too* compelling an illusion would make its (female) readers believe that improbable events could actually occur. Only in the gothic novels that proliferated in the 1790s did authors consistently try to efface signs of their own craft. That they did so might help account for both the popularity these novels enjoyed with readers who did not care about elevating the status of imaginative writing and the scorn heaped upon them by writers (like William Wordsworth) who emphatically did.

The value that reviewers and serious writers once ascribed to the kind of self-conscious aesthetic epitomized by *Tom Jones* and *The Prelude* may be difficult for modern readers to appreciate, for, as early as the end of the nineteenth century, the notion that self-effacing artifice was more "artistic" (as well as more appealing) than the alternative had achieved consensus, especially among self-declared champions of the novel. But it is important to remember that, during the decade of Trollope's greatest fame – the 1860s – the two most critically esteemed British novelists published works filled with exactly the kind of narrative intrusions that irritated Trollope's early reviewers. George Eliot's *The Mill on the Floss* (1860) and William Thackeray's *The Adventures of Philip* (1862) repeatedly remind readers that they are reading a novel and explicitly direct the reader's sympathies. That many readers now read even these novels as stories about "flesh and blood characters" means that, like the reviewers of *The Last Chronicle*, we have learned to overlook these self-consciously crafted features because we also favor "the wholesome rule of impersonality" to explicit reminders of craft.

To see the contribution that Trollope's Barsetshire novels made to this consensus, we need only compare the first five novels to *The Last Chronicle of Barset*. In each of the first Barsetshire novels, a narrator presides over the action; in a voice sometimes generalized by plural pronouns and sometimes individuated by direct references to himself, this narrator calls attention to the ways the fiction is crafted in order to direct the reader's sympathy (both for the characters and for the craft). Near the conclusion of *The Warden*, for example, the narrator dismisses Archdeacon Grantly by apologizing for his negative presentation; explicitly lamenting that "our narrative has required that we should see more of his weakness than his strength," the narrator suggests that he has deliberately obscured the character's more loveable qualities (*W* ch. 20). In *Barchester Towers*, the narrator doesn't wait until the end to announce that he presides over the novel's events. Instead of allowing the parallel courtships of the widow Eleanor Bold to proceed, the narrator preemptively reassures the reader that he will not sacrifice Eleanor to either the unctuous Mr. Slope or Bertie Stanhope, the impecunious artist who covets her wealth:

> But let the gentle-hearted reader be under no apprehension whatsoever. It is not destined that Eleanor shall marry Mr. Slope or Bertie Stanhope. And here, perhaps, it may be allowed to the novelist to explain his views on a very important point in the art of telling tales. He ventures to reprobate that system which goes so far to violate all proper confidence between the author and his readers, by maintaining nearly to the end of the third volume a mystery as to

the fate of their favourite personage. Nay, more, and worse than this is too frequently done. Have not often the profoundest efforts of genius been used to baffle the aspirations of the reader, to raise false hopes and false fears, and to give rise to expectations which are never to be realized? Are not promises all but made of delightful horrors, in lieu of which the writer produces nothing but the most commonplace realities in his final chapter? And is there not a species of deceit in this to which the honesty of the present age should lend no countenance? (*BT* ch. 15)

As an explicit comment on the novel's craft, this paragraph would not be out of place in Fielding's *Tom Jones*, and, in emphatically denouncing the tricks associated with gothic and other sensational novels, Trollope sides with novelists, like Fielding, who proudly revealed the machinery of their fictions.

Doctor Thorne takes such aesthetic self-consciousness one step further. In addition to repeated references to its own art (Frank Gresham "would have been the hero of our tale had not that place been preoccupied by the village doctor," *DT* ch. 1) and explicit authorial assurances ("I am too old now to be a hard-hearted author, and so it is probable that he may not die of a broken heart," *DT* ch. 1), *Doctor Thorne* opens with a prolonged backstory, which is so distended that it provokes an apology from the narrator:

I quite feel that an apology is due for beginning a novel with two long dull chapters full of description. I am perfectly aware of the danger of such a course. In so doing I sin against the golden rule which requires us all to put our best foot foremost, the wisdom of which is fully recognized by novelists, myself among the number. It can hardly be expected that any one will consent to go through with a fiction that offers so little of allurement in its first pages; but twist it as I will I cannot do otherwise ... This is unartistic on my part, and shows want of imagination as well as want of skill. Whether or not I can atone for these faults by straightforward, simple, plain story-telling – that, indeed, is very doubtful. (*DT* ch. 2)

Framley Parsonage, which was Trollope's first attempt at serial publication in a magazine, opens with an abbreviated, but no less self-consciously marked, version of the backstory that introduces *Doctor Thorne* ("But even yet more must be told of his good fortune before we can come to the actual incidents of our story," *FP* ch. 1). The most noteworthy examples of narrative intrusion in this novel, however, consist of passages of moral generalization, which simultaneously implicate readers in the weaknesses the characters exhibit and direct the reader's judgment of them. In explaining why Mark Robarts, the well-meaning but ambitious clergyman at the heart of *Framley Parsonage*, accepts an invitation to visit the Duke of Omnium's Chaldicotes House, the narrator involves the reader with the pronoun "we":

> It is no doubt very wrong to long after a naughty thing. But nevertheless we all do so. One may say that hankering after naughty things is the very essence of the evil into which we have been precipitated by Adam's fall. When we confess that we are all sinners, we confess that we all long after naughty things ... And there is nothing viler than the desire to know great people – people of great rank I should say; nothing worse than the hunting of titles and worshipping of wealth. We all know this, and say it every day of our lives. But presuming that a way into the society of Park Lane was open to us, and a way also into that of Bedford Row, how many of us are there who would prefer Bedford Row because it is so vile to worship wealth and title?   (*FP* ch. 4)

While *The Small House at Allington* opens with a less elaborate backstory than either *Doctor Thorne* or *Framley Parsonage*, this novel also contains explicit references to the crafted nature of the fiction ("I do not say that Mr. Crosbie will be our hero, seeing that that part in the drama will be cut up, as it were, into fragments," *SHA* ch. 2), and it carries over as well the addresses to the reader that insistently dispel the illusion of reality. In describing the jilted Lily Dale suffering at the hands of well-meaning neighbors, for example, the narrator appeals to the reader's experience:

> But Lily, though she put on it all so brave a face, had much to suffer, and in truth did suffer greatly. If you, my reader, ever chanced to slip into the gutter on a wet day, did you not find that the sympathy of the bystanders was by far the severest part of your misfortune? Did you not declare to yourself that all might yet be well, if the people would only walk on and not look at you? And yet you cannot blame those who stood and pitied you; or, perhaps, essayed to rub you down, and assist you in the recovery of your bedaubed hat. You, yourself, if you see a man fall, cannot walk by as though nothing uncommon had happened to him. It was so with Lily.   (*SHA* ch. 31)

In addition to such elaborate asides, the pages of *The Small House* are so littered with the narrator's "I" ("I regret to say," "as I have said," "I will only say," ch. 1) that it is impossible to forget his presence.

Given the prominence of such explicit signs of craft in the first five Barsetshire novels, how could *The Last Chronicle* make reviewers forget that they had once found these so offensive? The answer to this question – which also explains why the separate novels began to look like a series in 1867 – lies in two sets of features that *The Last Chronicle* deployed with unusual skill: first, the novel carries over and completes the stories of characters from other novels without changing these characters' natures; and second, the novel directs the reader's judgment with a new set of strategies that collectively render the action more dramatic. Taken together, these features helped make *The Last Chronicle* and all of the Barset novels that preceded it seem like a single panorama of living men and women.

The Last Chronicle revisits both major and minor characters from the other Barsetshire novels, but it does so without changing anything about these figures apart from their relative prominence in the novel. Using characters that are essentially the same over again while insisting that time has passed enabled Trollope both to capitalize on his reader's sense of familiarity with these figures and to economically import entire plots from other novels; in some instances, these imported plots perform the same function as the elaborate backstories in novels like *Doctor Thorne*, but, because they require no narrative elaboration, they provoke no authorial apology. Thus, when Lily Dale, who is one of the most important characters in *The Small House*, reappears in *The Last Chronicle*, she plays only a minor role, as the friend of Grace Crawley, whose father occupies the center of this novel's plot. When Trollope introduces Lily in *The Last Chronicle*, he invokes what happened in *The Small House* in two sentences, which do not explicitly guide the reader's response to Lily: "Grace had a cousin in London – a clerk high up and well-to-do in a public office, a nephew of her mother's – and this cousin was, and for years had been, violently smitten in love for this young lady. But the young lady's tale had been sad, and though she acknowledged feelings of most affectionate friendship for the cousin, she could not bring herself to acknowledge more." In the same chapter, in response to Grace's pleading for her cousin Johnny Eames, Trollope makes Lily speak for herself. She concludes the letter she writes Grace with an even more oblique reference to the past: "But when one thinks of going beyond friendship, even if one tries to do so, there are so many barriers!" (*LCB* ch. 6). Nine chapters later, Trollope returns to Lily Dale, and, quoting these words again, explicitly – but economically – solicits sympathy from the reader: "From which words the kind and attentive reader, if such reader be in such matters intelligent as well as kind and attentive, may have learned a great deal with reference to Miss Lily Dale" (*LCB* ch. 15).

The most important point about Lily Dale is that, as a character, she has not changed – even though alluding to her earlier history enables Trollope both to invoke that story and to allow readers (briefly) to think she might change. Having been jilted by Adolphus Crosbie, having rejected Johnny Eames, and having declared that her affections would never waver – all in *The Small House* – Lily is now available to provide an auxiliary focus for *The Last Chronicle*, which is more reliable, because more familiar, than Reverend Crawley, who is the primary focus of this novel. The fact that Lily does not change, in other words, in *The Small House*, in the time that has presumably passed between the action narrated in the two novels, or in the plot of *The Last Chronicle*, makes this character reflect upon the Reverend Crawley's inability to change without requiring the narrator to explain that consistency can be a virtue.

In addition to using major characters from another novel to import complex backstories into *The Last Chronicle*, Trollope revives relatively minor characters to elaborate the implications of actions initiated in earlier novels. Mortimer Gazebee, for example, first appears briefly in *Doctor Thorne* as the lawyer who marries the insipid Amelia De Courcy, whom Frank Gresham has declined to court. Now the legal representative of the De Courcy family, Gazebee makes an encore appearance in *The Small House*, where he weaves a web of marital obligation so tightly around Adolphus Crosbie that he nearly drives Lily Dale's one-time suitor to despair. In *The Small House*, the narrator describes the lawyer's relentless determination to protect the De Courcy family interest, but the lethal nature of the lawyer's embrace is not spelled out until *The Last Chronicle*, where the implicit metaphor of a spider is finally explicitly articulated: Mortimer is said to have worked for the De Courcys "as an inferior spider might be supposed to work" for its superiors (*LCB* ch. 43).

Those changes that do alter the recurring characters mostly involve age: characters like Griselda Grantly and Grace Crawley appear as children in the early novels, then return as adults in *The Last Chronicle*. In so doing, Griselda continues a history narrated more fully in another novel (*Framley Parsonage*), while Grace introduces a new center of interest. The character whose aging most obviously signifies that time has supposedly passed as Trollope was writing the novels is Mr. Harding, who is the focus of *The Warden*. Mr. Harding is mentioned in passing in *Framley Parsonage*, as "dear old Mr. Harding" (*FP* ch. 25), but his first significant cameo role comes in *The Small House*, where he is described in a way that indexes the passage of time. Already well-advanced in years in *The Warden*, the Mr. Harding of *The Small House* is "a little, withered, shambling old man," who walks with "an uncertain, doubtful step" (*SHA* ch. 16). Such descriptions anticipate the function this character plays in *The Last Chronicle*: with his death, Mr. Harding brings the novel and the series to a close.

By shifting the relative prominence of characters from novel to novel and by putting the character traits he has already established to various uses, Trollope was able both to create the impression that the lives of these characters continued even when the narratives stopped and to capitalize on information that readers had already gained from other novels. To a certain extent, such repetitions obviated the need to provide further narrative instruction about how to evaluate characters: a reader who had come to love Lily Dale by reading *The Small House* did not have to be taught to do so in *The Last Chronicle*. But recurring characters constitute only one of the strategies by which Trollope directed his reader's engagement in *The Last Chronicle*. A set of five related innovations also enabled him to minimize the narrative intrusions that had so irritated reviewers of the first Barsetshire novels. By keeping the narrator's presence to a minimum, Trollope was able to convince reviewers that the six novels were all of a part *even though* they are, in many respects, so different.

The first two strategies used to great effect in *The Last Chronicle* simply elaborate features that also appear in the earlier novels. First, the running chapter titles in *The Last Chronicle* tend to be more consistently interpretive or provocative than the generally descriptive titles of the earlier novels, two of which (*Framley Parsonage* and *The Small House*) did not even carry chapter titles in their original magazine format. Titles like "How Did He Get It?" (chapter 1) and "I Suppose I Must Let You Have It" (chapter 44) helped market the individual parts of the novel, which, in the unusual publication format of thirty-two sixpenny parts, required readers to decide weekly to continue buying the novel. Each of these chapters, which headed a new part, would not only have sustained readers' interest but also directed attention to the salient issue narrated in the new part. Second, free indirect discourse appears more frequently in *The Last Chronicle* than in the earlier novels. In the kind of passage in which the narrator of the previous novels typically intervened, the narrative of *The Last Chronicle* offers the dual perspective that free indirect discourse allows, so that readers could see, and judge, the character for themselves. In an early representation of the Reverend Crawley's tortured pride, for example, no narrator adjudicates between sympathy and judgment; instead, the narrative segues seamlessly from description to Crawley's thoughts, thus conveying the experience of his agony: "Dean Arabin had laughed at him because he had persisted in walking ten miles through the mud instead of being conveyed in the dean's carriage; and, yet, after that, he had been driven to accept the dean's charity! No one respected him. No one!" (*LCB* ch. 12).

Three more narrative innovations collectively render *The Last Chronicle* more "dramatic" than the previous Barsetshire novels. I use this adjective advisedly, for, implicitly or explicitly, theatrical performance was the model that critical reviewers of the first five novels repeatedly invoked. When the reviewer for the *Leader* chastised Trollope for the narrative intrusions in *The Warden*, for example, he explicitly cited drama as the ideal: if Trollope should doubt that "the illusion of the scene" was paramount, this reviewer insisted, "we refer him to the stage as an illustration. Did he ever see a great comedian talk to the audience over the footlights?" (*Crit. Her.* 37). In 1858, the *National Review* repeated this idea when he complained that "such intrusions are as objectionable in a novel as on a stage" (*Crit. Her.* 83). In *The Last Chronicle*, Trollope was able to enhance the dramatic qualities of his novel by combining extended passages of dialogue, many of which contain no narrative commentary and few speech tags; scenes that repeat and refine earlier, similar scenes or encounters; and passages in which characters judge each other, thereby encouraging the reader to evaluate both the character that passes judgment and the object of evaluation.

Trollope initially experimented with sustained passages of unmarked dialogue in *Nina Balatka*, the novel that immediately preceded *The Last Chronicle*. Trollope's decision to publish this novel anonymously, however, as well as its unfamiliar setting and unusual subject (it is set in Prague and deals with the love between a Jew and a Christian), conspired to marginalize this text, even though reviewers judged it to be "charming" because "simple" (*Crit. Her.* 267, 270). *The Last Chronicle* is thus the first of Trollope's major novels to be dominated by dialogue, and, even though its eighty-four chapters contain many descriptive, narrative, and even epistolary passages, some of the most important episodes are conveyed almost completely through dialogue. This is the case, for example, of both the scene in which Mrs. Arabin reveals to Johnny Eames that she gave Reverend Crawley the £20 check whose whereabouts drive the novel's plot (chapter 70) and the episode in which Mr. Toogood describes for Crawley the events he has tried so hard to remember (chapter 74). The first of these scenes, moreover, repeats numerous previous episodes in which other characters are either asked about the check or demand to know who has it. Various characters' inability to say where the check has gone becomes an index to their ethical reliability *even though* no one – including Mrs. Arabin and Reverend Crawley – could possibly trace the check's strange journey. Such repetitions, especially because they are not accompanied by a narrator's guidance, encourage the reader to sift the evidence the novel parcels out, both in order to evaluate the characters and to watch the effects of ignorance on their sympathy toward each other.

This last feature – Trollope's elaborate examination of the way characters judge each other – conclusively transfers the evaluative function once performed by the intrusive narrator to the interactions among characters and, by extension, between reader and text. Judging Reverend Crawley, as do the two Lady Luftons and Mark Robarts (from *Framley Parsonage*), Mrs. Proudie and the Archdeacon Grantly (from *Barchester Towers*), and Mr. Harding (from *The Warden*), characters simultaneously reveal their idiosyncratic prejudices, all of which have been established in earlier novels, and offer readers opportunities to see how their own, equally poorly informed opinions contribute to "the world's" judgment. By engaging readers in the activity the novel chronicles – evaluating Reverend Crawley and determining the responsibility he bears for the fate of the check – Trollope renders these characters nearly as real to readers as are the neighbors whom they judge every day.

By 1894, Henry James was able to theorize what had by then become a consensus about what made a novel "art." "Catching the very note and trick, the strange irregular rhythm of life, that is the attempt whose strenuous force keeps Fiction upon her feet. In proportion as in what she offers us we see life *without* rearrangement do we feel that we are touching the truth; in proportion as we see it *with* rearrangement do we feel that we are being put off with a substitute, a compromise and convention."[4] For James, the writer's ability to efface a novel's craft was part and parcel of the organic unity of the work. "A novel is a living thing," he declared, "all one and continuous, like every other organism, and in proportion as it lives will it be found, I think, that in each of the parts there is something of each of the other parts."[5] To at least one reviewer, looking back on Trollope's career after the novelist's death, the six novels of the Barsetshire series seemed to achieve precisely this effect, for each was simultaneously "complete in itself" and part of a single whole, which, as a whole, was "very like real life":

> We are set down in a country town, and at once make the acquaintance and become interested in our neighbours. Time goes on; and now and again a group which has been made prominent in one story disappears in the next ... Our favourites and our real friends, however, stay on, only we see more now of one and then of another of them ... The fate of our chief favourite, Lily Dale, is still unsettled when "The Small House at Allington" is finished, and we have to wait until the end of the "Last Chronicles [sic] of Barset" to learn that she never recovers from the cruel blow which she receives in the first of these last two tales. In the second, "The Last Chronicles of Barset," Trollope takes up the broken or unfinished threads of the whole series, and although there is an independent plot, the main interest of the book lies in the farewell view that it gives us of so many old and well-known friends.[6]

The consensus that a novel became art when it effaced its craft may have been nearly universal by the 1890s, but writers remained divided over whether Trollope had consistently achieved this goal. While many agreed that novels like *The Last Chronicle* made up for the intrusions that marred his other works, others – most famously, Henry James – refused to forgive Trollope for the "terrible crime" of acknowledging his craft: "He admits that the events he narrates have not really happened, and that he can give his narrative any turn the reader may like best."[7] That the six Barsetshire novels were treated as a single whole by many, however, suggests that, at least in this instance, Trollope had produced the most vital novelistic "organism" British readers had ever seen.

NOTES

1 John Locke, *An Essay Concerning Human Understanding*, 2 vols. (London: Everyman's Library, 1971), vol. I, p. 5.
2 Samuel Johnson, "Preface" to *The Plays of William Shakespeare, Samuel Johnson: Selected Poetry and Prose*, ed. Frank Brady and W. K. Wimsatt (Los Angeles and Berkeley: University of California Press, 1977), p. 312.
3 Samuel Richardson, *Clarissa, or The History of a Young Lady*, 4 vols. (London: Everyman's Library, 1962), vol. I, p. xiv.
4 Henry James, "The Art of Fiction," *Victorian Criticism of the Novel*, ed. Edwin M. Eigner and George J. Worth (Cambridge: Cambridge University Press, 1985), p. 206.
5 James, "Art," p. 203.
6 [Zoe Shipley], "The Novels of Anthony Trollope," *Dublin Review* 9:2 (April 1883), 323–4.
7 James, "Art," pp. 196–7.

4

WILLIAM A. COHEN

The Palliser novels

For Anthony Trollope, the political novel was both a subject of anxiety and an object of desire. A civil servant disappointed in his effort to become an elected legislator, Trollope aspired to write political fiction, yet he feared that his reading public would not like it. "I commenced a series of semi-political tales," he recounts in *An Autobiography* (1883); "As I was debarred from expressing my opinions in the House of Commons, I took this method of declaring myself ... In writing [these books]... I was conscious that I could not make a tale pleasing chiefly, or perhaps in any part, by politics. If I write politics for my own sake, I must put in love and intrigue, social incidents, with perhaps a dash of sport, for the sake of my readers. In this way I think that I made my political hero interesting" (*A* ch. 17). To be palatable, it seems, political medicine must be sweetened with romance, society, and sports.

What exactly did Trollope – and do we – mean by "political novel"? If it is a fictional account of professional politicians' public policy decisions and back-room machinations, the works in the Palliser series qualify. But as Trollope concedes, such a definition does not promise much to interest a broad readership. *Politics* by a more capacious definition, however, meaning "actions concerned with the acquisition or exercise of power, status, or authority" (*OED* s.v. 4.a.) can cover a wide range of plots and character dramas, and in this sense it resonates deeply with the Palliser novels. For while these works are in part concerned with the professional lives of fictive politicians, government policy and party loyalty, election campaigns and jockeying for ministries, they are also at least as much about romance, marriage, and conflicts between parents and children – in short, about the traditional materials of the novel genre: private and domestic life. The challenge for Trollope was to get both kinds of stories into the same novels; the challenge for his readers is to understand the relationship between them.

In the public arena, the condition of plot is a conflict between two parties, Liberal and Conservative – or, as they are called in the "old phraseology" that the novels sometimes adopt, Whig and Tory (*PM* ch. 64). Yet the distinction between Liberals and Conservatives is often not much of a difference at all, as changes in various characters' party loyalties suggest. For example, the muckraking journalist Quintus Slide begins as a Radical in *Phineas Finn* (1869), then switches to support the Conservatives in *Phineas Redux* (1874), largely to settle personal scores. The latter novel describes representatives of the two parties as being "so near to each other in all their convictions and theories of life that nothing is left to them but personal competition for the doing of the thing that is to be done" (*PR* ch. 33). The antagonism provides an instance of what Roland Barthes terms the *ni-ni* ("neither-nor") principle: two apparently opposed alternatives establish and naturalize a world of possibilities in narrowly conceived, highly constrained terms.[1] While Trollope himself was a fierce Whig loyalist, the discussion of his so-called political theory in the *Autobiography* suggests a difference more of nuance than of substance between Liberals and Conservatives.[2] Both, Trollope writes, acknowledge that "inequality is the work of God," never to be overcome; Conservatives aim to impede any tendency toward class leveling, while Liberals mildly encourage it – but only in such a way as to ensure that it cannot advance. Neither actually advocates equality, "for the word is offensive, and presents to the imaginations of men ideas of communism, of ruin, and insane democracy"; the ideal, repeated throughout the series, is *liberty* rather than equality. The proximity of the two nominally opposing views helps to explain Trollope's memorable description of himself as a hybrid "advanced conservative Liberal" (*A* ch. 16), just as it suggests why the government that his hero, Plantagenet Palliser, leads as prime minister should be a coalition of the two parties.

The Palliser series establishes a reciprocal relationship between stories of public and private life – stories that might more suggestively be termed the political and the psychological. The novels at once psychologize politics and politicize psychology, showing the two realms mutually to allegorize, as well as substantially to interact with, each other. While the distinction between Conservative and Liberal positions in the professional political sphere is, in Trollope's description, rather insubstantial, the difference becomes more consequential if we apply his definitions to "politics" in the wider sense. Chapter 68 of *The Prime Minister* (1876), entitled "The Prime Minister's Political Creed," recapitulates the "political theory" enunciated in the *Autobiography*. Conservatives, the title character states, wish "to maintain the differences and the distances which separate the highly placed from their lower brethren ... With the Conservative all such improvement is to be based on the idea of the maintenance of those distances ... and that is to go on for ever" (*PM* ch. 68). In *propria persona*, Trollope writes in the

Autobiography that the "Liberal is opposed to the Conservative. He is equally aware that these distances are of divine origin, equally averse to any sudden disruption of society in quest of some Utopian blessedness; – but he is alive to the fact that these distances are day by day becoming less, and he regards this continual diminution as a series of steps towards that human millennium of which he dreams" (*A* ch. 16). The Palliser novels extend these opposing partisan credos well beyond the terms of class distinction in which they are here articulated. Conservatism, in the broader sense, is a principle of constancy, even conformity, while liberalism advocates for adaptation and progress. It is this fundamental tension that enables "politics" to relate not just to party and Parliament, policy and principle, but to the large plot elements and narrative movements, private as well as public, that constitute Trollope's series. The opposing forces of liberalism and conservatism regulate both individual desires and the domestic policies that govern relations within families and social worlds. They pertain, in other words, to the materials that form the bulk of the novels' plots, including dramas of courtship and jealousy, family conflict and competition, personal ambition and retribution, crime and sensation, and even sports such as hunting and shooting. The public, professional world of politics is traditionally gendered male, and the private, domestic one of romance female; while Trollope's series respects these divisions, it also complicates them, showing not only how men and women alike participate in both spheres but also how the very terms of the conflict apply equally to both.

The homology the novels establish between the public political struggles and those in the private realm, together with the pseudo-opposition between the two parties, has the combined effect of appearing to evacuate the works of political content. To contract professional politics to interpersonal dramas may make compelling fiction, but the result is that the content of the political positions becomes largely irrelevant to the stories themselves. John Halperin has richly documented the ways in which Trollope's novels draw upon and reimagine real contemporary political events and figures. While Plantagenet Palliser is not a fictional representation of any particular prime minister, the novels, as Halperin shows, reflect the qualities of many public people – including all the prime ministers who served in the 1860s and 1870s, Derby, Palmerston, Russell, and, especially, Disraeli and Gladstone – in his and other characters. (Although reference is made to Queen Victoria, she never appears as a character.) The novels vividly portray the political process, but they are hardly *romans à clef*, and in their overall effect they are largely neutral on substantial political questions (even allowing for the powerful mistrust they betray of Disraeli). Keeping up the volley of power between the two parties serves to show that the parliamentary machine grinds on, without requiring the novelist or the reader to commit to particular political positions.

While in all of these ways the Palliser series seems to empty the political novel of political content, another type of political meaning emerges, at an even broader level than the two I have mentioned, to which it actively contributes – one that we might term "ideology." Within the represented content, both the public and the private plots produce a mildly progressive, perhaps even a "liberal" vision of *ni-ni* conflict, proposing that a form of flexible accommodation permits a degree of change within the social and political orders. What I am calling the ideology of the novels, however, contradicts the progressive vision embodied in these local political contests with a deeper and more thoroughly entrenched conservative advocacy for preserving established structures of power. Ironically, as I will show, this conservatism works in part by promoting an idea of modernity that advances over an outdated old order and, in the process, it has some surprising effects on the gendering of public–private distinctions. Moreover, the novels' two distinctive formal attributes – repetition and extension – reinforce the effect: with the variations it spins on a relatively narrow set of plot possibilities in a segment of the English ruling class, the gigantic series promises a story that will never end. In so doing, it gives to the ongoing preservation of the established order a feeling of adaptation and development, providing an "exquisite combination of conservatism and progress" (*CYFH* ch. 24).

The first novel in the series, *Can You Forgive Her?* (1864), establishes the pattern of conflict between liberal and conservative principles through a series of overlapping love triangles. In each case, the woman at the apex of the triangle must choose between an appealing but unscrupulous man and an honorable but dull one. The choice of the novel's heroine, Alice Vavasor, between the rakish, untrustworthy man who tempts her and the mild, appropriate one, whom everyone in her social world recognizes as her proper suitor, is itself cast in explicitly political terms:

> When she did contrive to find any answer to that question as to what she should do with her life, – or rather what she would wish to do with it if she were a free agent, it was generally of a political nature. She was not so far advanced as to think that women should be lawyers and doctors, or to wish that she might have the privilege of the franchise for herself; but she had undoubtedly a hankering after some second-hand political manoeuvering. She would have liked, I think, to have been the wife of the leader of a Radical opposition, in the time when such men were put into prison, and to have kept up for him his seditious correspondence while he lay in the Tower. (*CYFH* ch. 11)

In an age before female suffrage, the conventional role of women in politics is as onlookers, advisors, champions, and sometimes intermediaries for their male relatives. Alice's tempting bad object, her cousin George Vavasor, serves briefly as a Radical MP, and the bland, good one, John Grey, is eventually a Liberal member (though by virtue of his wealth and elevated class station, he is every bit a traditional Whig oligarch). Yet the idea of politics in this passage is not so much ideological as phantasmatic: her hypothetical husband is a Radical because it would be a delicious romance to serve some great heterodox cause, not because she is attached to any particular doctrine of Radicalism. If Alice thus appropriates political causes to romantic ones, the drama of her marital prevarication hinges on a choice between conservative and liberal options, broadly conceived. Her ultimate decision to obey the wishes of her family adheres to the conservative principle of preserving and sustaining wealth and class, rather than squandering them on rebels like George.

Trollope organizes the novel in what might be called a symphonic form, whereby the large themes and smaller motifs play out with variations across different dimensions of the plot, frequently echoing in different registers on the class scale. Alice's story is repeated first, in a tragic genre and a higher class register, by Lady Glencora Palliser, and second, in a comic genre and lower on the class scale, by Alice's Aunt Greenow. Lady Glencora's struggle is at a later phase than Alice's and serves explicitly as a cautionary tale: after a romance and near elopement with the dashing scapegrace Burgo Fitzgerald, Lady Glencora marries the eminently appropriate, cautious, and rather dull Plantagenet Palliser, heir to a dukedom and a fortune, who eventually rises to become prime minister. While Alice has yet to choose her path, Lady Glencora is a picture of a spirited young woman forced by her family into the grooves of conformity. That even after her marriage she nearly succumbs to the temptation of running off with Burgo is offered as evidence of the cost of a too-complete quashing of independence. Yet she ultimately finds a form of satisfaction in this marriage – happiness of a more moderate and temperate kind than the adventure with Burgo promised – which provides the novel's lesson. To adopt the terms in which Trollope describes his own political views, she illustrates an "advanced conservative Liberal" idea of married life: play by the rules, bend them a little, and in the end you will be rewarded. This too is finally Alice's fate, whereas the scoundrels at the radical end of the social spectrum (George and Burgo) are cast out from the future world of the novel, never to be heard from again.

While the stories of both Lady Glencora and Alice politicize psychology – in the sense that their romantic dilemmas come down to a conflict between conservative and liberal principles of adherence to social rules – Palliser himself, in this novel, psychologizes politics. Despite his general inattentiveness to home life, Palliser recognizes the crisis in his domestic affairs when news reaches him of his wife's imminent elopement with her lover; to save his marriage, he sacrifices the political career to which he is devoted, giving up his greatest ambition (to serve as Chancellor of the Exchequer) so as to spirit his wife away to the Continent and remove her from temptation. Public and private life are not only analogous; they also, as in this instance, directly affect each other. Similarly, George Vavasor switches his party affiliation from Conservative to Radical not because his views of society change but because he wants to spite his grandfather, the patron from whom he has become alienated: politics is nominal, depending on (and in turn provoking) family conflict rather than principle.

Phineas Finn and *Phineas Redux* (which Trollope, in the *Autobiography*, says "are, in fact, but one novel" [*A* ch. 17]) – switch from a female to a male protagonist, and the focus on parliamentary intrigue becomes far more direct; here we witness what might be called the politics of politics. Over the course of the two novels, Phineas has a series of romantic entanglements in tandem with repeated crises of political loyalty. In the first novel, he struggles over a party-line vote for a reform bill to disenfranchise certain pocket boroughs (one of which he occupies) and, later, over a vote for Irish tenant-right; in the second novel, the issue is Church disestablishment, a cause Finn supports, but against which he must vote because of party politics. Over and over, in these novels, Trollope exposes the absurdity of political strategy, whereby a party supports or opposes a measure that contradicts its articulated ideology simply because of political expediency. The Liberals, who advocate elimination of pocket boroughs, Irish tenant-right, and Church disestablishment, vote as a bloc against all these measures, while the Conservatives, who are opposed, vote for them. (These works often invoke real political positions, even if the issues represented are not precisely the ones before Parliament in the 1860s and 1870s.) The drama of Phineas's political education is learning to adhere to his party when it needs him – and determining when his convictions demand that he throw over the party and strike out on his own.

In the multilayered contest between, on the one hand, independence and conviction, and, on the other, loyalty and moderation, class and gender are decisive. Like unmarried women of all classes, a man such as Phineas, who lacks his own financial means, cannot afford to be independent. Because he depends on a government office for his living, he has no choice but to vote with his party; when he votes for Irish tenant-right in *Phineas Finn* the courage of his convictions costs him his salary and he must resign his seat. Unlike many of the other politicians represented, Phineas firmly holds on to his ideals. Trollope presents such integrity as a rare virtue, even if Phineas's patrons and supporters regard it as hopelessly self-defeating. The conflicts in his career parallel those of Lady Glencora and Alice Vavasor in domestic affairs, for in all these cases *independence* is the issue. Of Alice, Trollope writes, "All her troubles and sorrows in life had come from an overfed craving for independence" (*CYFH* ch. 43); and of Phineas, "He did wish that he had been a little less in love with independence" (*PF* ch. 67). Phineas's romantic career – as it moves over the course of the two novels from his courtship of Lady Laura Standish and then of Violet Effingham to his brief marriage to his Irish sweetheart, Mary Flood Jones, and finally to his long-deferred marriage to Madame Max Goesler – dramatizes and alters the shape of his political career. The first two women are beyond his reach, in terms of wealth and rank, but it is part of his bold independence (to his rivals, it reads as impudence) that he pursues such high-born beauties – just as he pursues a parliamentary career that more cautious advisors (such as the Lows) see as impractical and unattainable. In different ways, each of his two wives represents a form of appropriate, socially comprehensible pairing – just as he learns to be a loyal party adherent. Mary embodies retired domestic tranquility in his native Ireland, and while Madame Max is admittedly eccentric in the world of the novels – as a wealthy European widow (and possibly a Jew) – she and Phineas share a foreignness and an independence of character that makes them equally exterior to the elite society that is their purlieu. Both have the opportunity to join that society (she through marriage to the old Duke of Omnium, he through government employment), but together they represent a principle of difference. Their centrality to the Palliser world indicates its capacity to accommodate a wider range of ethnic and class configurations than a strictly orthodox idea of the British ruling elite might be imagined to include. Here is another version of conformity that learns to accommodate change, of independence that learns to conform.

Just as much of Phineas's plot occupies the nominally feminine sphere of romance, so are the women characters not only engaged in figuratively political struggles but also directly involved in the world of politics. Chapter 60 of *Phineas Finn*, titled "Madame Goesler's Politics," takes politics in the metaphorical sense, concerning the character's diplomatic effort to play off the old Duke's infatuation with her against Lady Glencora's effort to protect her family's claim on his title and wealth. But many women in these novels are intimately involved in political negotiations; for all of the agonized pining and disappointment on both Phineas's and Lady Laura's parts, for example, their relationship is decidedly political, in the sense that she secures him a seat (in her father's control) in Parliament, as Madame Max and Lady Glencora (now the Duchess of Omnium) later lobby for him to obtain government office. The clearest instance of female power as a blend of public and private arenas arises, however, in the labor of the Duchess of Omnium as the wife of the Prime Minister, in the novel of that name. The convergence of social and political worlds in *The Prime Minister* almost makes a mockery of the idea of separate spheres. While the Duke feebly holds together a coalition government, constantly feeling himself ill-suited for leadership, the Duchess – with supreme self-confidence and the lavish expenditure of her own fortune – rules over a domestic government, organizing invitations, guests, dinners, and parties at Gatherum Castle for her husband's political benefit:

> There was creeping upon [the Duke] the idea that his power of cohesion was sought for, and perhaps found, not in his political capacity, but in his rank and wealth. It might, in fact, be the case that ... his wife the Duchess ... with her dinner parties and receptions, with her crowded saloons, her music, her picnics, and social temptations, was Prime Minister rather than he himself ... It had, perhaps, been found that in the state of things then existing, a ministry could be best kept together, not by parliamentary capacity, but by social arrangements, such as his Duchess, and his Duchess alone, could carry out ... In such a state of things he of course, as her husband, must be the nominal Prime Minister. (*PM* ch. 18)

The novel often plays upon the gender inversion of a weak and ambivalent Duke managed by a Duchess (compared at several points to Lady Macbeth) who is ambitious and instinctively canny about politics and promotion: "I sometimes think, Plantagenet, that I should have been the man, my skin is so thick; and that you should have been the woman, yours is so tender" (*PM* ch. 42). Just as, in the realms of politics and romance, a minor adaptation of norms permits the established order to perpetuate itself, so here, in the arena of gender roles – where one might expect to see Victorian ideology at its most strictly regulatory – some play in the system is convenient to maintenance of the status quo. The Duchess's machinations, though unofficial, bear on real policy and patronage decisions; they are more manifestly political, and work more aggressively to benefit the Duke, than do his own cautious efforts. He admonishes her for what he sees as the vulgarity of her approach, and the charge offends her deeply, since she sees herself as advancing his interests at least as much as her own. When, however, her political efforts (such as promoting Ferdinand Lopez for office against the Duke's express wishes) fail, the charge sticks. While the female approach is to value appearances over substance, the male insufficiently appreciates appearances, as the Duke's insensitivity in awarding the garter to Lord Earlybird or expelling Major Pountney demonstrates. It is, in the end, impossible to sort out what is real substance and what is mere style, since they so thoroughly affect each other. Characterologically, he seems to adhere to convention and she to flout it – except that her boldness works in his interests, and that style itself is so often a matter of conformity.

A negotiation between adherence to convention and rebellion against it organizes both political and social life, and while the characters who stand at the far ends of the spectrum supply the engine for plot, they must, in the end, be either reformed or cast out from the world of "advanced conservative Liberal" values that Trollope's novels promote. Trollope often associates physical violence with men at the extremes, who are excluded from the broad middle-ground of flexible convention. He uses this characterization to condemn the old, outmoded order against which he distinguishes his vision of modernity – a vision that, perhaps paradoxically, is profoundly conservative.[3] If such violence does not destroy these characters, they must renounce it in order to be recuperated by sociability. In *Can You Forgive Her?*, George Vavasor, who, as we have seen, is both a Radical in politics and a pariah in the social sphere, embodies a type of male violence, beginning with the livid scar on his cheek, which becomes inflamed when his temper flares. In the course of the novel, he grows increasingly violent in his quest for Alice and her fortune: he starts a fist fight with his rival, John Grey; he treats Alice roughly (grabbing her arm, cursing at and insulting her); he knocks down his sister Kate, breaking her arm and threatening to murder her; he returns to John Grey and shoots a gun at him. Such violence, often rooted in delusion, places George so far beyond the social norms that he cannot be reintegrated, and at the novel's end he emigrates to America. In both *Phineas Finn* and *The Prime Minister*, young men (Phineas and Ferdinand Lopez, respectively) rescue others from garrotters; doing so serves to curry favor with the families of the women they court, and brings the men – both of foreign extraction – more nearly into the world of the English ruling class. The man whom Phineas rescues, Robert Kennedy, is also one of his rivals, and in the sequel, when Kennedy has married Lady Laura and begun to treat her roughly, he eventually becomes consumed with jealousy of Phineas, and shoots a gun at him, as the sign of his mounting insanity. Like George Vavasor, Robert Kennedy ultimately goes beyond the point from which he could be socially rescued; he loses his mind and dies soon thereafter, finally releasing his shattered wife. But while George is radical in his ideas about politics and society, Kennedy embodies a reactionary principle: his violence springs from rigid adherence to orthodox ideas of marital obedience, Presbyterian strictness, and inflexible morality. Unlike other married men, such as Palliser, he does not recognize how society has changed, and how those changes demand accommodation from him.

The third figure of unredeemed male violence is Lopez, in *The Prime Minister*; although his party affiliation is flexible (he stands for Parliament as a Liberal simply because the opportunity presents itself), his social position is so untenable that violence – in the form of suicide, by throwing himself before a train – becomes his only option. Self-interested and rapacious motives drive him to defy social norms, as they do George but, as an outsider, Lopez also works hard to fit in with the English society that mistrusts him. All of these men, unable to adapt themselves to the modern order, recur to violence and are ejected from the social world.[4]

Contrasting with the men who go beyond the pale of social acceptability are those who flirt with the extremes but ultimately draw back into a world of social norms. Such is Lord Chiltern, Phineas's rival for Violet Effingham in *Phineas Finn*, who seems at first like another George Vavasor, stepping beyond the bounds of upper-class propriety with both men and women by threatening violence. As with George, Lord Chiltern's violence is often characterized in sexual terms. Chiltern goes so far as to duel with Phineas, but he is eventually tamed into marriage, and he appears in subsequent volumes as a relatively ordinary figure in the society.[5] Chiltern's reformation condenses Trollope's larger point about violence: it belongs to an obsolete social order that has been superseded by a more bureaucratic, and implicitly feminine, modern age, where rivalries and competitions are carried out in the relatively displaced and disembodied form of consent to social regulations. The difference between Lady Glencora's lover and her husband manifests the contrast: while Burgo attempts to woo her physically and elope with her even after her marriage (implicitly relying on a form of male violence), Palliser unconsciously watches over her through the agency of his two "duennas" (Mrs. Marsham and Mr. Bott), gently guiding her back home without deigning to confront her over her contemplated adultery. The mild-mannered modern politician triumphs – without even seeming to try – over the superannuated chivalric rake. Modernity itself is shown to be a form of flexible accommodation, a way of preserving the social order, in domestic affairs as in Parliament. In its professionalized, disinterested repudiation of male violence, this modern world not only incorporates women as agents but itself derives from a feminized model of consent, adjustment, and propriety.

While modern masculinity moves beyond physical violence, and thus becomes a little more feminine, the modern woman, in attempting to negotiate the rules, endures an often wrenching form of psychic violence, and she too must learn to adapt herself to survive. Trollope's novels frequently focus on the plight of young women choosing among suitors; like the men, in both their domestic and political pursuits, the women strive to balance liberal and conservative drives. Those whose marital aims stray beyond their own class, nation, or status group – such as Lucy Morris, Violet Effingham, and Isabel Boncassen – must either adjust their own desires or reform the social and familial expectations they encounter. The conflict between an impulse to rebel and a wish to conform generates a psychological phenomenon in women of a certain class and temperament that Trollope dubs the "perverseness of obstinacy" (*CYFH* ch. 74). These women, notably Alice Vavasor and Emily Wharton, follow their hearts and make an initial bad choice for a man who lies outside the norms of propriety; having finally, through the repudiation or death of the man, moved beyond that choice and been offered a second chance, such heroines are paralyzed for a long time by their adherence to an idea of their own error. Misapprehending the dictates of "the world" in the first place, by choosing an inappropriate man (George Vavasor and Ferdinand Lopez, respectively), they misconstrue its rules all over again once they are released: they hold themselves to an impossible standard of purity, feeling permanently debarred from the social integration offered by the well-to-do, well-approved-of suitors (John Grey and Arthur Fletcher). As Alice finally consents to marry John Grey after many hundreds of pages of equivocation, Trollope writes:

> Of course she had no choice but to yield. He, possessed of power and force infinitely greater than hers, had left her no alternative but to be happy. But there still clung to her what I fear we must call a perverseness of obstinacy, a desire to maintain the resolution she had made, – a wish that she might be allowed to undergo the punishment she had deserved. She was as a prisoner who would fain cling to his prison after pardon has reached him, because he is conscious that the pardon is undeserved ... He was so imperious in his tranquillity, he argued his question of such love with a manifest preponderance of right on his side, that she had always felt that to yield to him would be to confess the omnipotence of his power. (*CYFH* ch. 74)

In both cases, the women feel themselves stained by their waywardness and inadequate to the men who court them. Such a conundrum could be read either as a misogynistic representation of female masochism or as a proto-feminist attempt to resist patriarchal demands. In either case, it registers as a fundamental failure to negotiate between individual impulse (a "feeling of rebellion") and socially managed exigencies ("imperious in [its] tranquillity... with a manifest preponderance of right"). Even when their desires conform to expectations, they fail to adopt the flexible approach necessary to return to the fold of sociality.

Such difficulties are compounded and, in part, explained by economic circumstances. George Vavasor and Lopez both pursue the heroines at least in part for their fortunes; the second suitors, Grey and Fletcher, are both wealthy providers for their wives. The distinction is even more evident in the histories of the financially independent widows in several novels (Aunt Greenow, Madame Max Goesler, and Lizzie Eustace), who can afford to be less conventional in their choice of second husbands. The struggle between independence and conformity loses its urgency when family fortunes and class propriety are not at stake, as is the case for these three widows. By contrast, the "tragic" fate of women without fortune who opt out or miss out on the chance for marriage (often through psychological unsuitability) provides a female equivalent to the men who, by virtue of their violent predilections, must be cast out from the stories. Such are the fates of Kate Vavasor, Lucinda Roanoke, and Mabel Grex, who all cling to their independence so fiercely as ultimately to wind up outside the social world, where they count for nothing.

Just as men and women have different kinds of access both to political power and to ideas about the reform and preservation of the social order, so too do characters of different generations. Or so, at any rate, does the final volume of the series, *The Duke's Children* (1879), suggest. In nearly every case in the prior novels, parents – if they are present at all – are weak and ineffectual. (In fact, part of the difficulty for Alice and Emily is that their widowed fathers have so little initial interest in their daughters' marital fates.) Up until the last volume, almost all the stories take the point of view of the younger generation; when parents and elders do appear, they seem outdated if not absurd. Minimizing the attention given to the older generations would seem to emphasize change over continuity. The shift in focus in the last volume, to the parent's perspective on his children's political and marital disobedience, suggests a loosening (if hardly an abandonment) of the rules governing aristocratic propriety. The younger generation's superficially exogamous marriages (in terms of class, rank, and nationality) at the end of *The Duke's Children* imply that an infusion of new blood will revitalize the old order.[6] As a number of critics have noted, however, the notion of a progressive development in the attitudes of the ruling class is at best minimal, at worst merely a cover for regressive retrenchment.[7] Both of the objectionable spouses (Isabel Boncassen and Frank Tregear) are ultimately forces for continuity, not change – she in her eagerness to submit to masculine prerogatives and English aristocratic decorum (by comparison with the fickleness and independence of her rival, Mabel Grex), he in his advocacy of Conservatism and the stability of the class system. The Duke's hopes for his children's marriages may be thwarted, but only because the younger generation wishes to remake itself in his image – as aristocrats who serve in Parliament. Ironically, one form that Lord Silverbridge's rebellion against his father takes is in recanting the family tradition of Liberal party membership: here is an oedipal rivalry in the explicit form of Conservatism (and even this parodic type of protest is finally overthrown by the novel's end).

The Duke's Children, in its attempt at highlighting change, shows the Palliser world's essential stability, suggesting that the balance between the principles of liberalism and conservatism, independence and conformity, has tilted toward the latter from the start. The seductiveness of Trollope's world lies in its ability to make repetition look like novelty, conservation like change. The fantasy of the novel-without-end, which the series' massive form sponsors, itself replicates this theme: there will, it seems, always be another novel, always another story of children rebelling against their parents, and of political parties handing off power to each other. It will always look a little different; it will always be pretty much the same. And it will go on and on. Such is an "advanced conservative Liberal" idea of the novel, as well as of politics. It is telling that the series ends, not with the rebellion of the children, but with the comfort of the parents.

NOTES

1 Roland Barthes, "La critique Ni-ni," *Mythologies* (Paris: Seuil, 1957); *Mythologies*, trans. Annette Lavers (New York: Hill and Wang, 1972), "Neither-Nor Criticism," pp. 81–83.

2 John Halperin, in *Trollope and Politics: A Study of the Pallisers and Others* (London: Macmillan, 1977), notes: "Until [Trollope's] last years he was an outspoken Liberal and an instinctive foe of the Conservative party and of what he conceived its few principles to be. This does not mean that Trollope, in today's terminology, could be described accurately as 'liberal.' On the contrary – though he was certainly 'advanced' on some issues, his was essentially a conservative temperament. The Liberal party of the time was no more 'liberal' than the Conservative party. Indeed, the oldest great landowning families in mid-Victorian England were Whigs; and the most radical measures of the nineteenth century were enacted by Tory ministries" (pp. 9–10).

3 In the world of professional politics, Monk and Turnbull are Radicals; the only sustained representation of radical working-class political agitation is in the account of the mob that gathers around Turnbull's carriage to support the secret ballot in chapter 24 of *Phineas Finn*. Arthur Pollard discusses the Duke of St. Bungay as the representative of the most inflexible, established tradition of Whig oligarchy in *Trollope's Political Novels* (Hull: University of Hull, 1968), pp. 17–18.

4 One more figure in this lineage might be Joseph Emilius, another villainous foreigner who originates in the satiric world of *The Eustace Diamonds* and lives mostly outside the upper-class social milieu of the other novels; his signal act of violence is to commit murder in a central plot event of *Phineas Redux*.

5 Some critics have suggested that Chiltern's occupation as Master of the Brake Hounds may serve to sublimate his violent impulses; see Priscilla L. Walton, *Patriarchal Desire and Victorian Discourse: A Lacanian Reading of Anthony Trollope's Palliser Novels* (Toronto: University of Toronto Press, 1995), pp. 98–99, relying in part on Robert Polhemus, *The Changing World of Anthony Trollope* (Berkeley: University of California Press, 1968).

6 That this new blood is itself charged with a progressive spirit of republican meritocracy is hinted in Lord Silverbridge's choice of the American Isabel Boncassen. Her father says to him, "If the Duke of Omnium will tell us that she would be safe as your wife, – safe from the contempt of those around her, – you shall have her. And I shall rejoice to give her to you, – not because you are Lord Silverbridge, not because of your rank and wealth; but because you are – that individual human being whom I now hold by the hand" (*DC* ch. 70).

7 Walton reviews prior scholarship on this topic; she argues, in part, "The order that is restored, here, does not change or alter the status quo . . . To 'open' the structure to include Tregear is to reaffirm the very values his inclusion appears to place in jeopardy. And the rebellious female characters are shown to be suppressed and subdued as a result of these two marriages" (*Patriarchal Desire*, p. 141).

5

ROBERT TRACY

Trollope redux: the later novels

Late in 1859, Trollope left Ireland, where he had lived for eighteen years, and settled near London. He had enjoyed Ireland, but "had often sighed to return to England ... and with some little difficulty got myself appointed to the Eastern [Postal] District of England." His Irish years had made him almost an outsider to English life, and perhaps explain the nostalgic mood of *The Warden* and *Barchester Towers* as their author imagined the placid "dear county" from an Ireland resentful of British rule and, in the late forties, undergoing the agonies of the Great Famine (*A* ch. 8). Phineas Finn, newly elected to Parliament for an Irish constituency, is "very quick to learn" the customs and rituals of Parliament (*PF* ch. 9), perhaps recalling Trollope's own self-conscious re-entry into English life, and his determination to understand how the political and social worlds of London interacted, the subject matter of much of his future work. Marginalized in childhood, and in his Irish exile, he was now uniquely prepared to examine English society with the fascination of an outsider and a new self-confidence as an insider. Approaching his fifth decade, Trollope would become a more inclusive and a more ambitious novelist, in ways that make it critically useful to distinguish earlier and later categories of his fiction.

He had already published nine of his forty-seven novels. Three were failures, but the success of *The Warden, Barchester Towers*, and *Doctor Thorne* established him as a literary presence. On January 1, 1860 *Framley Parsonage*, Trollope's first novel to be published serially, began to appear in Thackeray's *Cornhill Magazine*, and he attended his first *Cornhill* dinner, recognition that he belonged in contemporary literary society. For a naturally gregarious and competitive man, this was of great importance. He believed "that a man who could write books ought not to live in Ireland,– ought to live within the reach of the publishers, the clubs, and the dinner parties of the metropolis" (*A* ch. 8). During the next few years he was elected to the Cosmopolitan and Garrick clubs, then to the Athenaeum, further evidence that he had achieved the boyhood goal he would record in his *Autobiography*, to be welcomed among those who had scorned him at Harrow and Winchester. In December 1864, he was among the founders of the *Fortnightly Review*, intended as a forum for serious critical discussion of literary and social issues. Later he founded and edited (1867–70) *St. Paul's*, a Liberal journal. The Trollope of the 1860s became a major participant in contemporary literary activity, increasingly more ambitious in his aims and more confident in his ability to accomplish them. Well before the end of the decade he was recognized, along with Dickens, Thackeray, and George Eliot as one of the major English novelists.

With his regular habits of composition, Trollope quickly adapted to serial publication, often in *Cornhill*, the *Fortnightly*, or *St. Paul's*, or in weekly or monthly parts. By 1867, with writing taking more of his time, he was earning enough from his fiction to sacrifice £500 of his future annual pension by resigning prematurely from the Post Office after thirty-three years. A year later he stood unsuccessfully for Parliament as a Liberal candidate.

These literary and extra-literary activities in the 1860s suggest that Trollope was restless despite his success, a state of mind he implies and almost regrets in his farewell to Barset in *The Last Chronicle of Barset* (1867). In *An Autobiography* he describes overhearing two clergymen, each reading an installment of a Trollope serial, condemning his use of certain characters from novel to novel. They were especially tired of Mrs. Proudie. Trollope assured them he would "'kill her before the week is over,'" and did so in an unexpectedly moving scene (*A* ch. 15). But in fact no novel featuring Mrs. Proudie was appearing while he was writing *The Last Chronicle*. The anecdote seems to dramatize and justify his own eagerness to try something new.

The later novels assert a willingness to experiment with new themes and settings. *Miss Mackenzie* (1865) deliberately omits an essential element of Victorian fiction, a love interest, and allows the spinster-heroine – she is thirty-five – to feel some sexual excitement. In *Nina Balatka* (1867), set in Prague, the families of Catholic Nina and her Jewish lover struggle to prevent a mixed marriage. The Nuremburg heroine of *Linda Tressel* (1868) is loved and cherished but destroyed by the aunt who guards her too rigidly. Trollope further experimented by publishing both novels anonymously, to find out if his books sold only because he was already popular. *He Knew He Was Right* (1869) is an extended study in obsessive jealousy, as Louis Trevelyan's mistrust of his wife brings him to madness. *Harry Heathcote of Gangoil* (1874) draws on some of Fred Trollope's experiences running a sheep ranch in New South Wales, and depicts the lawlessness and isolation of the Australian "outback." *John Caldigate*

(1879), partly set in the Australian gold fields, also about religious opposition to a marriage, introduces accusations of bigamy that send the hero to prison for a time, a painstaking amateur detective, and other elements reminiscent of Mrs. Braddon's sensational fiction. *The Fixed Period* (1882) imagines an English-speaking republic in the South Pacific around 1980, where by law any citizen who reaches the age of sixty-eight (Trollope was sixty-seven) must be painlessly executed, as a way of putting property into younger, more vigorous hands. Steam bicycles travel three miles in seven minutes, and cricket is played with a "steam bowler" (*FixP* ch. 4). The protagonist of *Mr. Scarborough's Family* (1883) is bedridden throughout the novel, but manipulates his two sons and his lawyer to control which son will inherit his estate. Altering texts to control "reality," he is a study in the similarities between the plotting of a novelist and that of an unscrupulous schemer.

The unconventional settings and characters of these novels suggest Trollope's creative restlessness and his readiness to introduce new settings and character types in the second half of his career. But most of them remain comparatively unpopular in the Trollope canon, unlike those novels of English life that he produced in tandem with them during the same period: *Orley Farm* (1862), the Palliser series (1864–80), *The Belton Estate* (1866), *The Claverings* (1867), *The Vicar of Bullhampton* (1870), *The Way We Live Now* (1875), *The American Senator* (1877). Trollope's more successful experiments retained English setting and characters but he developed new fictional techniques, a greater ease in telling his stories, and a readiness to deal with larger and perhaps more personal issues.

Of the five Trollope novels Michael Sadleir considered "faultless (in a technical sense)" *Doctor Thorne, The Claverings, The Belton Estate, Sir Harry Hotspur of Humblethwaite*, and *Dr. Wortle's School* (Sadleir 375), only *Doctor Thorne* (1858) was written before Trollope resettled in England. Novels written after that show an increasing skill and confidence. In *The Last Chronicle of Barset*, the novel that marks his transition from a good novelist to a great one, he organizes several parallel and interrelated plots to present Victorian society in all its moral and political complexity. Trollope's farewell to Barset on the last page of *The Last Chronicle* recognizes that the "dear county" he had so vividly realized was no longer believable. He had carefully kept Barset free of factories, a resentful working class, and other manifestations of the contemporary world. In the sixties more dangerous forces were abroad than the reforming zeal of John Bold and the comic dislocations represented by Mrs. Proudie and Mr. Slope, greater evils than the clerical appetite for lucrative appointments with sketchy duties, greater issues than the need for family approval before Frank Gresham and Lord Lufton could marry women they love.

Trollope said farewell to Barset because he had ceased to be interested in the kind of novel the Barset series represents. Before writing *The Last Chronicle*, he began his second cycle of sequential novels with *Can You Forgive Her?* (1864), the first of the "Palliser" or "Parliamentary" novels that combine the marital history of Plantagenet Palliser and his wife, Lady Glencora, with the intricacies of parliamentary politics and the assumptions that govern society. The centrality of the Palliser cycle to Trollope's later work, and its carefully devised unities and analogous use of multiple plots, invite us to consider it a single extended work of fiction, lavishly displaying Trollope's mature skill and preoccupations. I have chosen to concentrate on this sequential text to discuss Trollope's later fiction. Intensely private in its examination of the Palliser marriage, panoramic in its portrayal of public life, the Palliser cycle is Trollope's own Gatherum Castle, perhaps too vast, too extravagant, sometimes uncomfortable, but an explicit claim: this novelist has changed the literary landscape, he cannot be ignored. Many of its major episodes, especially those involving the interconnections of money, love, and rank, have frequent analogues elsewhere in his later novels. The reappearances of Senator Gotobed (*The American Senator*) and Dolly Longestaffe (*The Way We Live Now*) in *The Duke's Children*, of Sir Damask and Lady Monogram (*The Way We Live Now*) in *The Prime Minister*, connect these novels to the Palliser cycle and suggest that Trollope's characters all move in a contiguous world, where parliamentary politics and high society interact.

The Palliser cycle is the ultimate serial novel in the great era of serial fiction. In *Can You Forgive Her?*, *Phineas Finn* (1869), *The Eustace Diamonds* (1872), *Phineas Redux* (1874), *The Prime Minister* (1876), and *The Duke's Children* (1880), Trollope examines the marriage of Plantagenet Palliser and Lady Glencora. Palliser's high-minded but plodding devotion to duty contrasts with Glencora's vivacity and impulsiveness, her occasional imprudence. Their uneasy relationship embodies a Victorian tension between civilization and its discontents. Trollope developed and sustained this episodic but unified chronicle of a twenty-five year marriage over sixteen years of his own career: a single vast work of fiction with individual novels as its chapters or serial parts. Committed to "the necessity of progression in character... how this woman would act when this or that event had passed over her head, or how that man would carry himself when his youth had become manhood, or his manhood declined to old age" (*A* ch. 17), he made time, real and fictional, a central element in his story.

The Palliser cycle develops like those long stories that Trollope told himself as a boy, carrying them on

> For weeks, for months ... from year to year ... binding myself down to certain laws, to certain proportions, and proprieties, and unities. Nothing impossible

was ever introduced ... I was myself, of course, my own hero. Such is a necessity of castle-building. But I never became a king, or a duke,– much less when my height and personal appearance were fixed could I be an Antinous, or six feet high ... But I was a very clever person, and beautiful young women used to be fond of me. And I strove to be kind of heart, and open of hand, and noble in thought, despising mean things.   (*A* ch. 3)

Plantagenet Palliser, rising Liberal politician, heir to the Duke of Omnium's title and fortune, plays an inglorious part in *The Small House at Allington* (1864), where he is briefly infatuated with another man's wife. Though Glencora is already engaged and powerfully attracted to the "beautiful, well-born, and utterly worthless" Burgo Fitzgerald (*A* ch. 10), "very fond of brandy ... said to be deep in every vice" (*SHA* ch. 55), the Duke and her guardians decide that she and Palliser will marry, and they do. "She had received a great wrong,– having been made, when little more than a child, to marry a man for whom she cared nothing," Trollope declares; "when, however, though she was little more than a child, her love had been given elsewhere. She had very heavy troubles, but they did not overcome her" (*A* ch. 10). This imposed marriage reverberates throughout the cycle, shaping the Pallisers' life together, and kept before us in various analogues.

In *Can You Forgive Her?* Palliser and Glencora have been married for a year and a half. Palliser is intelligent, ambitious, determined to use political power to make things better, but he is awkward in social situations, often unable to express his feelings, and without humor. His face is "almost insignificant" (*CYFH* ch. 22), and he is "very dull. He rather prided himself on being dull ... dull as a statesman, he was more dull in private life" (*CYFH* ch. 24). He has been told that Glencora was engaged to Burgo Fitzgerald, but "thought little about it, and by no means understood her when she said to him, with all the impressiveness which she could throw into the words, 'You must know that I have really loved him.' 'You must love me now,' he had replied with a smile; and then, as regarded his mind, the thing was over" (*CYFH* ch. 24). It is not.

Glencora is not yet twenty-one. She is lively, outspoken, spontaneous, sometimes indiscreet, and completely uninterested in the politics that absorb Palliser. Fitzgerald reappears, and urges her to come away with him. She knows this will disgrace her and he will waste her fortune, but she is sick with love for him, and frustrated desire. When Palliser kisses her "it was the embrace of a brother rather than of a lover or a husband. Lady Glencora, with her full woman's nature, understood this thoroughly, and appreciated by instinct the true bearing of every touch from his hand" (*CYFH* ch. 42). Trollope provides her with a *confidante*, Alice Vavasor, with whom she can discuss her frustrations and fears. Had it been possible, she would have eloped with Fitzgerald before her marriage:

> I should have gone with him then, and all this icy coldness would have been prevented ... it is better to have a false husband than to be a false wife ... it has been all false throughout. I never loved [Palliser]. They browbeat me and frightened me till I did as I was told; – and now;– what am I now ?... When I went to him at the altar, I knew that I did not love the man that was to be my husband. But him, – Burgo,– I love him with all my heart and soul. I could stoop at his feet and clean his shoes for him, and think it no disgrace! ... every hour of every day and of every night,– I am thinking of the man I love ... I am always talking to Burgo in my thoughts; and he listens to me – I dream that his arm is round me – ... I loathe myself, and I loathe the thing that I am thinking of. (*CYFH* ch. 27)

Glencora delivers this impassioned speech in the romantic setting of the Matching Priory ruins by moonlight – we are almost in *Lucia di Lammermoor* territory. Glencora is a new type of Trollope heroine, who responds to a lover sexually, and powerfully so. In 1867, the *Spectator* would praise Trollope for insisting "that the mind, the will, can regulate the affections." The woman who does not "regulate" her affections loses "true delicacy" and can be disgraced by "the gathering of mean intrigues and meaner intriguers round her."[1] In inventing Glencora, he questioned this contemporary belief. Glencora does attract mean intriguers throughout the Palliser cycle, and she never completely regulates her affections. After she scandalizes society by boldly waltzing with Burgo – he has a carriage waiting nearby and tickets for the Continent – she confesses to Palliser: "I do love Burgo Fitzgerald. I do! I do! I do! How can I help loving him? Have I not loved him from the first,– before I had seen you ... last night, I had almost made up my mind ... that I must go away with him and hide myself ... I would kill myself if I dared." "I do love you," Palliser unexpectedly responds. "Will you try to love me?" (*CYFH* ch. 58).

Glencora is persuaded "partly by her own sense of right and wrong," Trollope tells us, "and partly by the genuine nobility of her husband's conduct, to attach herself to him after a certain fashion" (*A* ch. 10). He gives up his chance to be Chancellor of the Exchequer to take her abroad and try to save their marriage. They do save it, "after a certain fashion." Both develop within it, Palliser to become Prime Minister, Glencora to become a great political hostess and a social arbiter. "She had attained this position for herself by a mixture of beauty, rank, wealth, and courage," Trollope remarks; "but the courage had, of the four, been her greatest mainstay" (*ED* ch. 80). Both feel that they have been cheated of love and passion. The marriage has been an arrangement, an acceptance of society's rules, a commitment, but they feel they have missed something.

Throughout the cycle Palliser and Lady Glencora move amid a dance of couples who re-enact variations on their story, introducing other women who prefer the "wild man" (sometimes merely poor, and so an imprudent choice) but eventually accept "the worthy man." In *Can You Forgive Her?* Alice Vavasor, like Glencora, must choose between a dark reckless cousin, almost Burgo's double, who describes himself as the "brandy" she really craves rather than the "milk diet" his worthy rival represents (*CYFH* ch. 5). Like Glencora, Alice ultimately makes the prudent choice. In a comic parallel plot, the Widow Greenow opts for "the more scampish of two selfish suitors" because he offers "a little romance" (*A* ch. 10; *CYFH* ch. 64).

Parallels to the story of Glencora and Palliser persist throughout the cycle, continually reminding us of their initial difficulties and the mutual sacrifices and complex financial interests on which their marriage rests. Phineas Finn, Irish, poor, but hardly wild, needs a rich wife if he is to have a parliamentary career. Love cannot be his only criterion, Lady Laura Standish declares, in an oblique comment on Glencora and on herself: "Even in a woman passion such as that is evidence of weakness, and not of strength" (*PF* ch. 71). Laura rejects Phineas for the prudent choice, only to find she has married a gloomy and jealous introvert. Violet Effingham repeatedly refuses her wild man but eventually accepts and tames him. When Phineas makes the hard but right choice on a parliamentary vote, he knows that he is sacrificing his political career, as Palliser risks his by declining office to save his marriage. Phineas quietly returns to Ireland and marries plain Mary Jones.

Lizzie Eustace, a rich young widow in *The Eustace Diamonds*, has both a "worthy" suitor and a "Corsair," but her careless way with the truth, even under oath, frightens them off. Glencora characteristically defends Lizzie against criticism, "instigated, perhaps, by a feeling that any woman in society who was capable of doing anything extraordinary ought to be defended"(*ED* ch. 47), and by Burgo's legacy, her persistent weakness for adventurers. Lizzie, Glencora's tawdry analogue, admires her as "my beau-ideal of what a woman should be – disinterested, full of spirit, affectionate, with a dash of romance about her" (*ED* ch. 62).

Returning to London and Parliament as a widower in *Phineas Redux*, Phineas undergoes an emotional and moral ordeal as intense as Glencora's agonies over Burgo Fitzgerald. Accused of murder, imprisoned while awaiting trial, he broods over his ambitions and where they have brought him. Exonerated, he finds it difficult to take up life again, and begins to doubt the value of political participation. Phineas has been altered by his experiences. No longer the brash, optimistic young man who idealized Parliament, he has come with Trollope to understand better how things work. Lady Laura reappears, to repent of rejecting Phineas and admit her "strong, unalterable, unquenchable love for" him (*PR* ch. 12), but he marries Madame Max Goesler, whose wealth will support his parliamentary career.

The Prime Minister is nominally about Palliser as head of a coalition government, essentially about Glencora's eagerness to play a political role. "I fear I shall never make you a politician," he had said to her, early in their marriage, a phrase Trollope hoped readers of *The Prime Minister* would remember (*CYFH* ch. 42). Now she becomes enthusiastically political. "I'd listen to every debate in the House myself, to have Plantagenet Prime Minister," she proclaims (*PM* ch. 6); "They should have made me Prime Minister" (*PM* ch. 56). At times she seems to think they have.

For Palliser and Glencora the "domestic circumstance" that caused him to decline office long ago still haunts their marriage (*PM* ch. 6). Society remembers "a queer story once ... some lover she had before she was married. She went off to Switzerland ... Palliser ... followed her very soon and it all came right" (*PM* ch. 10). Trollope keeps the rocky start of the marriage before us by another analogue. Glencora is drawn to Ferdinand Lopez, another dark adventurer, because he reminds her of Fitzgerald. She encourages him to marry Emily Wharton for her money (*PM* ch. 24), and disobeys Palliser by backing him in an election, provoking an embarrassing press campaign against the Pallisers. Ruined politically and financially, Lopez commits suicide, and an abashed Glencora convinces Emily to marry the worthy man she had earlier spurned.

"It was my study that" Plantagenet Palliser, Duke of Omnium and his wife, "as they grew in years, should encounter the changes which come upon us all," Trollope tells us in *An Autobiography*:

> The Duchess of Omnium, when she is playing the part of Prime Minister's wife, is the same woman as that Lady Glencora who almost longs to go off with Burgo Fitzgerald, but yet knows that she will never do so; and the Prime Minister Duke, with his wounded pride and sore spirit, is he who, for his wife's sake, left power and place when they were first offered to him;– but they have undergone the changes which a life so stirring as theirs would naturally produce. To do all this thoroughly was in my heart from first to last; but I do not know that the game has been worth the candle. (*A* ch. 10)

We may wonder if Trollope, writing Glencora's agonized confession amid the ruins of Matching Priory in 1863–64, was quite as sure that she "knows she will never" go off with Fitzgerald as he was when he recalled the scene in *An Autobiography* eleven years later.

Trollope anticipated Proust in examining how time and social change affect his characters, yet leaves them essentially the same. He wondered if any reader would perceive how carefully he had developed his leading characters over the entire Palliser cycle, how he keeps their pasts continually before us, how they grow and alter from novel to novel, yet remain unmistakably the same. "Who will even know that they should be so read?" he asks. It is a rare moment of self-doubt, but he adds, "in the performance of the work I had much gratification . . . I look upon this string of characters . . . as the best work of my life . . . I think that Plantagenet Palliser stands more firmly on the ground than any other personage I have created" (*A* ch. 10).

Glencora is dead at the beginning of *The Duke's Children*, but Trollope continues his ambitious fiction to show us Palliser as a widower, how the compromises that had kept the couple together always had limits, and how Burgo Fitzgerald always made their marriage a triangle. Palliser feels utterly alone. "There had been no other human soul to whom he could open himself," he realizes; "He had so habituated himself to devote his mind and his heart to the service of his country, that he had almost risen above or sunk below humanity. But she, who had been essentially human, had been a link between him and the world" (*DC* ch. 1).

Now he must cope with three children, temperamentally more hers than his. Lord Silverbridge, their eldest son, has already got into "scrapes" and been sent down from Oxford. Glencora had deplored the scrapes, "but with the spirit that produced the scrapes she fully sympathized. The father disliked the spirit almost worse than the results" (*DC* ch. 1). Soon Silverbridge loses £70,000 through shady racetrack associates. He falls in love with Isabel Boncassen, unsuitable because she is American, whose grandfather was once a laborer in New York.

Before her death, Glencora had encouraged their daughter Mary's engagement to Frank Tregear, who is neither rich nor titled. "It is quite impossible," Palliser declares when he learns about it. "You must conquer your love. It is disgraceful and must be conquered" (*DC* ch. 8). But Mary will not repeat her mother's sacrifice, and refuses to give up her lover, this time successfully. She has Palliser's "cool determination" together with Glencora's "hot-headed obstinacy" (*DC* ch. 24).

All the tensions that have existed throughout the marriage re-emerge. Palliser continually sees analogies to Glencora's early infatuation in the inappropriate choices his children have made. In Glencora's encouragement of Mary's "most pernicious courtship" he recognizes "a repetition of that romantic folly by which she had so nearly brought herself to shipwreck in her own early life" (*DC* ch. 5). Having located a suitable husband for Mary, "he would endeavor to console himself with remembering the past success of a similar transaction. He thought of his own first interview with his wife. 'You have heard,' he had said, 'what our friends wish.' She had pouted her lips, and when gently pressed, had at last muttered, with her shoulder turned to him, that she supposed it was to be so" (*DC* ch. 46). Glencora may have told her own story to Mary, perhaps to Silverbridge (*DC* ch. 2, 14). In encouraging Mary's engagement to Tregear, Glencora does not just support her daughter's choice. Tregear "put her in mind of another man on whom her eyes had once loved to dwell. He was dark, with hair that was almost black" (*DC* ch. 3). Palliser's battle is with Glencora, not their children.

Palliser is particularly outraged because Tregear – a penniless man in search of a rich wife, a Conservative, and resembling Burgo Fitzgerald – has tainted Mary by attracting her love: "When this foolish passion of hers should have been stamped out, [she] could never be the pure, the bright, the unsullied, unsoiled thing, of the possession of which he had thought so much." Fathers sometimes find it difficult to surrender a daughter to a husband. Palliser's vocabulary here – *pure, unsullied, unsoiled* – is less about Mary than about his resentment that he was not Glencora's first love:

> had she not in the same way loved a Tregear, or worse than a Tregear, in her early days? . . . had he not been feeling all his days, that Fate had robbed him of the sweetest joy that is given to man, in that she had not come to him loving him with that early spring of love, as she had loved that poor ne'er-do-well? How infinite had been his regrets . . . Fortune had been unjust to him because he had been robbed of that . . . He had felt it for years. Dear as she had been, she had not been quite what she should have been but for that. And now this girl of his, who was so much dearer to him than anything else left to him, was doing exactly as her mother had done . . . [Tregear] might be made to vanish as that other young man had vanished. But the fact that he had been there, cherished in the girl's heart,– that could not be stamped out. (*DC* ch. 7)

This is an astonishing passage, in its intensity, in the depth of Palliser's resentment, and in the sudden unexpected light it sends down the long vista of the Palliser marriage. He has transferred an obsession from Glencora to Mary. This man, so controlled, so sensible, is deeply romantic. He has been inwardly nursing a grievance all these years. At the end of the Palliser cycle, Trollope invites us to re-examine all that we have come to assume about the Palliser marriage, and about Palliser's sacrifice to preserve it and Glencora's determination to "go straight" so long ago. "Palliser is thoroughly true to her," concludes Trollope in *An Autobiography*; Glencora "is imperfectly true to him" (*A* ch. 10).

Like Trollope, Palliser and Glencora have told themselves a story about themselves, and sustained it for weeks, months, years. In Glencora's story she has made a great sacrifice. Having done so, she runs no risks when she takes up a handsome dark young man who needs a patroness. Plantagenet tells himself a story in which Glencora has never completely obeyed that "forsaking all others" ordained by the marriage service. She has taken up dark adventurers. He sees her encouragement of Tregear and Mary almost as dishonoring him. Each remembers their life together in a different way.

Palliser eventually consents to Mary's marriage with Tregear, and Silver-bridge's with the American girl. As he stands at the altar giving Mary away, he seems a man "who now took special joy in the happiness of his children, – who was thoroughly contented to see them marry after their own hearts. And yet, as he stood there on the altar steps giving his daughter to that new son and looking first at his girl, and then at his married son, he was reminding himself of all that he had suffered" (*DC* ch. 69). He will re-enter politics, but the old zest is gone. And the old grief remains.

Though the "Palliser" cycle is primarily a detailed and extended study of a marriage, it also selectively examines contemporary political issues: extending the franchise, tenant rights in Ireland, disestablishing of the Church, Irish Home Rule. Trollope drew recognizable portraits of the two rival giants of the day, Disraeli (Mr. Daubeny) and Gladstone (Mr. Gresham), and of such lesser lights as Lord Derby (Lord De Terrier) and Lord Palmerston (Lord Brock). He despised Disraeli, but Gladstone, who resembles Palliser in his high sense of duty and his lack of humor, was one of his political heroes until 1882, when he wrote *The Landleaguers* to attack Gladstone's Irish policies. Though Trollope tried and failed to be elected to Parliament in 1868, the Palliser cycle allowed him to express "my political and social convictions" (*A* ch. 10). He had received "a running order ... for a seat in the gallery ... for a couple of months" from the Speaker to study the procedures of the House of Commons for the Palliser cycle (*A* ch. 17). Readers who have served in Parliament have testified to the accuracy of his parliamentary types and procedures, his ability to convey in certain scenes the feel of the House during a great debate or a sudden crisis.[2]

Disraeli in *Sybil*, Dickens in *Bleak House, Hard Times*, and *Little Dorrit*, and Mrs. Gaskell in *North and South* had established the "condition of England" novel as a genre, combining a melodramatic plot with a critique of how England was governed in an age when a newly industrialized society could compare its efficient machines to the antiquated machinery of government. Trollope was not much interested in the poor or in efforts to improve their lot. He was suspicious of reformers' schemes for human or social betterment, believing that change should come about gradually, step by step. This is essentially the political creed of Plantagenet Palliser, Trollope's idealized self-portrait.

Trollope's political novels do not argue for any particular change or reform, but instead show us how England is really governed, by an implicit agreement among political leaders that reform is to come slowly. Conservative or Liberal, their responsibility is to maintain order. The novels are about life at the top, among the great nobles who still sometimes determine who sits in Parliament from constituencies where they are major landowners, despite the Reform Bills of 1832 and 1867: at twenty-two, Silverbridge is enthusiastically elected for a family seat. Palliser believes in equality to come, but maintains his own family's privileges now.

By focusing on the Palliser cycle as Trollope's most varied and sustained work, and treating its novels as parts of that work rather than independent achievements, I have left little room for *The Way We Live Now*, Trollope's most successful application of the panoramic method in a single novel. Melmotte, the "Napoleon of Finance," has a financial empire only on paper. He presides over an orgy of speculation, extended by analogy into the worthless books Lady Carbury writes, and the worthless IOUs young aristocrats circulate at their club. Trollope's concern is with the decay of public and political morality that makes a Melmotte possible, but he adds a new element: there is a dangerous willingness to admire such a man because he believes himself above the law. Trollope, like Dostoyevsky's Raskolnikov, had read Napoleon III's *Histoire de Jules Cesar* (1865–66), which argued that great men are not bound by moral laws. We know the effect of this doctrine on Raskolnikov; Trollope believed "that no country can really thrive under a Caesar."[3]

In one of the great set pieces of the book, Melmotte, as a representative English merchant and Member of Parliament, hosts a banquet for the Emperor of China. Trollope draws our attention to the awful isolation of the Emperor, a stranger in a strange land, and compares it to Melmotte's isolation. Trollope saw the social isolation that destroyed his father and blighted his own childhood as the greatest evil. When we remember that he confers a certain isolation on Palliser and Glencora, each of them alone in their resentments, we can recognize how constant a theme isolation is in the later novels, and how it lies in wait amid the bustling panorama that is Trollopian society. Robert Kennedy's descent into madness, the even bleaker descent of Louis Trevelyan (*He Knew He Was Right*), and glimpses of other isolated or obsessive characters suggest how Trollope associated brooding over real or imagined injuries with a self-destructive tendency.

Aware of her own sacrifice, Glencora rescues Emily Wharton from the perpetual widowhood to which she has pledged herself. Palliser fears that

Mary will die of grief if he isolates her from Tregear, as he believes his duty demands. Sir Harry Hotspur determines to reunite the family estate and title by marrying his daughter to his nephew, but the daughter pines away when the heir's worthlessness is revealed, and the estates go to a distant relative. Indefer Jones loves his niece and respects her suitor, but believes his duty is to leave family property to one who bears the family surname; in *Cousin Henry* (1879), Henry Jones duly inherits. But when Henry finds a later will, he cannot bear to leave the room where it is hidden, and finally, half mad with fear, he gives up the secret. For these novels of obsession Trollope avoided the panoramic method. They usually depend on isolating the protagonist and watching intently as he or she deteriorates. Contrasting as they do with the panoramic novels, they portray the sad alternative to that association with one's peers that Trollope hoped for and found when he settled in London and was able to explore and celebrate both personally and as a writer.

NOTES

1 Unsigned review of *The Claverings, Spectator* 40 (May 4, 1867), 498–99.
2 Introduction to *The Prime Minister*, ed. L. S. Amery (Oxford: Oxford University Press, 1973), p. viii.
3 Robert Tracy, *Trollope's Later Novels* (Berkeley: University of California Press, 1978), p. 170.

6

LISA NILES

Trollope's short fiction

On November 17, 1858 Anthony Trollope sailed for the West Indies on postal business. The trip, which culminated in his first visit to North America, marked a new phase in his writing career. While in New York he called at the offices of *Harper's New Monthly Magazine* and, with an eye ever focused on the financial opportunities afforded by writing, offered to produce several short "tales" for their magazine, thus turning his travels to yet another productive purpose. Trollope had already begun writing non-fiction accounts of his excursions and would use this expedition as a source for *The West Indies and the Spanish Main* (1859).[1] *Harper's* printed two of his stories: "The Relics of General Chassé," a farce set in 1830s Antwerp, appeared in the February 1860 issue and was followed in August by "The Courtship of Susan Bell," a love story set in Saratoga Springs, New York. Having found a new outlet for his fiction, Trollope ploughed forward in typically industrious fashion, authoring a total of forty-two stories between 1859 and 1882. His career as a short-fiction writer began after his success as a novelist was well on its way; of his eight novels thus far, *The Warden* (1855) and *Barchester Towers* (1857) had lodged Barsetshire firmly in the reading public's imagination, and *Framley Parsonage*, the third install-ment of the series, would appear in 1860 to both critical and popular acclaim.

One might expect that the author who petitioned for additional volumes in the already capacious triple-decker form – "Oh, that Mr. Longman would allow me a fourth!" – would find the constraints of short fiction stifling (*BT* ch. 43). His critics hinted at this possibility: the *Spectator's* reviewer observes of *Tales of All Countries*: "No writer requires more the freedom and continuity of an extended narrative, in order to produce his best effects."[2] It would appear that the pieces intended to be mere supple-ments to Trollope's income proved difficult to execute, demanding an economy of scope that rarely presented itself to the series novelist. In 1876 Trollope was offered the exceptionally large sum of £150 to write a story for the Christmas issue of the *Graphic*.[3] Having agreed to the request, he expresses his dread in fulfilling it: "I feel with regard to literature somewhat as I suppose an upholsterer and undertaker feels when he is called upon to supply a funeral. He has to supply it, however distasteful it may be." Noting the deadline that looms a mere three weeks away, Trollope bemoans a case of severe writer's block: "I have in vain been cudgelling my brain for the last month. I can't send away the order to another shop, but I do not know how I shall ever get the coffin made." Trollope's comparison of the profession of authorship to trade reaches its humorous pinnacle here. But what is particularly striking is how different this attitude toward the story is from his discussion of *The Prime Minister* two paragraphs later, when he declares that he "returned with a full heart" to the Palliser series, whose governmental characters "had been very easy to describe and had required no imagination to conceive" (*A* ch. 20). Whereas short-story writing submits to the "distasteful" analogy to the business of death, the series novel meets with a joyous reception, offering as it does the ease of self-reproducing characters.

This restrictive view of an end-driven short story standing in opposition to the more open-ended pleasures of the novel, however, is myopic at best. While the short story, with its singularly focused plot and compressed space, suggests a privileging of endings, Trollope's short fiction often resists closure, mediating a far more complex narrative strategy. In the first published tale, "The Relics of General Chassé," we catch a glimpse of the complexity to come. The story's plot revolves around a dandified clergyman losing his trousers, but the plot's comic interest hinges on the narrator never naming the object outright. Instead, we are offered euphemistic approximations – "relics," "an article," a "virile habiliment," "the regimentals." The narrator's elaborate, extended refusal to name the trousers as such gestures toward a move Trollope makes in much of his short fiction: that of ambivalence toward the form itself. Through repetition and continual revision – never achieving that final promise of clarity – Trollope resists the restrictive conventions of the short story. Thus when he gets "the coffin made," it houses expansive possibility rather than narrative closure.

John Bowen claims for the short story an outcast, marginal status: a form featuring outcast figures, short fiction is frequently overlooked in critical analysis.[4] For Trollope this marginalization proved liberating. We see fewer conscientious clergy and middle-class heroines and more conniving spinsters, cross-dressing women, working-class heroes, adulterers, prisoners, outcasts, drunkards, and madmen. From the homoeroticism that skirts the edges of "The Turkish Bath" (1869)[5] to the sadistic and suicidal marriage plot of "La Mère Bauche" (1861); from the impotent husband in "Mrs. Brumby" (1870) to the dipsomaniac wife in "The Spotted

Dog" (1870) – these stories show a freer, less restrained hand than that visible in many of the novels.

"Mrs. General Talboys" (1861), which was rejected by W. M. Thackeray's *Cornhill* for its indelicacy and finally appeared in the *London Review*, is one such example. Writing to Thackeray, Trollope acknowledges: "An impartial Editor must do his duty. Pure morals must be supplied. And the owner of the responsible name must be the Judge of the purity. A writer for a periodical makes himself subject to this judgement by undertaking such work; and a man who allows himself to be irritated because judgement goes against himself is an ass" (*Letters* 1:127–28).

Yet Trollope does allow "himself to be irritated," offering an irresistible jibe at Thackeray by holding up his literary rival Dickens as the only "pure English novelist, pure up to the Cornhill standard" in contrast to Thackeray's own novelistic production. (Of course, Trollope cannot allow even apparent praise of Dickens to stand here. He then remembers "Oliver Twist and blushed for what [his] mother & sisters read in that fie-fie story.") Trollope then feels compelled to issue an impassioned plea "in defence of [his] own muse": "I will not allow that I am indecent, and profess that squeamishness – in so far as it is squeamishness and not delicacy – should be disregarded by a writer." While he acknowledges that Thackeray "must especially guard the Cornhill," Trollope writes: "You speak of the squeamishness of 'our people,'" yet "history perhaps should be told even to the squeamish" (*Letters* 1:128–29). And this slightly reticent declaration, with its *perhaps-edness* in the midst of an otherwise assured diatribe, best expresses Trollope's ambivalence toward the very restraints he acknowledges operate upon the periodical contributor. Outwardly aware of the possible necessity for repression, Trollope often subverts that necessity formally rather than thematically by working against narrative conventions. And so it is with "joking apart," that Trollope declares himself "quite satisfied" with Thackeray's decision, while he simultaneously defies the verdict with this petulant claim: "I trust to confound you by the popularity of Mrs. Talboys" (*Letters* 1:128–29). Its popularity was a long time in coming, as the story's initial publication aroused what Laurence Oliphant, editor of the *London Review*, described as "universal" distaste among his subscribers (*Letters* 1:141).

"Mrs. General Talboys" narrates a summer spent in Rome by Ida Talboys, an outwardly respectable English wife and mother who expresses extreme libertinism in her views on marriage. Swept away by desire for her and "her own indiscreet enthusiasm," the Irish artist Wenceslas O'Brien, himself a married man, beseeches Ida to run away with him to Naples. Although she professes indignation and violently refuses by giving O'Brien "a knock in the ribs," a hint of successfully accomplished adultery in mid-life taints the narrative in a way that Lady Glencora Palliser's possible elopement with Burgo Fitzgerald in *Can You Forgive Her?* never can. When defending himself against an accusation of impropriety, a sympathetically rendered O'Brien declares, "'I give you my honour that I did it all to oblige her,'" implicating Mrs. Talboys in the process of clearing his own name.[6] The story was most likely rejected because of its uncritical reference to illegitimacy and allusion to adultery; yet, the subtext of middle-aged female desire surfaces potentially as even more repugnant to Trollope's readers. If O'Brien did, in fact, do "'it all to oblige'" Mrs. Talboys, he is affirming a passion which violates a domestic ideal grounded in the refusal of sexual desire in the middle-aged, maternal body.

Trollope's stories not only offer what John Sutherland calls "the unexpected image of a morally embattled writer, one at odds with, and sadly hampered by, the 'squeamishness' (his word) of the times";[7] they also challenge assumptions about the conventions that structured the nineteenth-century short story. Initially appearing in fifteen magazines and two collections for the women's activist Emily Faithfull, Trollope's stories were often written to order – shaped to meet the needs of a particular periodical's bent or editor. Sutherland notes that "Trollope conceived his short stories in bundles, and in terms of long-running contract relationships with particular magazines (a strategy which allowed him to 'target' audiences)" (*Early Short Stories* ix). They were also reprinted in book-length collections; five volumes were published between 1861 and 1881.[8] Trollope himself provided the topical lens through which to read many of the stories by giving three of the collections proscriptive titles: the two-volume *Tales of All Countries* and *An Editor's Tales*, which draws on his experiences both as a writer and as an editor. Following Trollope's lead, the Trollope Society reissued the complete short fiction in a five-volume set in the late 1990s, with the following titles: *Christmas Stories, Editors and Writers, Tourists and Colonials, Courtship and Marriage,* and the miscellany catch-all, *The Journey to Panama and Other Stories.*[9] Ellen Moody in her moderated Internet discussions on Trollope-l, classifies the stories even more precisely, offering seven groupings: "Tales of All Countries," "Of Love Courtship and Marriage," "Irish Tales," "Christmas Tales," "Archibald Green Stories," "Burlesques," and "An Editor's Tales."[10] Read in the context of these headings, each story takes on an association with the formulaic conventions that shape particular topics – those that adhere, for example, to the marriage plot or the travel story. But even Moody's most precise designations allow for the possibility of unfixedness, as she cross-references those tales which belong "to more than one category." This cross listing speaks to a critical, yet challenging, strength of Trollope's stories – their resistance to categorization. Both within and across the collections, there are stories that initially appear to fit clearly within a particular narrative framework but ultimately *do not fit* – those which do not align themselves comfortably alongside a prescribed narrative conceit.

Marked by ambivalence with regard to content and form, by marginalized characters and indignant reception, Trollope's short fiction resists clear classification. In what follows, I examine stories that both invoke and challenge the conventions associated with the Christmas story, the travel narrative, and the editor's tale. My aim is to show the multi-layered complexity of these pieces – to offer up the readerly thrill of uncovering Trollope's most radical narrative experimentation.

No toys for Tiny Tim: Christmas with Trollope

To set Trollope's own Christmas stories against a Victorian tradition, I turn to Charles Dickens's *Christmas Books* (1852), which includes the now-legendary "A Christmas Carol" (1843) among its offerings. Dickens prefaces the collection with a statement of purpose, claiming he desires "in a whimsical kind of masque, which the good humour of the season justified, to awaken some loving and forbearing thoughts, never out of season in a Christian land."[11] These "loving and forbearing thoughts" exemplify the Christmas setting as a site of over-determined sentimentality, one which results in self-sacrifice, benevolence, and Christian charity (when given to the deserving poor, of course). Once reframed through Dickens's narrative lens, Christmas became infused with heightened expectation – a reification of Victorian values – particularly as it reflected a middle-class vision of benevolence through the domestic ideal: the industrious father, the nurturing mother, and the near-beatific child gathered together in grateful forbearance. Trollope acknowledged Dickens's role as the bearer of this standard: "A Christmas story in the proper sense should be the ebullition of some mind anxious to instill others with the desire for Christmas religious thought, or Christmas festivities, – or, better still, with Christmas charity. Such was the case with Dickens when he wrote his two first Christmas stories" (*A* ch. 20). For Trollope, however, the Christmas story often bears little relationship to this formula of overt sentimentality.

Trollope wrote nine Christmas tales, eight of which were published in magazines and the ninth, *Harry Heathcote of Gangoil* (1873–74), offered as a one-volume novel. When describing his difficulty in writing "Christmas at Thompson Hall" (1876), Trollope complained bitterly about the "humbug implied by the nature of the order" to write a Christmas tale: "Nothing can be more distasteful to me than to have to give a relish of Christmas to what I write" (*A* ch. 20). This distaste may explain why Betty Jane Breyer in her edition of *The Christmas Stories* acknowledges that "whether Trollope himself would approve such a collection is open to question."[12] And indeed his seasonal stories draw on other concerns: the courtships of young, at times humorously star-crossed, couples in "The Mistletoe Bough" (1861), "Christmas Day at Kirkby Cottage" (1871), and "The Two Heroines of Plumplington" (1882); the hardships faced by an Australian sheep farmer in *Harry Heathcote*; or the possible destruction of an American family whose sons fight on opposing sides in the Civil War in "The Two Generals" (1863). Under the guise of seasonal settings, Trollope's holiday stories demystify the workings of female sexual desire, violence, and capitalism.

"Not if I Know It" (1882), Trollope's last completed story, approaches nearest to the turn of heart that Christmas tales should engender, although the benevolence is directed not at one in need but to a man "worth ten thousand pounds" (Thompson 959). George Wade lobs the churlish retort, "Not if I know it!" at his brother-in-law, Wilfred Horton, after Horton requests a reference regarding his financial soundness. Wade's insolent refusal threatens to ruin Christmas, and the plot turns on whether or not Mrs. Horton, Wade's sister, can reconcile her husband to her brother. Attendance at the local church service does that which is needful, engendering both men with a spirit of mercy. As they leave "the church," they are "ready in truth to forgive each other" (Thompson 957). Christmas is saved, Mrs. Horton's face beams with a smile, and we are led to assume that Mr. Horton's already substantial wealth will increase once his brother-in-law offers that reference to "The Turco-Egyptian New Waterworks Company" (Thompson 959).

By relocating the sentimentalized framework of forgiveness onto the unsentimental act of making money, "Not if I Know It" suggests that the holiday ideal of familial harmony is easily supplanted by the desire for financial success. Of course, Christmas stories often engaged the bourgeois world of finance. Dickens's Ebenezer Scrooge offers a didactic model of benevolent capitalism – the redistribution of wealth to those in need achieved through an over-determined act of repentance. Where Trollope's narrative exhibits transgression is in its treatment rather than in its topic; a sardonic subtext taints the tale, as the generosity of spirit exhibited by all gets put in service to the building (and keeping) of wealth rather than charitable self-sacrifice.

Christmas more often served as a temporal anchor to the narrative rather than an inspiration for behavioral change, underscoring the persistent secularity of Trollope's holiday tales. Such is the case in "Catherine Carmichael: or, Three Years Running" (1878), a story set in the rough gold-digging terrain of Hokitika, New Zealand. On "Christmas Day. No. 1," young Catherine Baird buries her alcoholic father and must marry fifty-year-old Peter Carmichael, a man who is "odious to her" (Thompson 885), when the man she loves, John Carmichael, Peter's younger cousin, offers no alternative. Her husband dies on the eve of the third Christmas, but as "she would not admit to herself to have been the wife of a man whom she had ever hated" (Thompson 900), Catherine refuses any inheritance, insisting it go to John, Peter's closest relative. The problem of Catherine's disposition is quickly solved, however, when John Carmichael returns and proposes marriage, thus returning to Catherine the inheritance he declares is rightfully hers. As she looks out over her first husband's grave, her husband-to-be asks, "Kate, will you take it, if not from him, then from me?" (Thompson 902). Repeatedly commingling death with desire, the narrative offers a series of detours through the conventional marriage plot with a Trollopian twist. Catherine marries first out of financial expedience; as "she was only a burden" (Thompson 887), her pragmatism virtuously resigns to rationality over emotion. Such a marriage of convenience, particularly one of a young girl and an older man, is a commonplace in Victorian fiction. Yet Trollope narrates the second marriage, expressive of Catherine's desire, as yet another rational choice. Only by framing the proposal through the necessity of Catherine's economic survival – "Whither will you go? Where will you live?" (Thompson 902) – does Trollope represent a marriage based solely on female desire. The inheritance – the "it" that Catherine would not accept from Peter but will from John – stands in for the sexual pleasures Catherine will take from her new husband. So the marriage plot repeatedly interrupts the expression of Catherine's desire – deviating from the trajectory toward consummation – to place in its stead the ugliness of financial need and the restriction of choice available to unmarried women.

Finally, "Christmas at Thompson Hall," one of Trollope's most delightful tales, offers up a series of farcical events worthy of P. G. Wodehouse. The Browns, an English couple living abroad, travel through Paris to reach England in time for Christmas with her family. During their stay at the Grand Hotel, the wife enters in the wrong hotel room in the middle of the night and mistakenly applies a mustard plaster to a man she believes to be her invalid husband. The result is a series of comic accusations, denials, admissions, retreats, and, finally, a reunion of sorts between the wronged man, who turns out to be the Browns' future brother-in-law, and Mrs. Brown herself. The farce itself offers a forum to narrate sexual anxiety in public and private spaces, highlighting both the hotel and the country house as repositories of sexual tension and possible transgression.

Rendering the moment of recognition in epic tones, the narrator satirically exposes the repressive forces that turn this scene from accident to indiscretion:

> Not Priam wakened in the dead of night, not Dido when first she learned that Æneas had fled, not Othello when he learned that Desdemona had been chaste, not Medea when she became conscious of her slaughtered children, could have been more struck with horror than was this British matron as she stood for a moment gazing with awe on that stranger's bed. (Thompson 689)

This "British matron," assuredly free from the impulsive passions of a Medea or a Dido, should leave the room once she realizes that this "stalwart stranger" (Thompson 692) could not possibly be her husband. Yet she lingers, if only momentarily: "She watched him for a moment longer, and then, with the candle in her hand, she fled. Poor human nature! Had he been an old man, even a middle-aged man, she would not have left him to his unmerited sufferings" (Thompson 690–91). But of course he is a desirable, potent young man, and Mrs. Brown herself closes off the possibility of the impossible attraction. She retreats, leaving "the grand proportions of that manly throat" to a "discomfort" that "at the worst would not be worse than hers had been" (Thompson 689, 692).

Yet when the Browns and Mr. Jones meet again in the country house, Mrs. Brown is no longer afforded the option of retreat. The case of mistaken identity makes for an embarrassing confession at Christmas dinner, as she acknowledges "her fault with true contrition" in front of the entire family (Thompson 710). Rather than a maudlin scene of tears and forgiveness, we get instead Mrs. Brown's cousin "almost rolling off his chair with delight" at the thought of it. And this cousin offers the moral of the story: "It only shows that what I have always said is quite true. You should never go to bed in a strange house without locking your door" (Thompson 710). The tale ends with a darkly comic fear. Every house is, in this tale, "a strange house" in the gathering of strangers together under the same roof. And in that "strange" space, you must be attuned to the possibility of violation. You must lock your door. This ending, which raises the specter of domestic policing, surveillance, and sexual threat, certainly offers a very different effect than that expressed by Dickens's narrator in "A Christmas Carol." Rather than Tiny Tim's observation, "God bless Us, Every one!" these characters might offer the less charitable plea, "God protect us from every one!"

Do all roads lead to England?: Trollope's "Tales of All Countries"

Trollope's travels have garnered significant critical interest in recent years, as James Buzard's, Nicholas Birns's, Gordon Bigelow's, and Amanda Claybaugh's chapters in this collection attest. In *An Autobiography*, Trollope enthused that he "could fill a volume with true tales" of his adventures (*A* ch. 7), and in the two-volume *Tales* alone, all but two of the stories are set outside England, with "The Parson's Daughter of Oxney Colne" (1861) and "The Mistletoe Bough" (1861) as notable exceptions. Many of the stories take place in colonial settings, including the Holy Land, Egypt, Costa Rica, and the West Indies. Continental Europe receives its fair share of representation, as the backdrop for tales such as "The House of Heine Brothers in Munich" (1860) and "The Chateau of Prince Polignac" (1861). America also offered a continuous font of inspiration, including "Miss Ophelia Gledd" (1863), a tale of a young socialite modeled on Trollope's friend, Kate Field. Finally, Ireland lent itself as a tantalizing setting to several stories, two of which are narrated by Archibald Green, a quasi-autobiographical figure for the young Trollope, who tells of his own youthful embarrassment in the face of cultural difference.[13]

Avid readers of travel fiction might have expected the obligatory description of "local colour," but, as Donald D. Stone observes, Trollope depicted un-English settings with quite a different purpose in mind: "Where a Romantic writer would have rhapsodized over the mountain settings in 'La Mère Bauche,' for example, Trollope sketches in the Pyrenees only so that his heroine can have something high enough to fling herself from."[14] Stone's witticism points to a key function of the foreign in Trollope's stories. Marie Calvert's suicide, rendered in grim, Balzac-ian fashion, is not one of French piquancy, but one of repressed desire colliding with the expectation of marital obligation. Indeed these mountains do give Marie "something high enough to fling herself from," and that mundane rationale is precisely the point.

Fundamental to the concept of the foreign is that it is always a space of projected desire – of othering. What Trollope's travel fiction offers is a displacement of the un-narratable, but very English, domestic anxieties onto these alien settings. While this use of the foreign as an ideological space of displacement is not unique to Trollope, the widely varied topics his stories engage through this singular trope demand a reconsideration of these narratives as much more than merely "tales of all countries."

While these stories afforded Trollope the opportunity to exercise an imperial impulse, elevating Englishness in the face of other countries' failings, he often chose instead to expose the follies of his countrymen.

"John Bull on the Guadalquivir" (1860) offers a glimpse of Trollope the traveler at his most self-deprecating.[15] The story begins with a young Englishman, John Pomfret, wooing a Spanish beauty, Maria Daguilar. No impassioned Latina, Maria shows a practical "turn of mind," while her suitor secretly longs for a spot of romance (Thompson 145). We quickly learn, however, that the outcome is never in doubt – in the first paragraph Pomfret notes that Maria is "sitting on the other side of the fireplace" (144) as he writes his tale. That "flower of romance" (Thompson 144), notably absent in the courtship, is then suggested by the idea of a picturesque setting. Sailing to Spain to receive Maria's answer to his proposal, Pomfret travels with an expatriate living in Xeres, Thomas Johnson. On the boat to Seville, they mistake a Spanish nobleman for a bull fighter because of his elaborate dress. Wishing to investigate further, Johnson accosts the Marquis D'Almavivas "with that good-natured familiarity with which a thoroughly nice fellow always opens a conversation with his inferior" (Thompson 148). Pomfret proceeds to examine his clothing, to which the Marquis bemusedly submits: "I was emboldened to hold up his arm that I might see the cut of his coat, to take off his cap and examine the make, to stuff my finger in beneath his sash, and at last to kneel down while I persuaded him to hold up his legs that I might look to the clocking" (148–49). The scene ends with Pomfret tearing one of the buttons off the Marquis's coat and the Marquis refusing to accept payment for it, voicing his denial in fluent English. The story of the "two vulgar men" (Thompson 156) makes its way through the town, and Pomfret must own his embarrassingly English behavior not only to his intended but to the Marquis himself, who graciously accepts his apology.

The hilarity of Pomfret's social blindness, seeing nothing amiss in his treatment of the Spaniard – "I had got fast hold of him by one ankle, and was determined to finish the survey completely" (Thompson 149) – underscores what for Trollope is a very serious matter: economic pragmatism. The exoticism of the Marquis's costume merely provides the opportunity to showcase the narrator's obsession with value. He wants to "finish the survey" in order to determine with unflinching accuracy the clothing's cost. Having done so, he offers the prosaic declaration that any man wearing an outfit in which the buttons alone are worth "more than forty pounds" is "an uncommon ass" (Thompson 148). Turning the desire for romance back in on itself, Pomfret shows that it is vulgarity – exhibited through the decidedly unromantic assessment of pounds and pence – which comprises Englishness. This story, one of Trollope's comic delights, offers a travel tale geared toward the English reader in which English identity itself is undergoing revision. So when we learn that Mrs. Pomfret "would not . . . be well pleased were any one to insinuate that she were other than an Englishwoman" (Thompson 144), we know that Trollope would not dare do so. Ironically the Spanish bride – the charmingly pragmatic corrective to her husband's vulgarity – represents the best of Englishness.

Set in Bermuda, "Aaron Trow" (1861) is a tale of violence and brutality that reverses readerly expectations surrounding race, violence, and justice. Trow, a hardened prisoner, eludes capture for weeks after a dramatic escape. While on the run he attempts to rob Anastasia Bergen, a white timber dealer's daughter. When she declares that she has no money in the house, he rapes and brutally beats her. Rather than submit, Anastasia savagely resists. Meeting violence with violence, she bites his hand and grabs his hair, refusing to release her grasp even when he stabs her, leaving her covered in her own blood. Trow is subsequently killed in a ferocious manhunt led by Anastasia's fiancé, but his ghost remains "as part of the creed of every young woman in Bermuda" to serve as a spectral reminder of brutality and its ends (Thompson 291).

In the story, Trollope not only takes on the taboo subject of rape; he situates the event in a radical context, providing a chillingly sympathetic portrait of the rapist. Displacing the otherness of racial tensions in Bermuda onto the white prisoner Trow, Trollope suggests that it is the predominantly white Western socio-economic structures, not blackness, that most threaten the Victorian ideal of femininity Anastasia represents. For Trow is not the fiend one might expect: "Had the world used him well, giving him when he was young ample wages and separating him from turbulent spirits, he also might have used the world well" (Thompson 279). Trow's threat to Anastasia – "I will do worse than murder you. I will make you such an object that all the world shall loathe to look on you" (Thompson 307) – eerily suggests an act of reflexive violence, as Trow himself has become that very "object," with "the look of a beast ... to which men fall when they live ... as outcasts from their brethren" (Thompson 279). Most disturbing is the repeated insistence on the sameness of Trow, Anastasia, and her mild-mannered fiancé, Caleb Morton. When faced with violence, each responds violently, and the narrator describes their rage in hauntingly similar terms, eliding any difference between the genders, between the classes, between national identities. So it hardly surprises that when Morton drowns Trow in a dramatic struggle in the river, the "justice" of the killing is marked by ambivalence, as Morton himself does not believe "that there had been anything in that day's work of which he could be proud;– much rather of which it behoved him to be thoroughly ashamed" (Thompson 291).

Finally, "The Widow's Mite" (1863) adds yet another twist to Trollope's travel formula, offering a marriage plot that depends upon an English bride-to-be's successful relinquishing of her national identity. Nora Field refuses to purchase a wedding trousseau for her marriage to a wealthy American, choosing instead to donate the monies to the Lancashire textile workers who are economically displaced as a result of the American Civil War. Her wedding clothes – a very domestic symbol indeed – forge a connection between the abstraction of a foreign war and the material fact of local suffering. In this story, the wedding dress mediates national difference and the tensions of a global economy, as Nora claims that she must and will relinquish her Englishness once married to Frederick F. Frew. Beneath Nora's seemingly trivial insistence on offering relief to her starving countrymen by wearing a plain, drab dress lurks the unspoken anxiety about the possibilities of a disrupted life in a war-torn country. The drabness of her clothes, soon forgotten in the excitement of the wedding day, serves as a reminder of the solemnity of the national identification she is preparing to adopt. In its transitional, transnational status, "The Widow's Mite" emblematizes what each of these travel tales intimate: the fluidity of the concept of foreignness itself. To quote Michael Sadleir, "all of what is known as 'local colour,'" was "to Trollope the grease paint on the actor's face – a final touch to help the illusion, but trivial beside the personality of the actor himself" (Sadleir 178).

An editor on the margins

It seems fitting to conclude an essay focused on Trollope's narrative strategies with a brief consideration of those stories purporting to render transparent the machinations of the literary marketplace. Trollope's work on both sides of the periodical fence – in addition to being a contributor, he was the editor of *St. Paul's Magazine* for three years – provided him with ample stories about the trials and tribulations of aspiring writers. *An Editor's Tales* presents those experiences from the first-person perspective, most often narrated through the editorial (and perhaps monarchical) pronoun "we." With this intensely autobiographical focus, one might expect Trollope's editorial stories to slide into solipsism, offering platitudes on the correctness of the editorial perspective or the worthiness of the writer. What they do offer is something quite different; these tales expose the literary marketplace as a site of desperation, poverty, insanity, alcoholism, degradation, and grinding tedium.

In stories that propose to show how the integrity of the periodical must be maintained, such as "The Panjandrum," "The Turkish Bath," "The Adventures of Fred Pickering," and "Mrs. Brumby," the policing function of the editor is overrun by the persistent pathos of the would-be authors. Yet the marginalization of their aspirations ironically reclaims them through their prominence in the stories. And, by aligning himself with these writers, Trollope's editor reclaims a part of himself as well. These deviants represent a collective body that resists consolidation into the literary marketplace; and the characters themselves come to represent the role of Trollope's short fiction. They reroute our expectations in new directions, offering productive moments of resistance to narrative expectations.

"Josephine de Montmorenci" depicts one of Trollope's most memorable literary misfits. The editor of the *Olympus Magazine* receives the manuscript of a sensational novel, "Not So Black as He Is Painted," from a mysterious woman, who styles herself Josephine de Montmorenci. While he rejects the manuscript, he wishes to uncover the siren who keeps writing to him with a wit and verve he is sure must accompany great beauty. Finally granted an audience with her, Mr. Jones discovers a disabled crone, Polly Puffle, and not the temptress he imagined. In an interesting turn, Polly's loss of sexual power creates a space for economic power, as Jones agrees in a moment of sympathy to publish the novel, which, ironically, is quite successful. Josephine functions in the narrative only as a projection of the editor's consciousness – she is only other, existing as a symbol of desire. Yet Polly does exist, refusing the othering that would displace her and embracing the empowerment her marginalized position now offers her. Through Polly's character, Trollope engages many of the topics he takes up repeatedly in his short fiction. Anxieties about sexuality, economic power, social policing, domesticity, and foreignness: all are turned to unexpected purpose in this comedic gem.

Perhaps it is no accident that the stories which take as their topic the art of story writing itself resist easy analyses. For as this foray into the vast oeuvre that is Trollope's short fiction has shown, these tales offer almost limitless possibility in their creativity – in their sheer indulgence of Trollope's fancies. In demonstrating their complexity and independent literary merit, Trollope's stories reveal the imaginative possibilities behind and beyond more familiar fictional forms. Trollope's short fiction shows a very different side of one of Victorian England's busiest authors.

NOTES

1 Trollope wrote *The New Zealander* in 1855–56, although it remained unpublished until 1972.
2 Unsigned review of *Tales of All Countries, Second Series* by Anthony Trollope, *Spectator* (May 1863), Supplement pages 20–21.
3 The story is "Christmas at Thompson Hall."

4 John Bowen, "Collins's Shorter Fiction," *The Cambridge Companion to Wilkie Collins*, ed. Jenny Bourne Taylor (Cambridge: Cambridge University Press, 2006), p. 37.

5 Mark W. Turner offers a compelling reading of "The Turkish Bath" and gay cruising in *Trollope and the Magazines: Gendered Issues in Mid-Victorian Britain* (Basingstoke: Macmillan, 2000). Kate Flint also takes up this tale in her consideration of queerness in this volume.

6 Julian Thompson, ed., *Anthony Trollope: The Complete Shorter Fiction* (New York: Carroll & Graf, 1992), pp. 207–8. All short story citations are taken from this edition, which is referred to throughout as "Thompson."

7 John Sutherland, ed. Introduction. *Early Short Stories by Anthony Trollope* (Oxford: Oxford University Press, 1994), pp. vii–xxiii, ix.

8 *Tales of All Countries: First Series* (1861), *Tales of All Countries: Second Series* (1863), *Lotta Schmidt and Other Stories* (1867), *An Editor's Tales* (1870), and *Why Frau Frohmann Raised Her Prices* (1881).

9 The Trollope Society set is a reprint of Betty Jane Breyer's earlier collection, with a new introduction by Joanna Trollope. See Betty Jane Breyer, ed., *Anthony Trollope: The Complete Short Stories*, 5 vols. (Fort Worth: Texas Christian University Press, 1979–1983). Rpt. by the Trollope Society (1996–2000).

10 See www.jimandellen.org/trollope/shortstory.html and Ellen Moody, *Trollope on the Net* (London: Hambledon, 1999).

11 Charles Dickens, *Christmas Books*, ed. Ruth Glancy (Oxford: Oxford University Press, 1998), p. v.

12 Breyer, *The Complete Short Stories*, vol. 1, p. i.

13 Archibald Green also narrates "Miss Ophelia Gledd."

14 Donald D. Stone, "Trollope as a Short Story Writer," *Nineteenth-Century Fiction* 31 (1976), 26–47, p. 31.

15 Trollope insisted that the story was based on an incident that actually happened. See *A* ch. 5.

7

JENNY BOURNE TAYLOR

Trollope and the sensation novel

"Among English novels of the present day, and among English novelists, a great division is made," Trollope famously argued in *An Autobiography*:

> There are sensational novels, and anti-sensational; sensational novelists, and anti-sensational; sensational readers, and anti-sensational. The novelists who are considered to be anti-sensational are generally called realistic. I am realistic. My friend Wilkie Collins is generally supposed to be sensational ... All this I think is a mistake ... A good artist should be both, – and both in the highest degree. (*A* ch. 12)

Trollope drafted *An Autobiography* in 1875–76, when the critical consensus in favor of "higher realism" had been established for some time. His chapter on "English novelists of the present day" stresses the social and moral responsibility of the novelist, setting the leisurely unfolding of events over striking effects, and pitting "the elucidation of character" over "the construction and gradual development of a plot." "When I sit down to write a novel I do not at all know and I do not very much care how it is to end," Trollope observes. "Wilkie Collins ... plans everything on, down to the minutest detail, from the beginning to the end ... The construction is most minute and most wonderful. But I can never lose the taste of the construction" (*A* ch. 13).

There may be an element of truth in Trollope's contrast between himself and Collins: between his own dense, multiple plots dominated by an overarching authorial persona and the latter's use of multiple voices and contrasting forms of narrative testimony. But his use of such contrasts is primarily rhetorical and, throughout his writing career, Trollope increasingly draws on "sensational" techniques. As Walter M. Kendrick has argued, "opposites are always economically interrelated" in Trollope's fiction, which works "in shifting, dynamic relation to the clichés of his contemporaries."[1] This chapter will explore the dynamic relationship between his methods and concerns and those of his explicitly sensational contemporaries: briefly noting their respective positions as professional novelists within a rapidly expanding literary marketplace, discussing their narrative methods, and focusing on their treatment of shared concerns. Trollope's writing shares with sensation fiction a concern with *legitimacy* in both its narrow and its wider senses, particularly in the late 1860s and 1870s. Both probe the limits of formal law and dominant customs as they affect the transmission of property, the definitions of sanctioned and unsanctioned birth, marriage, and the position of women within and outside it. Both investigate the boundaries of social propriety and the line that separates criminal and respectable behavior. Both explore the performative nature of social identity, the ambiguity of human motivation, and the tensions that lurk within apparently stable mid-Victorian middle- and upper middle-class families in a world in which the residual power of landed wealth is disrupted by emerging economic structures and social roles.

The sensation novel was often perceived as a symptom of cultural decline in part because it transgressed class boundaries in terms of its audience, importing the melodramatic effects of the penny magazines into the middle-class household. "She may boast, without fear of contradiction, of having temporarily succeeded in making the literature of the kitchen the favourite reading of the drawing room," W. F. Rae wrote of Mary Elizabeth Braddon's *Lady Audley's Secret* (1862) in 1865.[2] The 1860s saw the beginning of the proliferation of specific markets within this expanding readership, with the growth of children's fiction and the domestic novel as well as the growing division between "popular" and "serious" fiction, in part shaped by magazine and journal serialization. But these divisions had yet to harden, and while Trollope's early fiction was praised by the *Times* critic E. S. Dallas in 1859 as perfect "Mudie" material – his stories of middle-class domestic life (in contrast with the "moral contagion" of the sensation novel) being ideal material for the powerful Evangelical magnate of the circulating libraries – Trollope and Collins would have shared many readers, and Dallas might have modified his anodyne view of Trollope's later career (*Crit. Her.* 103–4). Both writers, for example, serialized stories in the *Cornhill Magazine* during the 1860s, and both had to negotiate a rapidly expanding and competitive literary industry, with its pressures of (weekly or monthly) serial publication, the three-volume format and the lending libraries, and an increasingly globalized market.[3]

Trollope and Collins dealt with these opportunities and challenges in different ways, but their situations have many points in common. Trollope was nine years older than Collins and died seven years earlier, but both spanned a momentous period in the history of the novel, beginning their careers in the late 1840s in the era of Dickens and Thackeray

(*The Macdermots of Ballycloran* appeared in 1847; *Memoirs of the Life of William Collins, Esq., R. A.* in 1848), and ending them in the 1880s, as Hardy and Stevenson were in the ascendant and just before the three-volume novel format fell apart. Although their literary apprenticeships were very different, both came from literary and artistic families (though Collins's family never suffered the financial disasters that plagued Trollope's childhood), and both lived in households dominated by powerful and creative mothers. Each of them was highly professional, combining a workmanlike attitude to his writing as a craft with a sense of the novel's higher aesthetic function. And while the sensation novel was notoriously attacked in the *Quarterly Review* for its cynical mass-production of fiction as a commodity – "A commercial atmosphere floats around works of this class, redolent of the manufactory and the shop" – Henry Mansel's comments have a bearing not only on Lady Carbury's efforts at historical romance in *The Way We Live Now* (1875), but also on Trollope's assessment of his own working practices in *An Autobiography*.[4]

Narrative structures and strategies

Trollope's writing shares with sensation fiction a range of responses to mid-Victorian modernity, and this emerges in the narrative methods as well as the social and psychological concerns of his fiction. With some significant exceptions, both Trollope's novels and those of his overtly sensational peers have contemporary settings, being as Mansel put it, "laid in our own days and amongst people we are in the habit of meeting," and placing traditional preoccupations with property, inheritance, and marriage within the everyday modern world of the railway and the telegraph.[5] In contrast with Dickens and George Eliot, who tend to set their stories in the recent past (usually thirty years, or a generation, earlier), Trollope, like Collins and Braddon, sets his plots in the immediate, or almost immediate present, reinforcing the presence of his fictional world, often through specific topical references. The opening of chapter 87 of *He Knew He Was Right* (1869), for example, makes a humorous reference to the diplomatic dispute over nationality that led to the passing of the 1870 Naturalisation Act, and while the political subplot of *Ralph the Heir* (1871) has echoes of George Eliot's *Felix Holt* (1866) in its accounts of electoral corruption, it is explicitly set in the context of the Second Reform Act of 1867, not, as in Eliot's case, its 1832 forerunner. It is this immediacy that fuels Trollope's sense of the excitement of modern life, and the links between the public and private spheres. "If Parliament were an Olympus in which Venus and Juno never kissed, the thing would not be nearly so interesting" notes the narrator in

Can You Forgive Her? (1865). "But in this Olympus ... exciting changes occur which give the whole thing all the keen interest of a sensational novel" (*CYFH* ch. 42).

This emphasis on the immediate undercuts the critical value-system which posits sensation as the necessary "other" of realism in various ways. The term "sensation fiction" was held together by series of critical anxieties rather than forming a stable genre – it was a hybrid narrative mode, combining elements of gothic romance, melodrama and domestic realism. But Trollope's brand of realism was equally hybrid, combining overt author-ial intervention with the detailed ethnographic representation of the minu-tiae of daily life and the investigation of consciousness and subjectivity, and also drawing on Gothic and melodramatic modes. While Trollope doesn't reproduce the narrative relativism of Collins's multiple narrators, his multi-plotted stories nonetheless suggest a complex multifaceted reality springing from an intense sense of the significance of detail, in which emotional extremity is often generated through immediate physical response. Sensation fiction was attacked for "preaching to the nerves" of its readers (in Henry Mansel's phrase), but Trollope often deploys similar effects. The gradual decline of Louis Trevelyan in *He Knew He Was Right*, first into monomania, then into insane delusion, is monitored above all by the index of his bodily condition. In *The Eustace Diamonds* (1873), Lizzie Eustace's growing terror of detection is also realized through immediate sensation: "With a horrid spasm across her heart, which seemed ready to kill her, so sharp was the pain, Lizzie recovered the use of her legs and followed Mrs Carbuncle into the dining room" (*ED* ch. 52).

"He who recounts these details has scorned to have a secret between himself and his readers. The diamonds were at this moment locked up within Lizzie's desk," notes the narrator immediately after the discovery of the apparent theft in *The Eustace Diamonds* – a text, which, with its interplay of the fetishization of women and jewels, is often seen to be a parody and riposte to Collins's *The Moonstone* (1868) (*ED* ch. 48).[6] Trollope had deliberately defused narrative suspense in *Orley Farm*, his earlier story of a woman with a secret which appeared two years after Collins's *The Woman in White* (1859–60) and the same year as Braddon's *Lady Audley's Secret*, in 1862. "I venture to think, I may almost say to hope, that Lady Mason's confession at the end of the last chapter will not have taken anybody by surprise," states the narrator near the beginning of the second volume (*OF* ch. 45). Trollope later seemed to regret this deliberate revelation, noting that "the plot of *Orley Farm* is probably the best I have ever made, – but it has the fault of declaring itself and thus coming to an end too early in the book" (*A* ch. 9). Such narrative transparency seems to be his greatest point of contrast with Collins and Braddon. But even this distinction breaks down if we compare Trollope's text with Collins's *No Name*, which appeared the same year as *Orley Farm*, and where the Vanstone sisters' illegitimacy is revealed near the beginning of the novel. Collins's justification of this maneuver could be Trollope's own. "All the main events in the story are purposely foreshadowed, before they take place," he states in the Preface to the novel, "my present design being to rouse the reader's interest in following the chain of circumstances by which these foreseen events are brought about," as the novel explores the complexity of the ambiguous heroine, Magdalen Vanstone, who like Mary Mason, struggles between contradictory impulses.

Conversely, if we reject as artificial the distinction between plot and character (as Collins does in the 1861 Preface to *The Woman in White*), further interconnections emerge in which "surface" effects generate particular forms of psychological interiority. Contemporary physiological psychologists such as Alexander Bain, William Carpenter, Thomas Laycock, and G. H. Lewes all stressed the intimate interconnections between mind and body, putting physical sensation, emotion, and intellectual response on a continuum rather than in opposition during the 1850s and 1860s, and emphasizing the complexity of human motivation and the power of unconscious mental activity.[7] These psychological developments are closely bound up with the novel's wider interest in internal mental states and their role in shaping character and behavior that Trollope, Collins, and Braddon have in common with other mid-Victorian novelists such as Elizabeth Gaskell, Charlotte Brontë, and George Eliot. Collins and Braddon share with George Eliot a preoccupation with secrecy as the manifestation of the power of repressed memory and the fascination with nemesis, which binds detective fiction to classical tragedy, and which Hardy would explore so devastatingly.

Despite his narrative transparency and broadly comic view of human actions, the suppressed events of the past also haunt and disrupt the present in Trollope's novels, often through the perverse actions of the protagonists themselves. Lady Mason successfully forges the codicil to her husband's will bequeathing Orley Farm to Lucius her son, but perversely fails to completely destroy all the evidence, so that the resentful lawyer Dockwrath is driven to discover her conspiracy when Lucius deprives him of his land. The eponymous anti-hero of *Cousin Henry* (1879) is unable to destroy the will which disinherits him, haunted by the fear that the past will return and destroy him. In *Ralph the Heir* the novel's comic counterplot of legitimate Ralph's courtship of the tailor's daughter Polly Neefit is set against the hubris of the old squire Gregory Newton, who attempts to override his own transgression of having fathered an illegitimate child by struggling to overturn the entail his own father had imposed on the estate. In this concern, not with secrecy as such so much as the effects of repression or denial, Trollope manifests what E. S. Dallas described in *The Gay Science* (1866) as the opposite trait of novels of character: "man is represented as made and ruled by circumstance, the victim of change and the puppet of intrigue," as narrative tension hinges on characters being placed in extreme situations, situations which grow nonetheless out of ordinary events, as they do in sensation fiction.[8] "Everything is legitimate, natural and possible, all the exaggerations of excitement have been carefully eschewed," Margaret Oliphant wrote, praising *The Woman in White* in 1862; and Trollope, too, pushes "legitimate" situations and emotions beyond their normal boundaries so that they turn back on themselves, questioning the legal, social and moral authority on which they had initially rested.[9]

Legitimacy, property, and marriage

This authority is questioned in Trollope's probing of what Henry James described as "those most mysterious of mysteries, the mysteries that are at our own doors."[10] While his fiction depends heavily on the comic use of marriage as a means of closure and resolution, these plots almost always exist alongside counterplots of unhappy or uncertain marriages – of struggles that are often more powerful sources of narrative tension than thwarted courtship. Many of the novels of the late 1850s and 1860s – *Doctor Thorne* (1858), *Castle Richmond* (1860), and *The Belton Estate* (1865) to name but a few – explore the legal, social, and emotional consequences of various forms of illicit liaisons; and the fall-out from unorthodox relationships highlights the often contradictory claims of formal law, dynastic imperative, and romantic love. However, from the late 1860s Trollope becomes increasingly concerned with the slipperiness of the codes of marriage and legitimacy and, with it, the instability of social identity itself. "There is nothing more difficult to decide than questions of legitimacy," remarks the solicitor Mr. Frick in *Lady Anna* (1874), and Trollope, like Collins, plays on the undecidability of personal legitimacy to explore the relationship between birth status and wider forms of economic, political, and symbolic power (*LA* ch. 21).

In testing the limits of marriage itself as a social and legal institution and the social and legal status of children, Trollope, like Collins and Braddon, is articulating and reworking current concerns and anxieties. The debates in Parliament that had surrounded the 1857 Divorce Act demonstrated how powerful patriarchal concerns with legitimacy remained deeply embedded in the revised legislation (which stipulated that while husbands could gain divorce on the ground of adultery alone, wives had to prove in addition bigamy, cruelty, or incest).[11] The wider discussions in the press surrounding both the Divorce Act and the unsuccessful first Married Women's Property Bill had attacked the ancient common law of coverture as an anachronism, and the question of what the rights and responsibility of marriage might be continued to be debated throughout the 1860s.

These questions became entangled with the equally thorny question of what actually constituted both marriage and legitimacy in a complex national and global context. The 1858 Legitimacy Declaration Act, which identified the newly formed Divorce Court as a forum for establishing cases of doubtful legitimacy, in practice highlighted the complex and contradictory relationship between a person's legitimacy and their status as a British subject. The incommensurability of conflicting codes of marriage both within the United Kingdom between England, Scotland, and Ireland, and between Britain and its present and former colonies surfaced again in cases such as the Yelverton bigamy scandal, which drew attention to the chaotic state of the marriage and property laws, which the Royal Commission of the Laws of Marriage in 1868 (and which Collins robustly attacked in his campaigning novel of 1870, *Man and Wife*) unsuccessfully attempted to address.

Trollope explores this ambiguity surrounding marriage in *John Caldigate* (1879), which is discussed in more detail elsewhere in this volume. Like Braddon's *Aurora Floyd*, this is a cross-class bigamy novel. Euphemia Smith, who had been Caldigate's informal spouse during his early life in Australia, threatens his status as a respectably married English landowner by claiming the legal validity of their former relationship. Though the danger of this disturbing colonial liaison is removed when it is discovered that Euphemia (in a classically sensational move) has altered the date of a letter in which Caldigate addresses her as his wife, the moral and legal obliquity of the story remains. Informal colonial partnerships were often accepted as valid marriages in English courts and the narrative makes clear that just as Caldigate's position and wealth as an English gentleman rested on his dubious colonial exploits, so his younger self had lived with Euphemia to all intents and purposes as his wife – that the distinction was purely a formal one – just as Paul Montague in *The Way We Live Now* had a moral obligation to his former American mistress, Mrs. Hurtle.

John Caldigate is presented as the victim of a scheming woman and her partner, in which the anarchic life of the colonies threatens English patrilineal stability. But Trollope is equally fascinated with the results of legally ambiguous liaisons, with the unstable boundary that separates the legitimate child and the bastard. Illegitimacy pervades mid-Victorian fiction and for Trollope, as for Elizabeth Gaskell and George Eliot, it highlights the sexual double standard and the inexorable return of the past. These concerns are picked up in Trollope's fiction, but in the 1870s and early 1880s it is the slippery legal boundary between legitimacy and illegitimacy exploited by Collins that becomes the means of probing the instability of the law and the performativity of social identity.[12] In *Ralph the Heir, Lady Anna* (1874), *Is He Popenjoy?* (1879), and *Mr Scarborough's Family* (1883) the question of legitimacy is also inextricably bound up with plots and plotting, further exposing the disingenuousness of Trollope's own dismissal of narrative intricacy in *An Autobiography*.[13] Although Trollope usually ends up explicitly supporting the "Burkean" values of genealogical continuity based on legitimate descent, the convolutions of his plots in practice undermine them.

As with Collins's *Armadale* (1866, in which the two central protagonists share a name) *Ralph the Heir* hinges on the contrasting position of the two Ralph Newtons – the heir of the title and his illegitimate cousin. The novel sets the feckless heir against the virtuous bastard; the rigidity of English common law and the artificiality of the entail against the ties of blood and affection. Ralph the legal heir morally delegitimizes himself by squandering the estate through taking out endless loans against his uncle's death, whereas Ralph the bastard is the perfect English gentleman – a fantasy of patrilineal continuity who is also the victim of the hubris which follows his father's attempt to alter the legal line of descent. At the same time the very duplication of the name makes "Ralph Newton" a tenuous identity, as the novel eats away at the possibility of any higher authority in a world where everybody survives by "growing into some shape of conviction from the moulds in which they are made to live ..." (*RH* ch. 41).

In contrast, *Lady Anna* and *Is He Popenjoy?* (1878) each hinge on the legal instability of the legitimate–illegitimate distinction. But while both novels are centrally concerned with the tensions between moral, legal, and natural right that this uncertainty highlights, the "older" concern with patrilineal inheritance of the legitimacy plot is supplemented and ultimately displaced by power struggles within and surrounding marriage itself. Unusually for Trollope, *Lady Anna* is a historical novel, opening in the immediate aftermath of the French Revolution, then brought forward to the 1830s. Though it is very different from Lady Carbury's sensational history *Criminal Queens* in *The Way We Live Now*, it also tells the story of the obsessive quest for legitimacy of an older woman, Josephine Murray, who, like Lady Mason in *Orley Farm*, will stop at nothing to shore up the social identity and status of her child. Trollope plays on the rhetoric of radical melodrama as well as sensation fiction here: the Earl, Anna's father, who pronounces his relationship with Josephine void in the novel's opening, is a "Gothic" aristocratic libertine, and Josephine and Anna are protected in the first part of the novel by the radical tailor Thomas Thwaite, who sees their claim as emblematic of the fight against aristocratic privilege. This link between personal and political legitimacy is transformed in the main body of the novel, as the fight over Anna's status in the Court of Queen's Bench is made into a sensational media event and also highlights her position as a woman, an object of exchange rather than an inheritor of wealth. The Whiggish compromise that Anna marry the young Earl, suggested by the solicitor-General Sir William Patterson, is rejected by Anna – who has pledged herself to Thomas Thwaite's son Daniel – and the "sensation" of the case is bound up with the romance plot spun round it by public opinion. But while Trollope depicts Josephine as engaged in an increasingly obsessive and pathological attempt to force her daughter to marry the new earl, he also defuses the simple polarities of melodrama. The new heir is no aristocratic villain but a personable young man, and a modern middle-class profes-sional, and in a final twist Daniel Thwaite, whom Anna finally marries and emigrates with, has all the makings of a repressive and controlling husband. This is an uneasy closure which many critics found unpalatable: "we trust that nothing may happen, even in Australia, to make Lady Anna regret that she married Daniel Thwaite the Cumberland tailor," commented *The Times* (*Crit. Her.* 389).

The performance of gender identity and the boundaries of the self

"The story with which I must occupy the time of the court . . . is replete with marvels and romance," states the Solicitor-General at the beginning of *Lovel v Murray* in *Lady Anna*. "I shall tell you of great crimes and of singular virtues, of sorrows that have been endured and conquered, and of hopes that have been nearly realised." As Trollope makes clear, Sir William Patterson's statement deliberately plays to the gallery – "the audience in the Court of Queen's Bench listened with breathless attention" – and while Sir William both acts as the conductor of the case and underwrites the expedient pragmatism of the law, *Lady Anna* also gently satirizes the dramatic possibilities of the courtroom (*LA* ch. 28). Sensational trial scenes, particularly those in which beautiful women are exposed and probed on the public stage, can be traced back to Scott's *The Heart of Midlothian* (1818) and were a key sensational feature of the 1860s and early 1870s, as Anthea Trodd has argued.[14] Ellen Wood's *Mrs Halliburton's Troubles* (1862), Eliot's *Felix Holt*, Charles Reade's *Griffith Gaunt* (1866), and Collins's *The Law and the Lady* (1875), as well as Trollope's own *Orley Farm* and

The Eustace Diamonds, use the literal and figural unveiling of women in court to blur the boundaries between public and private identities and reveal hidden emotions and motives. Influenced in part by highly dramatic contemporary cases, such as the much reported 1857 trial of Madeleine Smith, a middle-class young woman accused of poisoning her lover, but acquitted by the jury in part by her display of ladylike refinement, Trollope, like Reade and Collins, uses the sensational court scenes to test the limits of feminine performance.

Trollope fully exploits the dramatic resources of the trial scenes in *Orley Farm* and *The Eustace Diamonds*, both novels in which powerful women commit crimes in order to hold on to property which they feel they have a right to. In common with the powerful and dangerous women of much sensation fiction, they both raise questions about women's legitimacy in a world of overwhelming patrimonial power – a world in which it is not possible for women both to have and to be – and in both novels the ostensible act of theft displaces and, at the same time, implicitly stands for sexual transgression and the question of illegitimacy in its more specific sense. In both novels the courtroom is explicitly presented as a stage on which two women act out very different versions of femininity, suggesting contrasting notions of authenticity and performance. Lady Mason "raised her veil and never removed it again till she had left the court ... She had dressed herself with great care ... Her face was very pale, and somewhat hard; but no one on looking at it could say that it was a countenance of a woman overcome either by sorrow or by crime. She was perfect mistress of herself ..." (*OF* ch. 64). Yet this self-possession is radically at odds with Mary Mason's unstable representation in the novel as a whole; and her use of illicit means to pursue a natural and moral, if not a legal right, places her close to Collins's perverse heroine Magdalen Vanstone in *No Name*. Both women dissemble to realize a claim against unpleasant and parsimonious lawful heirs (in Mary Mason's case this is complicated by Lucius's position as younger son); both are set against saintly and compliant other women (in *Orley Farm* Edith Orme); both teeter on the edge of breakdown. And, like Isabel Carlyle in Ellen Wood's *East Lynne* (1861), Lady Mason is portrayed as a "fallen" woman in ways that force the reader to reassess that familiar stereotype, not through sexual transgression but through her private display of guilt and remorse.

While sympathy is elicited for Lady Mason by Mr. Furnival (who defends her despite suspecting her guilt), Lizzie Eustace puts on an affecting performance of feminine weakness and modesty in court, attempting to stay veiled and "bursting into tears and stretching forth before the bench her two clasped hands with the air of supplicant. From that moment the magistrate was altogether on her side, – and so were the public" (*ED* ch. 74). Lizzie's successful manipulation of public opinion is an aspect of the narrator's wider representation of her character as being as hard and immutable as the diamonds she clings to, and throughout the novel the jewels (which she often hides in a box beneath her skirts) operate as an extension of her value as a sexual object as well as desiring subject.[15] Lizzie comes close to such sensational villainesses as Lucy Audley in Braddon's *Lady Audley's Secret*; like Lucy she is sexually alluring, manipulative, and a consummate actress, and is portrayed by Trollope as twisting patriarchal values to her own ends. While the diamonds become hateful objects to Lizzie, the novel nonetheless displays the anxieties surrounding women's ownership of property; and their slippery status (they are neither clearly real nor personal property, neither exactly heirlooms nor paraphernalia) enacts Lizzie's disturbingly liminal status both inside and outside the family. Her position, too, is not simply contrasted with a saintly counterpart, but triangulated, set against two women placed uncomfortably within structures of homosocial exchange. Lucy Morris, the novel's "treasure," is Lizzie's virtuous counterpart, but her status as a poor middle-class woman is equally liminal and uncertain; while Lucinda Roanoke, the strong-minded horse-riding heiress in the style of Braddon's eponymous Aurora Floyd, is driven to the edge of madness by agreeing to a hateful engagement, from which she finally rebels – but in a way that can only be interpreted by her family as hysterical.

Trollope thus shows marriage as the source of destructive power struggles in a world in which, in the words of *John Caldigate's* Euphemia Smith, "A woman has to show a little spirit or she will be trodden absolutely into the dirt" (*JC* ch. 6). But even more powerfully he dramatizes the stresses that patriarchal structures and rigid class and gender roles place on men. Trollope's fiction is full of examples of insecure, weak or motiveless masculinity, and he places this lack of drive within the economic, psychological, and sexual pressures of the family far more explicitly than either Dickens or Collins do. It is men apparently possessed of power and status, more than women who seek it, who are most likely to perversely fail to fulfil social expectations, who fall into repetitive patterns of incontinent self-destruction which they are apparently unable to control, and who teeter on the edge of rationality: legitimate Ralph Newton, Felix Carbury, and Mountjoy Scarborough, being only three of the most obvious examples. At the same time Trollope, like Collins, shows how easily apparently upright forms of masculine behavior can become pathological – how the seemingly stable world of marriage can become the site of morbid masculinity when the rights of husbands over wives are too successfully internalized. The increasingly obsessive behavior of George Germaine in *Is He Popenjoy?* is one example, as the struggle of the nominal legitimacy of the infant heir is displaced by the struggle between the family's younger brother, his strong-minded wife and her scheming father. But above all it emerges in Trollope's devastating story of obsessive jealousy, *He Knew He Was Right*.

He Knew He Was Right turns the plot of the mad wife – developed in Charlotte Brontë's *Jane Eyre* (1847) and in *Lady Audley's Secret* and Ellen Wood's *St Martin's Eve* (1866) – inside out by extending and adapting the central sensational device of emerging insanity.[16] "Madness may intensify any quality, courage or hate, or jealousy or wickedness," noted the *Spectator*, discussing sensation fiction in 1866, remarking that in *St Martin's Eve* "Mrs Wood wants to paint jealousy in its extreme forms, and she has not of course the power to create Othello, or to paint, as Thackeray or Trollope might have done, the morbid passion in its naturalistic nineteenth-century dress."[17] P. D. Edwards has suggested that Trollope may have taken this comment as a cue, and *He Knew He Was Right* echoes Eliza Lynn Linton's story of an obsessionally jealous husband, *Sowing the Wind* (1867).[18] The *British Quarterly Review* described the novel as a psychological study of "a dangerous monomania; its origin in wilful caprice, its strengthening through perverse obstinacy, and its consummation in misery, madness and death," and Trollope makes a complex intervention in contemporary discussions of this mental condition (*Crit. Her.* 333).

Growing out of the older concept of melancholia, monomania was a slippery concept in the burgeoning field of psychological medicine – it could mean both a particular obsessional disorder or the beginnings of a full-scale bout of moral insanity. This wider definition, and the difficulties of understanding mental disorder that it raised, lay behind the influential French physician J. E. Esquirol's *Mental Maladies* (1845), which described monomania not as a reversion to a savage state so much as the direct product of modernity. Monomania "embraces all the mysterious anomalies of sensibility, all the phenomena of human understanding, all the consequences of the perversions of our natural inclinations, and all the errors of our passions," Esquirol writes. "The more the understanding is developed, and the more active the brain becomes, the more is monomania to be feared."[19] Trollope exploits this slipperiness in a way that relates closely to contemporary anxieties that monomania itself elicited about moral responsibility and the limits of masculine self-control. In *He Knew He Was Right* the workings of Trevelyan's mind become an interpretative problem within a narrative explicitly set up as a psychological case study. "I do not know that in any literary effort I ever fell more completely short of my own intention than in this story," Trollope later wrote in his *Autobiography*, stressing that he had wished to "create sympathy for an unfortunate man who ... is unwilling to submit his own judgement to the opinion of others" (*A* ch. 17). Yet in remorselessly following Trevelyan's monomania to its final end Trollope achieves a sophisticated set of perspectives, which again take up and reconfigure the narrative techniques and tropes of sensation fiction.

Trevelyan's desire to control and dominate his wife represents an anachronistic patriarchalism; but the conditions which foster his increasingly irrational obsessions – the private detective and the postal service – are resolutely modern. With the development of secular society, Esquirol writes, "it is the police which troubles feeble imaginations, and establishments for the insane are peopled with monomaniacs who, fearing this authority ... [think] themselves threatened, pursued and ready to be incarcerated by agents of the police."[20] Trollope introjects this structure of paranoia: it is Louis, pursued by his own demons of jealousy, who employs the ex-policeman Bozzle to spy on Emily, and Bozzle's initial bureaucratic efficiency and culture of suspicion is in turn finally undermined by his own wife. Trevelyan refuses to "submit his judgement to the opinion of others"; but his position is refracted through their opinion, and his behavior (like Sir Perceval Glyde's behavior in *The Woman in White*) is initially tolerated if not approved by polite society. Above all *He Knew He Was Right* both analyzes and mimics Trevelyan's condition in its very narrative structure, as the representation of Louis's mental state is achieved through shifts between interior monologue, free indirect discourse, and omniscient narration.

Trollope's fiction can thus be read as reworking his argument in the *Autobiography* and complicating it. Scott's *The Bride of Lammermoor* and Charlotte Brontë's *Jane Eyre* "charm us not simply because they are tragic," he insists, but "because we feel that men and women of flesh and blood ... are struggling amidst their woes" (*A* ch. 12). In many of his own novels, too, we are drawn into empathizing with many of the extremities of his characters. But Trollope's fiction does much more than illustrate his critical arguments. In his resolutely contemporary settings, his concern with the ambiguities of marriage and the position of women; his interest in the narrowness of the boundary between the legitimate and the illegitimate, and the normal and the pathological; he challenges the critical consensus that defined higher realism against its sensational other. His fiction not only makes use of "sensational" techniques, but makes us question and recast the literary categories that we use to make sense of the rich, complex, and hybrid nature of all mid-Victorian fiction.

NOTES

1 Walter M. Kendrick, *The Novel-Machine: The Theory and Fiction of Anthony Trollope* (Baltimore and London: Johns Hopkins University Press, 1980), pp. 49–51.

2 W. F. Rae [unsigned], "Sensation Novelists: Miss Braddon," *North British Review* 43 (September–December 1865), 205; see also, Kate Flint, *The Woman Reader 1837–1914* (Oxford: Clarendon Press, 1993).

3 See, for example Mark W. Turner, *Trollope and the Magazines: Gendered Issues in Mid-Victorian Britain* (Basingstoke: Macmillan, 2000), Graham Law, "The Professional Writing and the Literary Marketplace," *The Cambridge Companion to Wilkie Collins*, ed. Jenny Bourne Taylor (Cambridge: Cambridge University Press, 2006), and Deborah Wynne, *The Sensation Novel and the Victorian Family Magazine* (Basingstoke: Palgrave Macmillan, 2001).

4 Henry Mansel [unsigned], "Sensation Novels," *Quarterly Review* 113 (April 1863), 483.

5 Mansel, "Sensation novels," 486.

6 On the connections between the two novels, see Anthea Trodd, *Domestic Crime in the Victorian Novel* (Basingstoke: Macmillan, 1989), pp. 40–42 and Aviva Briefel, "Tautological Crimes: Why Women Can't Steal Diamonds," *Novel* (Fall 2003), 135–57.

7 For an overview of these debates in relation to mid-century fiction, see Jenny Bourne Taylor "Body and Mind," *The Cambridge Companion to English Literature 1832–1914*, ed. Joanne Shattock (Cambridge: Cambridge University Press, 2009), pp. 184–204.

8 E. S. Dallas, *The Gay Science* (London: Chapman & Hall, 1866), 2 vols., vol. II, p. 293.

9 "Sensation Novels," *Blackwoods Edinburgh Magazine* (May 1862), 566.

10 Henry James, "Miss Braddon," *The Nation*, November 9, 1865, 595.

11 See Mary Lyndon Shanley, *Feminism, Marriage and the Law in Victorian England* (Princeton: Princeton University Press, 1989).

12 For a wider discussion, see R. D. McMaster, *Trollope and the Law* (London: Macmillan, 1986).

13 For a fuller discussion of Trollope and illegitimacy, see Jenny Bourne Taylor, "Bastards to the Time: Legitimacy as Legal Fiction in Trollope's Fiction of the 1870s," *The Politics of Gender in Anthony Trollope's Novels*, ed. Margaret Markwick, Deborah Denenholz Morse, and Regenia Gagnier (Aldershot: Ashgate, 2009), pp. 45–60.

14 Trodd, *Domestic Crime*, pp. 130–55.

15 See Briefel, "Tautological Crimes," p. 140.

16 For an analysis of the novel as a reworking of *Jane Eyre*, see Deborah Morse, "'Some Girls who Come from the Tropics': Gender, Race and Imperialism in Anthony Trollope's *He Knew He Was Right*," *Politics of Gender*, ed. Markwick, Morse, and Gagnier, pp. 77–98.

17 "Madness in Novels," *Spectator*, February 3, 1866, 135.

18 P. D. Edwards, *Anthony Trollope, His Art and Scope* (New York: St. Martin's Press, 1978), pp. 114–16.

19 J. E. Esquirol, *Mental Maladies: A Treatise on Insanity* (1845), *Embodied Selves: An Anthology of Psychological Texts 1830–1890*, ed. Jenny Bourne Taylor and Sally Shuttleworth (Oxford: Clarendon Press, 1998), p. 256.

20 *Embodied Selves*, p. 257.

8

KATE FLINT

Queer Trollope

They're a queer lot, – ain't they, – the sort of people one meets about in the world?

Lord Carruthers (*ED* ch. 75)

Trollope's fiction contains a number of characters who are described as "queer." In *Barchester Towers*, the Archdeacon talks to his wife about the new vicar, the Reverend Francis Arabin, who is coming to stay with them. "'He's very queer, isn't he?' asked the wife. 'Well – he is a little odd in some of his fancies; but there's nothing about him you won't like ...'" (*BT* ch. 14). Attending a dinner at Gatherum Castle in *Doctor Thorne*, Frank asks his clergyman friend Mr. Athill about the other guests: "Who is that funny little man sitting there...? I never saw such a queer fellow in my life" – the object of scrutiny is the former apothecary, Mr. Bolus (*DT* ch. 19). In the same novel, Frank remarks of his sister's fiancé, the ambitious and unreliable Mr. Moffat, that "for an engaged lover he seems to me to have a very queer way with him." To a modern reader, the nature of this queerness seems plain enough: "he was a nice, dapper man," we are told, with "very nicely brushed" dark hair, carefully trimmed whiskers, "very white" hands; he has a limp handshake, he simpers, he speaks in "a pretty, mincing voice." He seems remarkably reticent for a supposedly enthusiastic suitor: "Frank, poor fellow! who was of a coarser mould, would, under such circumstances, have been all for kissing" (*DT* ch. 15).

In Trollope's fiction, for a man to be effeminate, unmasculine, indicates that he lacks the kind of straightforward, honest, if impetuous personality that the author bestowed on many of his most favored male characters. But "queer" did not carry exactly the same connotations in Trollope's time as it does today. From the mid-sixteenth century, it initially signified someone or something who was in some way contemptible or worthless, increasingly implying that they were untrustworthy (if a person), or counterfeit or forged (if a banknote). To be queer was to be unreliable, questionable, suspicious, strange, unusual – not what one seemed to be. By the middle of the nineteenth century, the word had also started to carry the meaning of eccentric or unconventional. Certainly by the 1890s, it was used in a specifically homosexual context (at the time of the Wilde trial, the Marquess of Queensberry employed it in a letter, thereby suggesting that this sense of "queer" already had conversational circulation) – but it does not seem to bear this unambiguous weight in Trollope. However, its deployment to indicate someone who does not seem – in whatever difficult-to-define way – to correspond to social norms is not totally out of keeping with the reclamation of the word from 1990 onwards. In this recent usage, "queer" comes to describe someone who sees themselves as positioned outside the heteronormative – that is, anyone whose sexual preferences are not exclusively heterosexual (and this includes the asexual and the autosexual), or heterosexuals whose practices or proclivities place them outside the mainstream. But even if it is often used as an inclusive term for the GLBT community,[1] those who have claimed it most enthusiastically have very often done so because it allows them to free themselves from identity politics, and from maintaining that one's sexual being is an indivisible, core part of one's given make-up. "Queer" describes what one does (or doesn't do), not who one *is*. Judith Butler, one of the critics whose work has been most foundational to queer theory, has argued for the importance, moreover, of "the contingency of the term:"[2] in other words, that it both carries with it an element of the unpredictable, and that it is of the nature of "queerness" that it is dependent upon, or conditional upon, something else.

This idea of contingency is highly useful when it comes to considering "queer Trollope." I am using the term with one eye on current usage, understanding it, in this essay, primarily in relation to expressions of same-sex desire, whether between women or men. But I also take such constructions of desire as contingent upon mid-nineteenth-century social practices, and in relation to what was, or was not, conceived of at the time as aberrant from the norms of sexual arrangements and self-presentation. Trollope's literary career predates the pathologization of same-sex desire that, in the last decade of the nineteenth century, allowed commentators to see it as oppositional to, rather than as a variety of, normative sexual activity and affectionate preferences. Such pathologization led directly to the labeling of people's sexual orientations, drawing a clearer line than hitherto between the non-normative and the normative. Certainly, buggery was an offence (even if the death penalty for this activity, whether between men or a man and a woman, was abolished in 1861); but the Labouchère amendment, creating the offence of "gross indecency" – the first specifically anti-homosexual law in Britain – was passed three years after Trollope's death, in 1885.

It would initially seem that there is something decidedly queer, or at least perverse, in reading Trollope's fiction with an eye for queerness. His writing has from very early on been described as though it is synonymous with normalcy, with moral probity, with healthiness – as George Eliot put it, on receiving a copy of *Rachel Ray* in 1863, something "which has impressed me very happily in all these writings of yours that I know ... is that people are breathing good bracing air in reading them ... They are like pleasant public gardens, where people go for amusement, & whether they think of it or not, get health as well" (*Letters* 1:238). But there were, as Trollope was well aware, plenty of same-sex liaisons, whether enduring or fleeting, taking place in the society in which he moved and about which he wrote. And, in the sprawling, proliferating cast list that results from what Robert Polhemus termed Trollope's anxious desire to record "the blurring flux of life,"[3] there are numerous examples of women and men whose behavior and preferences are decidedly non-normative – if not downright queer, by any standard. These are of all kinds. They include the autoeroticism of Miss Mackenzie, in the eponymously titled novel, admiring her aging self in the mirror, her hand moving away from the grey hairs around her ears, and stroking her silky hair: "her hand touched the outline of her cheek ... She pulled her scarf tighter across her bosom, feeling her own form, and then she leaned forward and kissed herself in her glass" (*MM* ch. 9). They encompass the situation in which we finally encounter Lizzie Eustace, in *The Prime Minister*, living with a widow, Mrs. Leslie, who has "attached herself lately with an almost more than feminine affection to Lady Eustace" (*PM* ch. 48). But Trollope never presents such moments and circumstances in a sensational manner, far less as grounds for exceptional secrecy or blackmail or guilt. His queer characters do not feature as prominently as the major players in his courtship plots (Lizzie Eustace's appearance is a kind of catch-up afterword to her starring role in *The Eustace Diamonds*), and the longings, pragmatic maneuverings, betrayals, disappointments, frustrations, anticipations, embraces, and betrothals that accompany them. Yet they are nonetheless a presence – with, at times, their own small-scale dramas: they are part of a social continuum, rather than – for the most part – characters distinguished by an identity politics in some way or another predicated on their preferred choice of sexual partner alone.

The one obvious exception of a type that would seem to counter this generalization can be found in Trollope's deliberately overblown descriptions of vociferous supporters of women's rights. By emphasizing the fact that his most outspoken feminists, like the Americans Wallachia Petrie in *He Knew He Was Right* and Dr. Olivia Q. Fleabody in *Is He Popenjoy?*, had strongly masculine characteristics, Trollope may or may not also have been signaling their sexual preferences. Wally Petrie certainly seems to want to dominate her friend Caroline, who "had been the beloved of her heart since Caroline Spalding was a very little girl." She had hoped that "Caroline would through life have borne arms along with her in that contest which she was determined to wage against man" (*HKWR* ch. 72) but it was not to be. Trollope is not quite as unsympathetic to Wally as some commentators have claimed: he may portray her as an extremist, "so positively wedded to women's rights in general, and to her own rights in particular, that it was improbable that she should ever succumb to any man" and as ridiculously inflexible in her pompous and self-righteous rectitude, but he also tries to explain her as a national type, albeit one not likely to appeal to his immediate readership. "There are many such," he comments, "in America who have noble aspirations, good intellects, much energy, and who are by no means unworthy of friendship" (*HKWR* ch. 72). Nonetheless, the specific example of Miss Petrie offers him an opportunity for satire that he cannot pass up. Her resolute separatist feminism, expressed through her possessive feelings for Caroline as well as through her broader ideological pronouncements, is in the end, however, seen as something to be pitied as well as ridiculed, in large part because Trollope sees it as cutting her off from fuller social participation.

These ostentatiously masculine women are in some ways the counterpart to the effete and effeminate men – like Mr. Moffat – who are scattered through the pages of Trollope's fiction. What Trollope seems to be conveying through these male-gendered examples is a deficiency in manliness, and hence in attractiveness – whether to women or men. Their queerness is of a diffuse sort: it is, above all, manifested through their fastidious self-presentation – their grooming, their clothes – which resembles that of a Regency dandy, and as such is seen as highly suspect in a mid-nineteenth-century gentleman. More strongly, however, and in the case of both sexes, Trollope's antipathy is roused by the solipsism of the characters concerned. This is brought home by the figure of Francesca Altifiorla in *Kept in the Dark*. "She had her theories about women's rights, and the decided advantages of remaining single, and the sufficiency of a lady to stand alone in the world" (*KD* ch. 20). She, however, is resolutely heterosexual, or at least very prepared to give up her principles to marry a Baronet, only to revert, when ditched by him, to lecturing on feminism in the United States as a career move, thinking that "in one of those large Western Halls, full of gas" – it's unclear whether Trollope is thinking of the lighting system or the hot air of the women's movement – "and intelligence, she could rise to the height of her subject with a tremendous eloquence" (*KD* ch. 22).

Queer women are not, in the long run, identified in Trollope by such outspoken feminist positioning, but by far less self-seeking performances. Much more interesting than the obvious figures of satire, the verbal counterparts of contemporaneous *Punch* cartoons, are Trollope's "old maids" – especially those who are forthright in their avowals of independence, and yet who manage to sustain good friends and a respected place in their communities. To be sure, they are sometimes presented as entirely sexless: the Dean of Barchester's only daughter is a "gaunt spinster," Miss Trefoil, "a lady very learned in stones, ferns, plants, and vermin, and who has written a book about petals" (*BT* ch. 10). Far less desiccated is Miss Todd, one of the British visitors to the Holy Land whom we encounter in *The Bertrams* (1859) "a maiden lady, fat, fair, and perhaps almost forty; a jolly jovial lady, intent on seeing the world, and indifferent to many of its prejudices and formal restraints" (*B* ch. 9). She is said to have been modeled on Frances Power Cobbe, who made an eleven-month journey through Italy, Greece, Egypt, Palestine, and Syria in 1857, defying convention by camping alone in the desert (Sadleir 384n). Cobbe was to meet Mary Lloyd, her lifelong partner, in 1860, and although there is no hint of such a companion when Miss Todd reappears in *Miss Mackenzie* (1865), she is still bouncy and happy in her single, busily social life.

In *He Knew He Was Right*, Priscilla Stanbury provides a further, and more sustained, example of a woman who stands out for her lack of interest in marriage. Despite the fact that she lives very modestly, she refuses to give up independence and autonomy for material advantage, and she is ready to share this attitude, advising her niece Dorothy not to marry a man whom she does not love simply for money. Unlike Trollope's loud-mouthed feminists, she is prepared to listen to the views of others, and can, if necessary, admit to being wrong, but she is certainly not afraid to speak her mind. Among the issues about which she holds strong opinions is her own position with regards to marriage. Emily Trevelyan asks her, "Why should you not get married, as well as Dorothy [Priscilla's sister]?" "Who would have me?" she replies, saying first that she would want a husband who was both sensible and sensitive, and then continuing – as if recognizing the complete impossibility of these demands – "I am often cross, and I like my own way, and I have a distaste for men. I never in my life saw a man whom I wished even to make my intimate friend" (*HKWR* ch. 16).[4] In a novel that centers on a marriage gone terribly wrong, and that provides a number of further variations on the compromises that women can ill-advisedly make, Priscilla's point about knowing one's own mind when it comes to linking one's life to that of a man has resonances that go way beyond self-description.[5] Grabbing at any vaguely eligible man who will have one was a danger to personal happiness that Trollope repeatedly warns his women readers against through example. It was an act of panic reinforced by statistics: the 1861 census revealed a ratio of 1,053 women to every 1,000 men (a rise from 1,042:1,000 ten years earlier), with the greatest "surplus," of 209,663 women, occurring in the 20–29 age range: figures prompting, in 1862, such articles as W. R. Greg's "Why are Women Redundant?" and Frances Power Cobbe's "What Shall We Do With Our Old Maids?" To remain single was not necessarily an active choice.

But for some it was, and for a range of reasons. Lily Dale, of *The Small House at Allington* and *The Last Chronicles of Barset*, appears decidedly perverse, and emotionally masochistic, in her refusal to get over the perfidious Crosbie and opt, instead, for her devoted, and eminently suitable suitor, Johnny Eames. Nonetheless, her determination not to enter into a matrimonial compromise is also a spirited act of defiance on Trollope's own part, declining to pay back the reader's investment in the history of her love life by serving up a happy ending. It provides, moreover, an occasion for the narrator to advance the view that the heart is a capricious organ: that one cannot force oneself into accepting a particular love object just because convention, and indeed apparent suitability, makes it look to the outside observer that this is the right thing to do: "If the heart were always malleable and the feelings could be controlled, who would permit himself to be tormented by any of the reverses which affection meets? ... But the heart is not malleable; nor will feelings admit of such control" (*SHA* ch. 50).

Thinking outside convention: nowhere is this more startlingly put into practice than by Kate Vavasor, in *Can You Forgive Her?*, who acts as a kind of surrogate suitor for their cousin Alice on behalf of her brother George, speaking for him with more eloquent pleading than he can muster himself (she is, indeed, attached to him to an almost perverse degree: "The truth is, I'm married to George" [*CYFH* ch. 6]). When Alice gives her George's letter of proposal to read, Kate's response is fervent: "'Oh, Alice, may I hope? Alice, my own Alice, my darling, my friend! Say that it shall be so!' And Kate knelt at her friend's feet upon the heather, and looked up into her face with eyes full of tears." She goes on to complicate and confuse gender by posing a hypothesis: "is it not a letter of which if you were his brother you would feel proud if another girl had shown it to you?" (*CYFH* ch. 31). Sharon Marcus discusses this passage at some length in the course of an exemplary discussion of Trollope and the question of women and marriage in relation to this novel. She shows how mid-Victorian debates about divorce and marriage "indicate a general awareness of the plasticity of marriage." As legislators discussed how the terms of marriage between a woman and a man might be shifted, so "marriage" as a concept expanded in the vernacular understanding, and "acquaintances, friends, relatives and colleagues conferred marital status such as cohabitation, financial interdependence, physical intimacy, and agreements about fidelity";[6] moreover, Marcus goes on to demonstrate, the novel itself makes it very clear that although relationships between men and women achieve their best state in hierarchical marriage,[7] women have additional and varied forms of relationship open to them that could result in personal happiness.

As Marcus shows, Trollope was familiar, even friendly, with a number of women who were involved in lesbian partnerships. Through his mother and his brother, he knew members of the Italian Anglo-American expatriate circle of Florence and Rome, including Harriet Hosmer, Isa Blagden, Charlotte Cushman, Emma Stebbins, Cobbe, and Lloyd. Through them, too, he met Kate Field, another lesbian who became a friend and correspondent (Field never married, and thus Trollope's attraction to her was never validated through confirmation of her heterosexuality).[8] He was very supportive of Emily Faithfull and her Victoria Press, which sustained women writers, illustrators, and print compositors: he contributed "The Journey to Panama" to the Press's anthology, *Victoria Regia* (1861) and "Miss Ophelia Gledd" to *A Welcome* (1863) – the first a story about a woman whose inheritance allows her to remain single, and the second about a feisty Boston woman, unmistakably modeled on Kate Field (and ultimately married off).[9]

Very noticeably, Trollope's independent, and queer, women are inserted into stories that, in one way or another, pivot on the highly topical question of woman's role in relation to marriage. Women's queerness, however tolerantly, even sympathetically treated, is perennially positioned in relation to a heteronormative understanding of marriage and its place both within society and within mid-nineteenth-century novelistic plotting – and hence, however quietly and tacitly, helping to reinforce it *as* a norm – albeit a norm with alternatives. But in what ways does Trollope exhibit an awareness of *male* homosexual behavior – a topic not overtly imbued with the current urgency of the "marriage question"? Certainly, the society about which he writes is a very homosocial one – to use the term popularized by Eve Kosovsky Sedgwick in *Between Men* (1985). There are the friendships, often intense, formed by young men at college (usually, in Trollope's fiction, Oxford) – friendships consolidated through boating and hunting rather than shared study, and marked by a pattern of gods and acolytes, like the "little sect of worshippers" that formed around George Bertram at Trinity (*B* ch. 1). There are the bonds formed at work: the atmosphere in the offices of the Civil Service, Trollope tells us near the opening of *The Three Clerks*, is, in its patterns of favoritism and rivalry, much like that of public school. Throughout his fiction, men enter into deep and affectionate friendships with one another, the depth of the feelings perceived by Trollope – who at the same time recognizes their inexpressibility. He writes of Harry Gilmour's sentiments towards Frank Fenwick in *The Vicar of Bullhampton* that he "loved his friend dearly. Between these two there had grown up now during a period of many years that undemonstrative, unexpressed, almost unconscious affection, which, with men, will often make the greatest charm of their lives. It may be doubted whether either of them had ever told the other of his regard. 'Yours always,' in writing was the warmest term that was ever used" (*VB* ch. 62). And there are the numerous London clubs in which men of all ages meet and socialize – the Beaufort and Brooks', the Mountaineers, Pandemonium, and Peripatetics, and the dissolute Beargarden.

Yet if the homosociality of this society slid into any type of homosexual activity, or if the club members ever took a circuitous route home, visiting those "pleasant public gardens" for a different type of amusement from that which George Eliot had in mind, Trollope is silent on the matter. Nonetheless, he was far from blind to the existence of intense homoerotic attraction, as is vividly demonstrated by the relationship between Owen Fitzgerald and Patrick Desmond in *Castle Richmond*. Owen and Patrick are both portrayed as exceptionally attractive: their attraction for each other is readily comprehensible in the terms of classical history and mythology. Owen is introduced as "a very handsome man," tall, athletic, "with short, light chestnut-tinted hair, blue eyes, and a mouth perfect as that of Phoebus" (*CR* ch. 2), and this Apollonian reference is consolidated by the way in which he mentors the younger earl in horse-leaping and other sporting activities. As the youth grows into young manhood, he meets "no other friend to whom he could talk of sport and a man's outward pleasures when his mind was that way given, and to whom he could also talk of soft inward things, – the heart's feelings, and aspirations, and wants. Owen would be as tender with him as a woman, allowing the young lad's arm round his body, listening to words which the outer world would have called bosh – and have derided as girlish. So at least thought the young earl to himself" (*CR* ch. 34).

Rather than suggesting that there is something unusual or unhealthy about this, Trollope goes on to comment that "all boys long to be allowed utterance occasionally for these soft tender things; – as also do all men ..." (*CR* ch. 34). Through this classically inflected companionship, coupled with the fact that early in the novel, Owen falls for, and proposes to, the earl's sixteen-year-old sister, Trollope suggests that male sexuality is not readily compartmentalized into hetero-and homosexuality, but rather exists on a continuum – something made completely clear through the way in which Owen is compellingly attractive to – and attracted to – women and men alike (even if Patrick declares on several occasions that he will never marry). Indeed, Clara and Patrick's young widowed mother falls heavily for him, too, in the novel's quiet tragedy of a woman perceived to be too old to be considered marriage material at the age of thirty-eight. Clara's engagement to Owen comes to nothing – she marries his cousin instead. Since she is decidedly insipid, the proto-sensation fiction plot of bigamy and uncertain inheritances is far more interesting than the courtship dramas – until, that is, the close of the novel, when Patrick visits Owen to try to make him renew his courtship of his sister. It is clear that for Patrick, this is less a way of snagging a husband worthy of Clara than a means of trying to claim Owen for himself: the strength of the attraction between them is unmissable when Owen throws his arm over the earl's shoulder, presses him "with something almost like an embrace," and Patrick "squeezed Owen's arm with strong boyish love," and a little later throws himself on his breast in "a passion of tears" – Owen's own eyes are full of tears, too (*CR* ch. 34). In part, these are due to his continuing, romantic, chivalric attachment to Clara – but his affections are far from undivided: "'I, Owen Fitzgerald of Hap House, still love her better than all that the world else can give me; indeed, there is nothing else that I do love, – except you, Desmond'" (*CR* ch. 34). Clara is unreceptive to Owen's renewed proposal; and he, in turn, fails even to suspect that her mother would have been ecstatic to have been made an offer herself.

But this is not the end of the story. Patrick leaves Eton that summer, "in order that he might travel for a couple of years with Owen Fitzgerald before he went to Oxford. It had been the lad's own request, and had been for a while refused by Owen. But Fitzgerald had at last given way to the earl's love, and they had started together for Norway" (*CR* ch. 44). Most probably, Trollope saw Norway as a plausible outdoors destination (chapter 41 of *The Claverings*, "Going to Norway," features a fishing trip): it could in no way be associated with Mediterranean sybaritism.[10] Yet we learn neither where else they went, nor exactly what happens to them: "For two years Lord Desmond travelled with him, and after that Owen Fitzgerald went on upon his wanderings alone" (*CR* ch. 44): neither is inscribed into any future heterosexual relationship.

At the very least, *Castle Richmond* offers a clear invitation to read the bond between Owen and Patrick as one based on strong, and mutual, sexual attraction. Its rarity in Trollope's novels lies in the sustained way in which the narrative attention falls on these two men, rather than homosexuality being a matter for a veiled aside. To be sure, Trollope showed his awareness of men whose sexual preferences were solely, or largely, for other men. In *The Eustace Diamonds*, writing of the way in which Frank Greystock cannot stop himself from kissing Lizzie Eustace on three occasions even after he has engaged himself to Lucy Morris, the narrator comments how "It is almost impossible for a man, – a man under forty and unmarried, and who is not a philosopher, – to have familiar and affectionate intercourse with a beautiful young woman, and carry it on, as he might do with a friend of the other sex" (*ED* ch. 65). "Not a philosopher" – not, in other words, a Socrates or a Plato, synonymous with homosexual relationships.[11] That such practices were linked not only to the ancient world, but with the contemporary East is hinted at in *Barchester Towers*, where Bertie Stanhope is found, at the end of a garden party,

> comfortably ensconced in the ha-ha, with his back to the sloping side, smoking a cigar, and eagerly engaged in conversation with some youngster from the further side of the county, whom he had never met before, who was also smoking under Bertie's pupilage, and listening with open ears to an account given by his companion of some of the pastimes of the Eastern clime.   (*BT* ch. 42)

"The Eastern clime," in either its real or its imaginary form, infiltrates several of Trollope's short stories. It is, indeed, in his short stories that one finds his queerest writing of all. In "A Ride Across Palestine" (also known as "The Banks of the Jordan") (1861), the male narrator, calling himself Mr. Jones, travels from Jerusalem to the Dead Sea with a young man who introduces himself as "Mr. Smith" in a hotel – a bashful, somewhat self-effacing man for whom the narrator feels an instant attraction (the generic names alone stand as warnings of deception of one sort or another). Mr. Smith is modest – he doesn't wish Mr. Jones to rub brandy into his saddle-sore body; he insists that he prefers to bathe in his room rather than swim in public. When he puts out his hand to Mr. Jones who presses it in a token of friendship, "My own hand was hot and rough with the heat and sand; but his was soft and cool almost as a woman's. I thoroughly hate an effeminate man" – the narrator is suspiciously vehement in this assertion – "but, in spite of a certain womanly softness about this fellow, I could not hate him" (Thompson 179). A few minutes later, and after the narrator firmly proclaims his own liking for women, "We were silent again for a while, and it was during this time that I found myself lying with my head in his lap" (Thompson 179) – a curious disavowal of agency: he sleeps, wakes, finds Smith's hand on his brow. A few pages later, as their journey is coming to an end, he avows that he "loved him" – quickly qualifying this – "as though he were a younger brother" (Thompson 184). The reader has perhaps already guessed what the narrator has not – that Smith is a woman in disguise, fleeing from a guardian who wishes to marry her off. Jones regrets deeply that he deceived her by telling her, falsely, that he is unmarried – "In truth the one person really deceived had been myself" (Thompson 189). But in what way? By the obvious mistake of gender identity, or by his concealment, even to himself, of the true nature of his desires? Did Jones, at one level, suspect that Smith *was* a woman? Is this, therefore, a fantasy of heterosexual adultery, or of homoeroticism? Or might its queerness rest, in part, in the fact that the narrative certainly pivots around the transgressive, but the precise nature of this transgressiveness is diffuse, unnamable with any certitude?[12]

Whatever deception takes place in "A Ride Across Palestine" is made possible through the transformative effects of dress: Trollope's sartorial playfulness anticipates, in the most obvious of ways, Virginia Woolf commenting in *Orlando* that "often it is only the clothes that keep the male or female likeness, while underneath the sex is the very opposite of what is above."[13] Of course, Woolf was concerned with something more complicated – questions of identity and gender that pertain to the mind as much as to the physical body – but Trollope was well aware of the trust that one places in being able to read significance into dress. Nowhere does this become more obvious than in "The Turkish Bath" (1869) – a story, Trollope claimed, that was closely based on fact – and in which clothes disappear completely, offering no guide to class or relative affluence or background. A man – a man, moreover, whom the magazine-editor narrator realizes he has already noticed hovering around on the street outside – starts up a conversation with him in the all-male Jermyn Street Turkish Baths. This is a queer setting indeed, marked by "picturesque orientalism" and "very skilful eastern boys who glide about the place and create envy by their familiarity with its mysteries" (Thompson 514). Trollope's narrator describes in considerable detail how the clientele "divested ourselves of our ordinary trappings beneath the gaze of five or six young men lying on surrounding sofas" and wear their towels in different styles – one round "our own otherwise naked person," the other as a shawl, under the arm, as a turban – and thereby resembling "an Arab in the streets of Cairo" (Thompson 514–15). As Mark Turner has observed, this is a story marked by sexual tension, albeit of a teasing, unfulfilled nature, and powered by undercurrents of desire, financial need, and exchange. Being addressed by this strange man who (mendaciously) vaunts his cosmopolitanism, and offered a cheroot, the narrator appears intrigued, even excited by him. But this is no straightforward cruising: while the narrator might seem to expect, or at least hope for a sexual encounter, "the only thing offered to the editor is a manuscript."[14] Although, on the surface, this is a semi-comic story, at the editor's expense, as he comes to realize (when the man eventually visits him in his office) that he has been totally duped – the man is a fraud, a deluded madman – there are other stories, other scenarios, that lie tantalizingly close to the overt tale of deception.

One further short story, "The Telegraph Girl" (1877) is also unquestionably queer in the potential it offers for alternative social arrangements. Lucy Wilson, working as a "Telegraph Girl" in the Telegraph Office of the General Post Office, finds herself working, living without family, "'just as though she were a young man,' for it was thus that she described to herself her own position over and over again" (Thompson 763) – except that certain things she enjoys, like going to the theater, that would be acceptable for a young man, are beyond the bounds of propriety. The question of loneliness is solved by sharing a bedroom with another young woman from work, Sophy Wilson – although she is "almost disgusted" by pretty, feminine Sophy's interest in men and "the necessity of finding a husband" (Thompson 766). Although to all intents and purposes this is a heterosexual romance, albeit a slightly unorthodox one (Lucy eventually marries an older engineer in the same lodging house, despite Sophy's initial, and apparently successful attempts to capture his heart), Katie-Louise Thomas has explored the connection between female Post Office workers, and the ways in which they "earned roles as proto-lesbian heroines in fiction,"[15] not least through the parallels that are drawn between public duty and same-sex passion (Eliza Lynn Linton's hardly pro-lesbian *The Rebel of the Family*, in which GPO employee Perdita is temporarily thrilled by the prospect of the possibilities offered by a lesbian household, was published in 1880, three years after Trollope's story). Work – as it had done for so long in the case of men – offers possibilities for independence outside conventional marriage, for the development of moral self-sufficiency, and for the forging of relationships that have their origins in a structured world of public obligations, rather than within a domestic sphere.

It is significant, I think, that these three experimental fictions of Trollope's should take the form of the short story. This genre was especially amenable to the presentation of queer relationships – as was to become particularly apparent at the *fin-de-siècle* – because such writing, encouraging the social vignette, the puzzling, the unworked-through, thrived on inconclusive plots, and on leaving a great deal of interpretation up to the reader's speculation. In its frequent refusal to come to a clear-cut conclusion, to tie up loose ends, and to render motives and futures legible, it might, when considered in relation to the conventions of the Victorian novel, even be said to be a perverse form – queer narrative. No wonder that Trollope was at his most socially ludic in this developing mode, where he could set forth unconventional scenarios without any risk of them upending the ordinariness of the world that his novels depict.

Yet importantly, in these novels, Trollope does not exclude from sympathetic – as well as critical – attention those whose lifestyles do not exemplify heterosexual courtship, romance, and marriage. L. J. Swingle has rightly remarked that "fundamental differences of mind among people constitutes one of the primary laws of Trollopian territory."[16] Such differences, of affectionate objects as well as of mental operations, lie at the heart of Trollope's fascination with moral nuance, and with the unpredictability that one continually encounters among the apparently ordinary and everyday. Perversity – towards others, towards oneself, towards social expectations – is a perpetual feature of the ordinariness that Trollope records and invents. Intimately linked to such perversity are attitudes and practices that might unequivocally be called queer – whether by Trollope's own tenets, or by those of the twenty-first-century reader. Queerness, in other words, may stand out, provide the surprise or the oddity around which a short story can pivot. Yet even more notable, in the long run, is the degree to which it has been integrated into the daily fabric of Trollope's fictional world. Whether this queerness is seen as a part of a sexual continuum, or as something distinctly different – and Trollope's fiction allows for both possibilities – the varied manifestations of queerness in his writing allow one to believe in something that, from the vantage point of the twenty-first century, seems both utopian and achievable: that queerness can be seamlessly absorbed into the complex fabric of the everyday.

NOTES

My thanks to Alice Echols, for invaluable discussion and thoughtful reading of this chapter.

1 GLBT refers to gay, lesbian, bisexual, and transgender.
2 Judith Butler, "Critically Queer," in *Bodies That Matter: On the Discursive Limits of "Sex"* (New York: Routledge, 1993), p. 230.
3 Robert M. Polhemus, *The Changing World of Anthony Trollope* (Berkeley: University of California Press, 1968), p. 9.
4 For a measured discussion of Priscilla's sexual identity, see Ellen Moody, *Trollope on the Net* (London and Rio Grande: Hambledon Press, 1999), pp. 75–78.
5 Published just before John Stuart Mill's *The Subjection of Women* (1869), *He Knew He Was Right* was written when questions of women's role in marriage was very much a matter of current conversation, a point well made by Ruth apRoberts in her influential essay on the novel, "Emily and Nora and Dorothy and Priscilla and Jemima and Carry," *The Victorian Experience: The Novelists*, ed. Richard A. Levine, (Athens, OH: Ohio University Press, 1976), pp. 87–120.
6 Sharon Marcus, *Between Women: Friendship, Desire, and Marriage in Victorian England* (Princeton: Princeton University Press, 2007), p. 227.
7 Though certainly not their only state: there are various instances of prostitution mentioned in the novel.

8 For more about this circle, and about Kate Field, see Julia Markus, *Across an Untried Sea: Discovering Lives Hidden in the Shadow of Convention and Time* (New York: Alfred Knopf, 2000), pp. 62–64; Lisa Merrill, *When Romeo Was a Woman: Charlotte Cushman and Her Circle of Female Spectators* (Ann Arbor: University of Michigan Press, 1999), pp. 171–204; Martha Vicinus, *Intimate Friends: Women Who Loved Women, 1778–1928* (Chicago: University of Chicago Press, 2004), pp. 31–55; and Lilian Whiting, *Kate Field: A Record* (Boston: Little Brown, 1900), pp. 83–146.

9 See also Margaret F. King, "'Certain Learned Ladies': Trollope's *Can You Forgive Her?* and the Langham Place Circle," *Victorian Literature and Culture* 21 (1993), 307–26.

10 One might note in passing that the death penalty for male homosexual acts had been removed in Norway in 1842, just a few years before the novel is set.

11 For an elaboration of this point, see Margaret Markwick, *New Men in Trollope's Novels: Rewriting the Victorian Male* (Aldershot: Ashgate, 2007), p. 97.

12 For a queer reading of the tale – which, however, I think is over-confident in its readings of homoerotic imagery – see Mark Forrester, "Redressing the Empire: Anthony Trollope and British Gender Anxiety in 'The Banks of the Jordan,'" *Imperial Desire: Dissident Sexualities and Colonial Literature*, ed. Philip Holden and Richard J. Ruppel, (Minneapolis and London: University of Minnesota Press, 2003), pp. 115–31. See also William S. Cohen, "Deep Skin," *Thinking the Limits of the Body*, ed. Jeffrey Jerome Cohen and Gail Weiss, (Albany: SUNY Press, 2003), pp. 63–82, esp. pp. 67–73.

13 Virginia Woolf, *Orlando: A Biography* [1928] (New York: Harcourt, 1956), p. 189.

14 Mark W. Turner, *Trollope and the Magazines: Gendered Issues in Mid-Victorian Britain* (Basingstoke: Macmillan, 2000), p. 24. See also Mark W. Turner, *Backward Glances: Cruising the Queer Streets of New York and London* (London: Reaktion Books, 2003), pp. 73–78.

15 Katie-Louise Thomas, "A Queer Job for a Girl: Woman Postal Workers, Civil Duty and Sexuality 1870–80," *In a Queer Place: Sexuality and Belonging in British and European Contexts*, ed. Kate Chedgzoy, Emma Francis, and Murray Pratt (Aldershot: Ashgate, 2002), pp. 50–70, p. 51.

16 L. J. Swingle, *Romanticism and Anthony Trollope: A Study in the Continuities of Nineteenth-Century Thought* (Ann Arbor: University of Michigan Press, 1990), p. 26.

9

LAURIE LANGBAUER

The hobbledehoy in Trollope

We know Trollope as chronicler of the clergy, the parliament, and the Civil Service. Critics account for the form of his novels and his understanding of characterization, in fact, in terms of the category of "career" that was coming into its fore in England with the rise of professionalism in the nineteenth century – the self as determined and linearly plotted by the trajectory of a profession, the very notion of identity disciplined and shaped by institutions such as the Church or government.[1] In Trollope's novels, however, there is always a contrary fantasy. His novels also contain famous accounts of awkward youth – his "hobbledehoys" – who, no matter how much they want to fit in, remain *de trop*. They're terrible at their jobs, gauche in company – they cannot fit themselves onto any kind of straightforward path. They are sidetracked or arrested or just plain fail, even when it comes to the kind of basic development – such as growing up – that we think ought to unfold naturally.

These young ne'er-do-wells keep showing up in Trollope's novels – Trollope identifies Charley Tudor in *The Three Clerks* (1857) and Johnny Eames in *The Small House at Allington* (1864) and *The Last Chronicle of Barset* (1867) as hobbledehoys. But this kind of backward and ineffective young man appears throughout Trollope's fiction often and in many guises.[2] Readers recognize that hobbledehoys seem close to Trollope's heart; the partiality with which he regards them, we think, must tell us something important about Trollope's narrative intentions or social appraisal. But – just as with their parents, friends, and superiors in Trollope's novels – it can be hard for readers to know what to do with such young men. It can seem easier simply to throw up our hands and move on. We feel inclined to dismiss the narrator's marked sympathy for these graceless youths as a throwback – sentimental or annoying, cloyingly regressive, falsely nostalgic.

These errant scalawags seem in excess of any value they could possibly serve in Trollope's universe. We think they must at best demonstrate an escapist, ineffective recoil from capitalist ambition – they must point back as foils to the structures of England's professional world and the narrative form of the realist novel that remain unsupplanted and make them seem superfluous and their lack of direction so disappointing. But what if they point somewhere else, or question the teleology implicit in pointing altogether? In this alternative ethos, they provide the springboard for Trollope's writing by identifying the narrative impulse prompting it. Such gawky young people – as readers of Trollope's biographies know – are autobiographically inspired. They matter to his fiction because they console themselves (as he did) for their lack of direction precisely with pointless fantasy. They gesture less to the plottedness of career than to the idle fog of daydreams.

The hobbledehoy as a term already disrupts notions of proper development – it marks a period uneasily betwixt and between boy- and manhood. Hobbledehoys, Trollope's narrator tells his readers about Eames, "in truth … are not as yet men, whatever the number may be of their years; and, as they are no longer boys, the world has found for them the ungraceful name of hobbledehoy" (*SHA* ch. 4). "The chief fault … of young Peregrine Orme," the narrator tells us in *Orley Farm* (1862), "was that he was so young," still a boy at twenty-one, given to reckless spending and the immature pranks that get him expelled from college. And though the narrator declares, "I am not sure that those whose boyhoods are so protracted" aren't better than their more worldly, successful, or ambitious peers (*OF* ch. 3), Peregrine still suffers for his lack of purpose and achievement: he remains largely invisible, overshadowed in the novel and ignored by the girl he loves. Trollope seems to describe hobbledehoys according to the conventional benchmarks of growth and fruition – he says he prefers them to successful Apollos who have the world's esteem because their development, though "protracted" as in Peregrine's case, will nonetheless successfully conclude (as Trollope claims about Eames) in its "own good time" (*SHA* ch. 4). But the paths of these characters, like that of Eames's father – "a man of many misfortunes, having begun the world almost with affluence, and having ended it in poverty" (*SHA* ch. 4) – or of Trollope's other worldly failures, Septimus Harding and Josiah Crawley, at the very least question conventional notions of success. If Trollope's hobbledehoys succeed, it is because they repeat again and again the same failures.

"A novel," Trollope writes in his autobiography, "appeals especially to the imagination, and solicits the sympathy of the young" (*A* ch. 12). Trollope uses the term "hobbledehoy" to assert youth as intrinsic to the specific form of the novel. The temporal paradox of the hobbledehoy – neither boy nor man – extends adolescence beyond a fixed period in human development to figure instead fluid ways of structuring fantasy that persist lifelong, are reiterative rather than end-determined. In closely relating adolescence and the imagination, Trollope emphasizes the kind of persistence and open-endedness necessary to his ideas of the novel (the narrative impulse which also lends his novels so readily to series).[3]

The importance of "adolescence" as a conceptual category emerged in the social science of Trollope's time. The American psychologist G. Stanley Hall's first important paper on children appeared in the same year as Trollope's posthumous autobiography, 1883, following in the wake of European investigations conducted while Trollope was alive.[4] The title of Hall's definitive work, *Adolescence: Its Psychology and Its Relations to Physiology, Anthropology, Sociology, Sex, Crime, Religion, and Education* (1904), suggests the broad social sweep he located in the concept. But, like Trollope, he also closely related adolescence to daydreaming and fantasy.

Trollope's novels – including *The Three Clerks, The Small House, Orley Farm*, and *John Caldigate* (1879) – reflect on and complicate the first principles of end-determined narrative: these novels unsettle career success but also the marriage plot to which (heterosexual) adolescence tends. In them, the paradoxes of hobbledehoydom stand as critical threshold, refusing developmentalism, resisting closure, redefining dénouement. The hobbledehoy epitomizes what other critics have called patterns of repetitions characterizing Trollope's economy of writing. Their feckless inertia enacts habitual return to states that can never become prior. These stories of blundering adolescence counter the triumphant progressionalism of the nineteenth-century end-driven narrative that Trollope's novels are often taken to exemplify.

From the start, critics noted Trollope's interest in adolescence – his special focus on the "inner feelings of young ladies and young gentlemen" (*Crit. Her.* 205). Henry James's 1883 claim that Trollope "settled down steadily to the English girl; he took possession of her" is the most famous assessment, but as early as 1864 critics had proclaimed "this, indeed, is Mr. Trollope's peculiar theme" (*Crit. Her.* 203). Trollope was especially interested in the young heroes trying with varying success to take possession of his marriageable heroines, and he introduces the term "hobbledehoy" when describing the least matrimonially successful of the lot, Johnny Eames, who famously never gets Lily Dale. "The great blemish in 'The Small House at Allington,'" one critic complains, is "the character of ... Mr. Eames, whose development stopped at the asinine phase"; another laments "one has always felt that poor Johnny would never grow up into a marriageable hero" (*Crit. Her.* 211, 302). Hobbledehoys usually don't: neither Peregrine Orme nor Lucius Mason marries at the end of *Orley Farm*, and though John Caldigate does at his novel's beginning, the legitimacy of that marriage is always in question.

As Trollope writes in his autobiography, Eames – along with Charley Tudor in *The Three Clerks* – provides the most sympathetic of his repeated depictions of young men who bungle their goals. Indeed, any man in Trollope's novels who hasn't at least a trace of early blunder is meant for a cad. Trollope too had been "an idle, desolate hanger-on, that most hopeless of human beings, a hobbledehoy of nineteen, without any idea of a career, a profession, or a trade" (*A* ch. 2). But Trollope uses "hobbledehoy" both to describe and also implicitly to dispel the miseries of youth, since his response to this state also ironically ensures his later consolations.

The meaning of this term during Trollope's time encoded both blunder and promise. "Adolescence" was becoming the general term for the years after puberty but before adulthood. This phase was understood as unsettled and open-ended: "Early youth," Hall suggests, holds "great expectations. Life is mainly in the future ... The world is ideal, and possibilities are vast"; "character and personality are taking form, but everything is plastic."[5] Hobbledehoyhood, however, in Trollope's time referred to a subsequent moment, a state of tension when the promise of early adolescence seems about to demand or disappoint realization. "He was a boy, a youth, a hobbledehoy, a man," a contemporary explains.[6]

Hobbledehoyhood refers to particular qualities more than to a particular age, however. Like Trollope, other writers of the time assumed that this state could persist well past adolescence. The OED quotes the *Pall Mall Gazette* in 1891: "There is nowadays an immense public of hobbledehoys – of all ages." As part of its character, hobbledehoydom runs to extremes. Johnny Eames, Peregrine Orme – and the young Anthony Trollope too – build castles in the air one moment and thrash their opponents the next. Contemporary accounts agree: "Lawless youth is a problem in every country. The 'hobbledehoy' and 'the unmanageable girl' are the despair of too many parents," one article claims, while another touts "the hobbledehoy, shy, good-natured period of his life, when the male creature is neither boy nor man."[7] Emphasizing how inconsequential, even invisible, such labile and discomforted youth actually are, however, in the reigning scheme of things, one article speaks of creatures who "are apt to hide, like hobbledehoy children, when visitors call."[8]

Yet the hobbledehoy's wooly ineptitude secures the hidden potential Trollope sees in such unpromising material: it drives their tendency to build castles in the air. A hobbledehoy such as Eames or Charley Tudor daydreams what he cannot achieve: "and thus he feeds an imagination for which those who know him give him but scanty credit" (*SHA* ch. 4).

Trollope confesses that so did he, indulging fantasies for years, unbeknownst to those around him:

> Other boys would not play with me … [and yet] play of some kind was necessary to me then, as it has always been … Thus it came to pass that I was always going about with some castle in the air firmly built within my mind … For weeks, for months … from year to year, I would carry on the same tale … I have often doubted whether, had it not been my practice, I should ever have written a novel. I learned in this way to maintain an interest in a fictitious story, to dwell on a work created by my own imagination, and to live in a world altogether outside the world of my own material life. (*A* ch. 3)

He singles out Eames and Charley Tudor in his autobiography for special notice because of the similar force of their imaginations. Other struggling young men in his fiction – Alaric Tudor in *The Three Clerks*, Mason and Orme, John Caldigate – are valued more or less by how much they possess one.

"Puberty is the birthday of the imagination," Hall wrote,[9] spawning "castle building, and reverie."[10] He suggests that early "imagination is … a youthful condition of" future attainment.[11] For Trollope, however, hobbledehoyhood is not a developmental state to be left behind but an ongoing impulse: his successful heroes do not outgrow their adolescence, but maintain in adulthood the kind of creative distraction with which Trollope characterized himself. Trollope insisted that he remained a hobbledehoy – "something of the disgrace of my school-days has clung to me all through life," he writes (*A* ch. 1). He never outgrew his early miseries, but he also never outgrew his daydreams. Like Eames, who consoles himself for his loneliness by wandering off and indulging his imagination, Trollope locates his talent as a writer in his reveries. Trollope as adult too wanders "alone among the rocks and woods, crying at [his characters'] grief, laughing at their absurdities" when writing at his best, he claims (*A* ch. 10). The methodical plodding of literary careerism may be one narrative within Trollope's autobiography, but it is supplemented by this errant diversion, in which Trollope roams about crying and laughing, quarreling with and forgiving his imaginary companions (*A* chs. 12 and 17).

"There can, I imagine, hardly be a more dangerous mental practice" Trollope admits about his hobbledehoy daydreams (*A* ch. 3). Yet this statement in its form – "I imagine" – underscores that he is always actively engaged in this "dangerous" repetitive process: "I could be really happy only when I was at work," he says about his writing (*A* ch. 17). For Hall, such persistence of the imagination could be pathological, marking a late adolescent whose "dreams have passed beyond his … control and become

obsessions ... drunkenness of fancy." As if echoing Trollope, Hall acknowledges that such hidden fantasizing lies "unrevealed to others save in ...
clumsiness ... Here, near the verge of normality, belong many long-
continued stories."[12] Hall explicitly points to Trollope (who he thought
maintained enduring "pity" for the sufferings of youth) for prolonging his
adolescent daydreams into adulthood.[13] But Hall concedes that it can also
be "one of the marks of genius" when "the plasticity and spontaneity of
adolescence persists into maturity."[14] He suggests that, like other successful
authors, Trollope was able to conserve the "freshness [of his youthful
fantasies] on to full maturity, when he gave them literary form."[15] Within
the foundational psychological literature on adolescence, therefore,
Trollope comes to symbolize its persistently unsettled state, extending
beyond chronology into an ontogeny of imaginative plasticity. His own
triumphs as author, given his sorry beginnings, seem more fantastic than
the most romantic dreams of his imagined characters. The "full reality of
established intimacy" (*A* ch. 12) joining Trollope with his characters and
form with fantasy vindicates the resistance to normative development
encoded within Trollope's understanding of adolescence, and constitutes
the narrative of these novels.

The hobbledehoy refuses trajectories of development. Trollope exposes
such trajectories – seemingly fundamental to nineteenth-century narrative
and Victorian understandings of middle-class masculinity – as self-
interested delusion by juxtaposing his hobbledehoys' struggles to the
easy successes of opportunists such as Charley Tudor's cousin Alaric.
Charley ruefully accepts his boyishness, while Alaric, equally inexperienced
but more self-deceived, has great plans. In his raw ignorance, Alaric assumes
that life – his own, at any rate – is so plotted that he will ultimately mount
to the stars: "*Sic itur ad astra!*" (*TC* ch. 38). Critics recognized that Alaric's
only "object in life is to rise" (*Crit. Her.* 84). He thinks about little other
than constant advancement: "He never for a moment rested satisfied with
the round of the ladder on which he had contrived to place himself. He had no
sooner gained a step than he looked upwards to see how the next step was
to be achieved. His motto might well have been 'Excelsior!' if only he could
have taught himself to look to heights that were really high" (*TC* ch. 11).

Henry Wadsworth Longfellow's poem "Excelsior" (1841), with its alle-
gory of the single-minded youth ignoring life's distractions to attempt the
unconquerable summit, exposes the mid-Victorian conflation of adolescence and ascent. Hall speaks of adolescence as characterized by "secret
'excelsior' ambitions,"[16] ambitions Victorian culture tricked out with its
credo of inevitable progress. Trollope, like Charley Tudor, had been made

wretched, however, by his inability to live up to such impossible pieties: "Excelsior!" Charley thinks, "What had he to do with 'Excelsior?' What miserable reptile on God's earth was more prone to crawl downwards than he had shown himself to be?" (*TC* ch. 20). Charley takes seriously dictates about looking beyond himself to something better, though he knows he cannot live up to them; his incapacity to succeed saves him precisely where Alaric's confident reaching brings him low. Alaric's story demonstrates how easily "onward-and-upward" becomes corrupted into mere expediency, a watchword for getting ahead. The casuistry with which Alaric parses this slogan leads him astray: promoted to a Civil Service Committee, he invests in the very concern he has been charged to investigate: "'Excelsior!' said Alaric to himself with a proud ambition; and so he attempted to rise by the purchase and sale of mining shares" (*TC* ch. 15). Alaric is so blinded by this myth of personal evolution that he stumbles over the obvious and falls where Charley, by grace of his hobbledehoyhood, doesn't tread; Charley never even considers the temptations to gain that Alaric offers him.

The conventional plot of adolescent aspiration authorizing Alaric's opportunism and downfall also sways the youth around him. His young wife, invested unconsciously in her husband's ambitions; the heiress whose trust Alaric pilfers and the barmaid with whom Charley dallies, both with romantic ambitions of their own; even the heiress's mother, past her youth, who retains at any rate the "ambition to rule" those younger than herself (*TC* ch. 33): all invoke "Excelsior!" to advance their desires. The narrator tells us that, though Charley pledges himself to "Excelsior!" too, he so genuinely tries to "dream of higher things" (*TC* ch. 19) and is so humble about his inability to reach them that, unlike the others, "he did not dare to bring the word to utterance" (*TC* ch. 27), and hence escapes its taint. Alaric pursues a pretence of experience and sophistication; Charley looks not up and out, but in and back, discovering talents that were his all along.

Charley's promise to take "Excelsior!" as his motto happens offstage – connected to his friends' discovery that there was "that talent within him which, if turned to good account, might perhaps redeem him from ruin" (*TC* ch. 19) if only he would begin to write stories for magazines, turning to good account by turning out good accounts. Charley's mind reverts to this promise to write when tasked with his vow: "'Excelsior!' said Charley to himself ... Yes – now is the time to remember it, if it is ever to be remembered to any advantage. He went on ... determined to press home and put the last touch to" the story he has begun (*TC* ch. 20). But the talent of this hobbledehoy has been so well hidden that, along with his vow to hew to "Excelsior," this is the first the reader hears of it.

What seems like an authorial blunder, a problem of plot, however, actually provides a reflection on plot. The revelation of Charley's hidden talent, like his offstage vow, is not gradually developed but simply asserted. This gesture reveals Trollope's suspicion of over-investment in the concept of development; it underscores his sense that plot is overvalued: though it is "that which will most raise ... or most condemn [a book] in the public judgement ..." he writes, "to my own feelings, it is the most insignificant part of the tale" (*A* ch. 7). *The Three Clerks* was accused of other failings of linearity. Readers, for instance, resented Trollope's use of interpolated stories. Though Trollope was willing to pare away some of them (such as his essay on the Civil Service), he was tenacious in keeping intact the interpolation of Charley's first novel, the preposterous caricature "Crinoline and Macassar," with all of its own plot fiascos. This spoof is integral to the story because it reinforces that, at the story's end, when Charley begins his career as a serious writer, he hasn't transcended anything. His implied future marks not a rising but a repetition, a replaying of familiar material.

As a writer, Charley has transferred his adolescent energies to another sphere, not outgrown them. He's found a way to make people pay attention to his daydreams. Trollope marks the ambiguity of this accession with another self-reflexive gambit: he lets Charley rescue from drowning the girl he will ultimately marry, becoming a hero just like one in his own romances. Even as Charley accedes to maturity, he recedes into what the narrative signals he has always been: a carefully cultivated fantasy. Poised on the threshold of adult success, Charley remains firmly within the realm of hobbledehoy reverie. Fantasy pervades Trollope's realism because Trollope refuses a hierarchy between daydream and the novel: one cannot surpass the other when they are ultimately the same.

In negotiating rather than surmounting his hobbledehoyness, Charley figures Trollope's practice as writer. From the start, Trollope's contemporaries assessed Trollope in terms of juvenility. A review of his first novel (published when Trollope was already thirty-two) hoped that the book was a "juvenile essay," the writer still a boy, for "if he have already reached maturity of years, his case is hopeless" (*Crit. Her.* 546). Even when he was successful and emphatically middle-aged, reviewers like James continued to emphasize his callowness, complaining of *The Belton Estate* (1866) that "we seemed to be reading a work written for children" (*Crit. Her.* 258). Critics were exasperated at Trollope's juvenile insistence on comic names – such as Mr. Embryo or Mr. Younglad in *The Three Clerks* – no matter how much they underscored Trollope's themes (such as juvenility). They denounced them as "a trick which belongs ... to the lowest order of farcical absurdities" (*Crit. Her.* 87). They tied Trollope's supposed descent from the proper heights of fiction to his indifference to teleology: his "chapters of farce" are "part of the general want of method and plot" (*Crit. Her.* 100). Critics dismissed Trollope's narrative deviations as immature, irreverent, rather than recognizing in them a critique of reigning narrative presumptions.

The hobbledehoy resists, even ridicules, such norms, but what Trollope identifies as a certain "cruelty" in this insolence – as in Charley's backtalk to his boss Mr. Snape (*TC* ch. 2) – he also presents as a kind of rough justice (Snape is not kind to Charley either). Charley's first editor insists on every novel's need for a nemesis – and Charley's wife parodies that teleological edict in the mock-review with which she teases him, the interpolation of which ends *The Three Clerks*. This interpolation offers an episodic and unprecedented finale in Trollope's (or any other) fiction; it transforms the closure of Charley's marriage into the openness of his writing. In lamenting Trollope's refusal of closure, one reviewer wrote: "if ... the heroes of one novel reappear so constantly in the next, readers will begin to hope that funerals, and not marriages, [will provide] the *finale* ... [the hero] will beware of the nemesis that follows on good fortune, and expire before he reaches a third work of fiction" (*Crit. Her.* 124). The Tudors don't disrupt closure (as other Trollope characters do) by figuring in a later sequel; they simply ignore it altogether by running off in the midst of a hobbledehoy romp. Charley the writer chases after his wife the critic, the girl with whom he used to build one kind of castle and with whom he now builds another, pursuing her out of the room and out of the novel. The justice that metes out good fortune to the hobbledehoy in this novel – one of the few that allows him a happy marriage – refuses the very idea of the nemesis, implying that orthodox desires for finale and closure can only be retributive, necessitating a kind of death.

Orley Farm also contains unorthodox plotting, an authorial blunder as critics saw it, though Trollope suggests again that the best novels don't outgrow but recycle such seeming mistakes. *Orley Farm* turns on whether, as a young wife with a babe in arms, Lady Mason forged the codicil to her husband's will that leaves Orley Farm to her child rather than his older half-brother. Immediately challenged, the codicil stands; twenty years later the matter uncannily comes again to trial. Lady Mason's neighbors have little reason to doubt her innocence; no more do Trollope's readers. Yet, just as Charley Tudor admits in *The Three Clerks* that he bungles his plot with his handling of its heroine's secret, "told [too soon] at full length in the middle" of his novel (*TC* ch. 47), Trollope repeats the same confession about *Orley Farm*. Against all our expectations, he reveals that Lady Mason is as guilty of well-contrived plot and continuing subterfuge as Trollope seems to be of lax construction and hasty candor. Halfway through the book, touched by the proposal of old Sir Peregrine Orme, Lady Mason confesses her guilt. To *The Times*, the unforgivable mistake is not just Trollope's customary fault of letting "his secret out too soon," but also his thinking that such a great blunder could lie dormant twenty years (*Crit. Her.* 105, 160–63).

What breaks the period of latency for Lady Mason's crime is the broken latency of her son Lucius, the child for whom she schemed. Introduced at that adolescent threshold fundamental to Trollope's narrative, any promise of the hobbledehoy vanishes for Lucius, as it does with Alaric, through his ambition and striving, his "looking down from the height of his superior intellect on the folly of those below him" (*OF* ch. 33). In hopes of "doing something to lessen the dense ignorance of those around [him]" (*OF* ch. 26), Lucius enlightens them with his theories of "progress" (*OF* ch. 14), developmental plots which tend to culminate in his own superiority: Lucius lectures his mother, for instance, on Darwinist anthropology, unaware of her agony, as they sit in the evenings together (*OF* ch. 15). Even more than Alaric, he personifies the smug belief in the very plots his own story refuses him.

This blind entitlement sets the plot going when Lucius evicts from Orley Farm the tenant who, in revenge, renews the case against his inheritance. The revelations of his mother's guilt, of old Sir Peregrine's proposal and her longing to accept it, the idea that she has an existence separate from his, all merely disturb his sense of superiority without suggesting to him any other narrative than the bankrupt one of his own rise: "the idea that their fathers and mothers should marry and enjoy themselves is always a thing horrible to … the minds of the rising generation" (*OF* ch. 36). Even more than young Peregrine Orme, Lucius remains a child – remains, in how he views his mother, the very infant he was before the novel began, still demanding her absolute sacrifice of self to him. Like Charley Tudor, Lucius can do nothing but repeat his original fantasies, but, limited and impoverished, they lack the consolations of Charley's more generous canvas and bring none of the acceptance they provide Trollope's hobbledehoy heroes. Jilted and alone, Lucius disappears from the novel, transplanting his baffled indictment of his mother to another shore, not able to leave it or her behind.

Old Sir Peregrine Orme loathes young Lucius – resents him without knowing it because they are so similar, including their tendency to repeat mistakes. Sir Peregrine's main difference from Lucius is that his land and title seem to authorize his superciliousness. Both desire that Lady Mason mirror back to them their fantasies of manhood: their judgment, their innate superiority, their certainty. Because they possess none of these really, Sir Peregrine, like Lucius, longs for Lady Mason "as a child" (*OF* ch. 79).

Trollope is fonder of Sir Peregrine, partly because Sir Peregrine's years have taught him what Lucius never learns, the paradox that experience teaches nothing. Indeed, Trollope's greater imagination allows him to see the hidden stores of poetry within each, bespeaking the remnant of the hobbledehoy hiding in everyone:

> Young man, young friend of mine, who art now filled to the overflowing of thy brain with poetry, with chivalry, and love, thou seest ... that grim old man ...? Poetry, the feeling if not the words of poetry – is he not dead to it ...? Oh, my young friend! Thou art ignorant in this – as in most other things ... That old man's heart is as soft as thine, if thou couldst but read it ... The heart that is tender once remains tender to the last. (*OF* ch. 26)

Though Trollope insists that authors should represent "those changes which time always produces" (*A* ch. 10) in their characters, by such changes he implies differences of circumstance rather than substance. His novels are full of old men repeating the mistakes of their boyhood, just as old Sir Peregrine, withdrawn from the world at the story's end, asks his daughter-in-law and grandson to narrate its events for him all over again.

Trollope's stories are structured through recurrence. In *John Caldigate*, the continued recurrence of adolescence organizes the classic plot of the prodigal son. Caldigate, who meant to do great things at college, has racked up gambling debts instead. He fights with his father, sells off his inheritance, and sails for the Antipodes – "the world out there is upside down," Trollope says, and before a third of the book is done, Caldigate's fortunes indeed take miraculous turns (*JC* ch. 8). He seems to realize all his fantasies: he strikes it rich, buys back his inheritance, is reconciled with his father, and marries the unattainable girl of his dreams. "Things do come back to men," a mysterious woman tells him. Men can "have a resurrection," be recuperated after "a false step," "and, sinking at twenty-five or thirty ... come up ... at thirty-five as capable of enjoyment and almost as fresh as ever" (*JC* ch. 5). She seems to prophesy the entire plot of the book.

Trollope's publisher, John Blackwood, had problems with this plot: it had "a dangerous sameness throughout," so much so that it developed a kind of stutter; it stumbled midway, and repeated itself all over again (*Letters* 11:839). Things do "come back" in Caldigate's story, but, when they do, these resurrections are less triumphant apotheoses than the mechanical return of something undead. Caldigate redeems his undergraduate blunders, but then, years later, the whole cycle starts all over: the mysterious woman comes back to accuse him of abandoning her, he is tried for bigamy, convicted, and imprisoned. The problems of adolescence repeat themselves in Caldigate's middle-age. Trollope is careful to underscore this connection by giving the new troubles a slightly moldy undergraduate flavor: he meets his accuser in the grounds of his old college; when Caldigate tries to bargain with his blackmailers, an old college friend appears out of the blue to act as witness.

By making his older hero prodigal again, Trollope repeats a metaphor for adolescent recurrence from *The Three Clerks*: "Many a youth, abandoned by his friends to perdition on account of his folly, might have yet prospered, had his character not been set down as gone, before, in truth, it was well formed. It is not one calf only that should be killed for the returning prodigal. Oh, fathers, mothers, uncles, aunt, guardians, and elderly friends in general, kill seven fatted calves if seven should unfortunately be necessary!" (*TC* ch. 28). Caldigate is ultimately cleared but cannot escape our suspicion that he may retrace the prodigal's worn path again. Blackwood found the character "impossible to sympathize with ... a man who cannot look up or look out for help and does not feel his own weakness and that of all humanity is sure to break down in a pinch" (*Letters* 11:749). Caldigate remains incapable of learning from his mistakes. Adolescence in Trollope's work suggests that all mortals remain in this state, no matter what stories we tell ourselves about our ultimate redemption.

This late novel, like *The Three Clerks* or *Orley Farm*, demonstrates the recurrence of adolescence as inescapable. "What but the details distinguishes one of Mr. Trollope's novels from another?" Henry James asks (*Crit. Her.* 237). But it also stands apart from those novels by dwelling on one result of that recurrence – the melancholy of dreams that have outlasted their time. Critics wondered what Trollope was about "in making middle-age the synonym of silliness" (*Crit. Her.* 330). When Caldigate's partner resurfaces, a silly man in bright yellow trousers, though his mother hails him as another returning prodigal, his father "felt that the return of a son at the age of thirty, without any means of maintaining himself, was hardly an unalloyed blessing" (*JC* ch. 49). Trollope reflects a sense of his own belatedness: he had for years excoriated himself for the fecklessness that had kept him from starting to write until he was thirty; he waited a decade longer for any kind of success, and never in his lifetime received the respect he knew he merited. For such a writer, the insight that, though we can never surmount our mistakes, we may find ways to repeat them to good effect, went hand-in-hand with the knowledge that such understanding must always come too late.

Yet, because of such regrets, this novel confirms the inescapability of adolescent reiteration figured here as elsewhere through paradoxes of plot. Those accusing Caldigate of bigamy have demanded money they say he owes them. Though everyone around him cautions him against it, Caldigate accedes to their demands because he feels in some indefinable way that he does owe them. He is convicted largely because no one can understand why a man would pay blackmail unless he were guilty. But in having Caldigate pay that debt, Trollope indicts himself. Trollope devised that story line just as Caldigate paid the money – against all advice. Blackwood especially cautioned him that the unmotivated act would make his plot unbelievable. Like Caldigate, Trollope simply could not do differently: he was following a logic he could not change:

> I am bound to say that I never found myself able to effect changes in the plot of a story. Small as the links are, one little thing hangs on another to such an extent that any change sets the whole narrative wrong ... I may probably have been wrong. I shall think I have been if you say so. But I fear I cannot twist it otherwise. (*Letters* II:789)

This refusal repeats what Trollope had written twenty years earlier when asked to make changes in *The Three Clerks*: "It gives more trouble to strike out pages, than to write new ones, as the whole sequence of a story, hangs page on page" (*Letters* I:85–6).

That Trollope, who so often dismissed plot, nevertheless insisted on its demands, seems paradoxical. Caldigate's accusers, too, try to embroil him in "a wicked plot" (*JC* chs. 29, 35, 63), which he ignores by acceding to it. Caldigate has an irrational fantasy about paying the money: he thinks he would have given it had they not demanded it and insists that this motive should compel him to give it still, ignoring the reality that such demands convert gift into bribe. He pays the money out of his innocence, even though he knows it will confirm his guilt. Trollope seems to write out of compulsion too. Some critics suggest he was addicted to writing;[17] Hall suggests that adolescent imagination indulged too long turns into obsession. But both were working from a therapeutic model that Trollope rejected. To him, the problem itself was its own cure – or, rather, provided its own ongoing treatment, which was the best anyone could hope for. The trick is that such mistakes no longer keep him from writing but become the very reason for it. His insistence on his writing as a process – his motto *Nulla dies sine lineâ* ("No day without a line"), which cost his reputation so much posthumously (*A* ch. 20) – emphasizes this ongoingness.

Trollope was certainly not the first to imply that success could come only by dispensing with any conventional understanding of it. One might indeed win money and fame – as Trollope did – by embracing a child within who never grows up, is incapable of learning from his mistakes, is certain to repeat them. Trollope's embrace of this, however, could look a lot like just another version of the powers of positive thinking beginning to be promulgated during his time – albeit a particularly contrary and backward version. At its worst, this can seem the duplicitous suggestion that worldly success is available to everyone once we turn our backs upon it. But Trollope's hobbledehoys, though they explore this fantasy, never confirm it. On the contrary, the recognition of error means the relinquishing of guarantee. The moral of Trollope's autobiography is that neither steady work nor aimless woolgathering leads to success. Trollope tallies his words and tots up his profits because – windfalls – they record what he can never bank upon. "I tried my hand at it and I failed," he wrote about revising *John Caldigate*, "Such as it comes at first it must remain" (*Letters* II:815). Trollope's statements about form reiterate the substance of his plots. We must remain what we were at the first. Like his hobbledehoys, all Trollope can do is make the same mistakes – that is, indeed, his story.

NOTES

1 See Nicholas Dames, "Trollope and the Career: Vocational Trajectories and the Management of Ambition," *Victorian Studies* 45 (2003), 247–78.
2 Though "unfortunately hobbledehoy has no feminine" (C. J. Wills, "A Modern Eastern Martyr," *Good Words* 30 [December 1889], 812–20; 812), Trollope felt nevertheless there were girl hobbledehoys too: he tells us that Eames's sister (loving and bashful) is one, but never tells her story (*SHA* ch. 4). Many contemporaries refused to admit that girls went through an awkward stage (see Nicias Foxcap, "Hobbledehoys," *Belgravia* 5 [July 1871], 70–73), but those, like Trollope, who did acknowledge female hobbledehoys were not as sympathetic to them as he: the comic pages of the time define "the Feminine of Hobbledehoy" as "Hobbledehoyden", Anon, "Odds and Ends," *Judy, or the London Serio-comic Journal* (January 10, 1894), 17. "While fully alive to the shortcomings of the hobbledehoy," another review concurs, "we are inclined to think that girls, during the equivalent period of their existence, are even more difficult to manage," Two Books for Girls," *Saturday Review* 56.1 (October 6, 1883), 447–48. By 1917, accounts paralleled "the flapper and the hobbledehoy," Anon, "Untitled item," *Musical Herald* 834 (September 1, 1917), 272. By 1931, the girl who sits on table edges and smokes cigarettes has become a "brazen hobbledehoy" herself; Francis Lascelles, "This Week's Argument: Do We Want Co-Education?," *Saturday Review* 152.3962 (October 3, 1931), 425–26. Even for the Victorians, the "problem" seems largely to lie in refusal of gender stereotypes: the female hobbledehoy is bent on doing things girls usually don't – even if merely as a tomboy: for a normative account of marriage as the treatment for this difference, see Maarten Maartens, "John," *Temple Bar*, 119:471 (February 1900), 206–19. Part of some Victorians' reluctance to call girls hobbledehoys may lie in the term's roots: the linguist Anatoly Liberman translates one line of a 1557 account of the ages of man to read "between the fourteen and twenty-one suppress Sir Hobbard de Hoy. It can hardly be doubted that Sir Hobbard de Hoy is the Devil, the call of sex," "Extended Forms (*Streckformen*) in English," *Studies In The History Of The English Language II: Unfolding Conversations*, ed. Ann Curzan and

Kimberly Emmons (NY: Mouton de Gruyter, 2004), pp. 85–110, p. 102. Yet one writer, at least, agrees with Trollope in preferring a prolonged hobbledehoydom for girls too: "We want something to correspond with [the boy-stage of hobble-dehoy] in the girl system," Materfamilias, "Young Ladyism of the Present Day," *Bentley's Miscellany* 40 (July 1856), 475–76, 475. Related to the term's complications of gender are its class complications, for a "hobbledehoy" also came to denote a kind of adolescent factotum, a young uncouth male servant.

3 For the connection between adolescence and the novel, see Julia Kristeva, "The Adolescent Novel," *Abjection, Melancholia and Love: the Work of Julia Kristeva*, ed. John Fletcher and Andrew Benjamin (London: Routledge, 1990), pp. 8–23; for adolescents and Trollope, see Patricia Spacks, *The Adolescent Idea: Myths of Youth and the Adult Imagination* (New York: Basic, 1981), pp. 215–26.

4 G. Stanley Hall, "Preface," *Aspects of Child Life and Education*, ed. Theodate Smith (Boston: Athenaeum Press, 1907), pp. iii–ix, p. iii. Hall is referring to "The Contents of Children's Minds on Entering School," published originally in the *Princeton Review*, May, 1883.

5 G. Stanley Hall, *Adolescence: Its Psychology and Its Relations to Physiology, Anthropology, Sociology, Sex, Crime, Religion, and Education* (New York: London, 1916), 2 vols., vol. I, pp. 376, xv.

6 Anon, "The Odd Boy on a Self Made Man," *The Boy's Own Magazine* 218 (April 1, 1868), 64.

7 Anon, "The Curfew for Children," *The Woman's Signal* 242 (April 18, 1898); Anon, "The Rector's Daughter and the Squire's Son," *Fun* 1504 (March 6, 1894), 101.

8 Julia Ewing, "Among the Merrows: A Sketch of a Great Aquarium," *Aunt Judy's Christmas Volume for 1873*, ed. Margaret Gatty (London: Bell & Sons, 1873), pp. 44–57, p. 49.

9 Hall, *Adolescence*, vol. I, p. 313.

10 Ibid., p. 172.

11 Ibid., p. 534.

12 Ibid., p. 313. He is drawing on such conventional wisdom (ascribed here to Keats's preface to *Endymion*) that while "the imagination of a boy is healthy, and the mature imagination of a man is healthy ... between ... the soul is in a ferment, the character is undecided, the way of life uncertain, the ambition thick-sighted." Not enough artists "have been wise enough to destroy the tremendous productions of their hobbledehoy-hood" laments another contemporary, Anon, "Mozart-cum-Haydn," *Magazine of Music* 9:13 (January, 1893), 9.

13 Hall, *Adolescence*, vol. I, p. 563.

14 Ibid., p. 547.

15 Ibid., p. 581.

16 Hall, *Adolescence*, vol. II, p. 302.

17 P. D. Edwards, "Introduction," in Anthony Trollope, *An Autobiography* (New York: Oxford University Press, 1980) pp. v–xvi, viii.

10

DAVID SKILTON

The construction of masculinities

The world

More than in any other novelist, the construction of masculinities in Trollope involves the creation of a functioning fictional world in which individual characters are to live and act. It even involves the construction of the narrative voice or voices, and of the readership too. Trollope presents the life of individuals in a complex world, concentrating on the moral choices which individuals make in relation to that world. Ruth apRoberts shows that he pays attention to the minute particulars of each case, and that, although not a moral relativist in the sense of appealing to different standards in different cases, he espouses a situational ethics which takes account of the circumstances of the individual in each instance, which he examines as a case of conscience, rather than by drawing on moral or religious rules for guidance.[1] In this Trollope's characters are exercising what we might call their "secular consciences." Although deeply interested in "the gentleman" and values of gentlemanliness, Trollope is not a campaigning novelist. His chief subject is how best, given one's temperament and circumstances, to make life choices which enable one as far as possible to live a moral and fulfilling life in an admittedly imperfect world.

The world, therefore, is as important as the individual in this fiction, and the construction of masculinity is a social as well as an individual matter. Indeed we have to understand the society Trollope creates if we are to understand how men fit themselves to it, or fail to do so, and that society is far from monolithic. Such propositions as "the Victorians thought such and such" are generally misleading. Different from us they may have been, but uniformly like each other they were not. Trollope's great strength is that the social views and social standards he presents display multiple variations, and, within what some take to be a single narrative voice, there are a dozen different views or voices competing for attention. We should not look for Sophoclean characters in harmony or conflict with the world, but a continuing negotiation among the manifold alternatives which present themselves. So it is that masculinity is defined and produced in the fictional society as well as in the characters as individuals, and, as part of Trollope's supremely accomplished illusion of truth to life, it involves the author and the readership as well, enrolling them for the nonce in the same fictional but believable world.

Work on the construction of masculinity in the Victorian period tends to center on ideals such as Charles Kingsley's muscular Christianity and the "manliness" advocated in Tom Hughes's *Tom Brown's Schooldays* (1857), or on the later imperial mission and homosocial devotion of imperialism.[2] All critics agree on the disappearance of Regency elegance and decorum, which Dickens mocks in Mr Turveydrop, the dancing master in *Bleak House*, who is a grotesque relic of 1820s affectation, and which Thackeray mourns in his novels. There is a yearning too for a new form of chivalry, ridiculously acted out in a mock-medieval joust and revel at the Eglinton Tournament of 1839, organized by Archibald Montgomerie, 13th Earl of Eglinton at his castle near Kilwinning in Scotland. The same nostalgia fed into a thousand works of art, from minor historical romances to some of the most eloquent paintings of the age and Tennyson's *Idylls of the King* (1856–86). Along the way the colorful plumage in the male of the species is replaced by the earnest sobriety of "men in black."[3]

Trollope's works present the relations of middle-class men to their families and work from 1850 to 1882, years when work and domesticity were in most cases detached, with authorship a possible exception. The extremes of Evangelicalism had generally passed, and a father's status as head of the family was no longer in general a reflection of godhead in this world. Alongside domestic life, a middle-class man was expected to enjoy a homosocial life of work, club, sport, charity dinners, and so on, which constituted a quasi-bachelor life co-existing with family life but largely separate from it. By the end of Trollope's life there was a perceptible decline in marriage in his social class, and an expectation that many men would lead an entirely bachelor existence for life or until a late marriage, with clubs, bachelor flats, and the empire providing the scenes of their activities.[4] In the 1880s we see a new form of prose fiction aimed specifically at these new readers, in the "romances" of R. L. Stevenson and others, aimed at both men and boys.

The standards of "manliness" based on religion, nostalgia, and empire are not central to Trollope's vision of the world and how people strive to lead their lives. Although many of his good men show physical courage, they rarely share the mid-century religious earnestness of Tom Brown, and the medievalism, which is associated with the High-Church Oxford

Movement and Pre-Raphaelite aesthetic values, can be ridiculed even when espoused by sympathetic characters. Then again, neither Trollope nor his protagonists are enthusiastic imperialists after the late Victorian and Edwardian model. The colonies offer the opportunity for men to test themselves in making their way in the world, and are for Trollope, as for his fellow authors, a useful way of repairing characters' fortunes or removing them from the scene for a while. There is little sense of the mission and little of the systematic racism which we find in the last decades of the century. The replacement of the Regency buck by the Victorian gentleman is important because of Trollope's interest in attempts to live a moral and rewarding life in an imperfect world, and the qualities of a Victorian "gentleman" contribute as much as anything else to this effort. Neither old-fashioned deportment nor a trained and artificial chivalry will do for Trollope, manliness not being something that can be assumed deliberately or learned quickly. It is education and socialization, building on a good foundation of character:

> A man cannot become faithful to his friends, unsuspicious before the world, gentle with women, loving with children, considerate to his inferiors, kindly with servants, tender-hearted with all, – and at the same time be frank, of open speech, with springing eager energies, – simply because he desires it. These things, which are the attributes of manliness, must come of training on a nature not ignoble. But they are the very opposites, the antipodes, the direct antagonism, of that staring, posed, bewhiskered and bewigged deportment, that *nil admirari*, self-remembering assumption of manliness, that endeavour of twopence halfpenny to look as high as threepence, which, when you prod it through, has in it nothing deeper than deportment. (PR ch. 68)

The consequence is that Trollope does not present male characters and their development as something separate from their integration into society, and "manhood" is achieved by reaching a state in which a character fits without effort into his family and the society of men and women, and, importantly, into the masculine institutions of his fellows. The implication may be that different men reach "manhood" by different routes and with different results, but a common feature in those who are successful individuals comfortably integrated into masculine society and able to support a family and home is the capacity for hard work. Many critics see *An Autobiography* as Trollope's assertion of his own manhood through the description of his working life, publications, and earnings.

Trollope's fiction dramatizes major personal and social issues of the day as experienced by the professional middle class to which he belonged, and by others who shared their problems relating to morality, status, and prosperity – the same issues, that is, as he raises in relation to his own life in *An Autobiography*. Because these questions were recognized by his contemporaries as widely applicable, he was celebrated as a representative writer of his age, so that Richard Holt Hutton could assert in his obituary in the *Spectator* that his work "will picture the society of our day with a fidelity with which society has never been pictured before in the history of the world."[5]

Belonging

"Belonging" is the key to this matter, and from 1860 onwards, Trollope, the man, the civil servant, and the author, magnificently "belonged." He belonged to important homosocial institutions of his day, including numerous London clubs and the Freemasons, he hunted two or three times a week in the season, and he was seen at many a public and private dinner. But his sense of belonging had been hard won:

> In my school days no small part of my misery came from the envy with which I regarded the popularity of popular boys ... And afterwards, when I was in London as a young man, I had but few friends ... [E]ven in Ireland I had in truth lived but little in society ... It was not till we had settled ourselves at Waltham that I really began to live much with others. The Garrick Club was the first assemblage of men at which I felt myself to be popular.   (*A* ch. 9)

He was then forty-six. Dramas of exclusion and belonging are the stuff of his fiction, and not only found in his story patterns but in his narrator's relationship with his ideal reader, who is invited to enjoy a community of thinking and reading with the narrator, who quotes from the King James Bible, the Book of Common Prayer, Shakespeare, Milton, and other well-known sources, including Latin quotations which every schoolboy of Trollope's class will have learnt by heart. These act as what I have called elsewhere "handshakes of recognition" between the reader, narrator, and characters that they are all in the same "assemblage of men".[6] Even Trollope's aesthetics of fiction is built around the concept of an experience of life shared by the author, readers, and characters in the production and consumption of the work.[7]

In the 1860s there was a uniquely clear assumption of a close social identity between narrators, characters, and readers. Whether presenting *Framley Parsonage* in the character of a typical *Cornhill* reader, or writing *Phineas Finn* and its successors as a "method of declaring myself" politically, after failing at the Beverley election of 1868 (*A* ch. 17), Trollope was a middle-class gentleman addressing his equals. This unproblematic relationship was incomprehensible to a later generation, as Robert Louis Stevenson shows. "You are now come to that time of life," writes Stevenson's typical middle-class father to his son, "and have reason within yourself to consider the absolute necessity of making provision for the time when it will be asked, 'Who is this man? Is he doing any good in the world? Has he the means of being 'One of us?'"[8] For Stevenson and his contemporaries, a career in writing or art offered an escape from "being 'One of us.'" In contrast, Trollope's dearest wish and a motive in writing was precisely to be considered respectably bourgeois.

Modes of inclusivity

In presenting his bourgeois world, Trollope's narrator adopts the voices of many aspects of that world, reporting what other people in the fictional community think, and not telling us authoritatively that this or that opinion is justified. He does not openly endorse the statement at the opening of *The Prime Minister* that "it is certainly of service to a man to know who were his grandfathers and who were his grandmothers if he entertain an ambition to move in the upper circles of society," but leaves the reader to consider the matter, and agree that this was an important factor in mid-Victorian social acceptability (*PM* ch. 1). Still less does the narrator attack Lopez for being or being believed to be a Jew. This again is what is said of the character by others, and the anti-Semitic implications may or may not be shared by the narrator, while the reader is certainly not asked to agree with them in order to be admitted to the fictional "assemblage of men" which the novel creates. Trollope maintains a benignly ironic distance from the bundle of socially current views which the narrator reports – a technique the author learned from one of his favourite novels, *Pride and Prejudice*. It would be a dull reader who thought that Jane Austen herself believed that "it is a truth universally acknowledged, that a single man in possession of a good fortune, must be in want of a wife."[9]

This multivalency of the narrative voice suggests that conformity to masculine society will not entail uniformity of standards or opinions, but sufficient agreement on values to allow the constant negotiation of all these things, while a common cultural stock facilitates communication. Educational background makes acceptance into different "assemblages of men" more or less difficult. When in *The Last Chronicle of Barset* Josiah Crawley, the miserably poorly paid perpetual curate of Hogglestock, hears the lawyer, Mr. Toogood, refer to Mrs. Toogood, in a quotation from Dryden, as "the lovely Thaïs by his side," he wonders what kind of man can compare his wife to the courtesan who accompanied Alexander the Great on his Asian campaigns (*LCB* ch. 32). The answer is one who is not adequately educated in the classics.[10] It is a common educational background that enables his clerical superior, the wealthy Archdeacon Grantly, to acknowledge Crawley's belonging, in a scene which seems at first sight, when related by Crawley to his wife, to be cloyingly sentimental:

> "I would we stood on more equal grounds," I said ... "We stand," said he, "on the only perfect level on which such men can meet each other. We are both gentlemen." "Sir," I said ... "from the bottom of my heart I agree with you. I could not have spoken such words; but coming from you who are rich to me who am poor, they are honourable to the one and comfortable to the other."
> "And after that?"
> "He took down from the shelves a volume of sermons which his father published many years ago, and presented it to me ..." And thus the archdeacon had hit his bird on both wings.   (*LCB* ch. 83)

It is only when we read to the end of the passage that we learn that Grantly was consciously manipulating Crawley. Yet Grantly was not hypocritical, his purpose being the laudable one of making it possible to get on with his son's future father-in-law. The standard of acceptability is the readiness to be part of the social negotiations of inclusion, while the devices used in these negotiations are justified as much by pragmatic results as theoretical purity. In this, Trollope's account of masculinity is quite distinct from that of Thomas Hughes, for example, whose moral and Christian heroes all ought, it seems, as far as possible to think and act alike, and be able to justify their deeds and thoughts before the highest judgment seat. Yet, just in case other possibilities are forgotten, Trollope gives us a model of Christian humility and gentleness in Septimus Harding.

The institutions, the "assemblages of men," which Trollope uses as the instruments of inclusivity, are practical and conformist, but, like many English institutions, tolerate, even revel in, variety and eccentricity. The richness of Trollope's treatment of the clergy lies less in their religious observance and belief, about which we hear comparatively little, and more in the masculine society constituted by the Church, which made a fascinating study at the time partly because the terms of their belonging to secular "assemblages" were particularly complex, as in the case of Mark Robarts in *Framley Parsonage*, who behaves in too secular a fashion with his horses and his hunting when imitating the lives of the country gentry. He receives a hard lesson in economics when the bailiffs come to distrain his household goods, while, in the absence of his late father,[11] his moral faults are clearly pointed out by none other than Josiah Crawley, not then fully incorporated into the society of men. It is a triumph of Trollope's comic vision of inclusion when two novels later Crawley is enrolled by Archdeacon Grantly.

A man who cannot be assimilated, whether the fault is his own or not, does not develop a full-fledged social masculinity, and lone figures such as the earlier Crawley, or Louis Trevelyan, Indefer Jones or Melmotte, fail in this respect. Some are too distant from the recognized values of educated Englishmen, like Ferdinand Lopez in *The Prime Minister*, of whom John Feltcher says, "He's too clever, too cosmopolitan, – a sort of man white-washed of all prejudices, who wouldn't mind whether he ate horseflesh or beef if horseflesh were as good as beef" (*PM* ch. 16). Isolated figures do not occupy a place on the map of human affairs, and cannot exercise the "manly" virtue of work and beneficial interaction with the world, without which the Trollopian character can fall to pieces.

Social communication is aided by the use of quotations from a standard repertoire of sources, such as the Terence cited above. This device to help the expression of experiences and feelings may be equivocal – a sign of "manly" reticence or emotional inadequacy – but it acts as a shortcut in these negotiations. Its ambivalence is part and parcel of the complex of qualities know as Englishness, as James Fitzjames Stephen explained: "This sturdy mixture of frankness when they do speak, with a perfect willingness to hold their tongues when they have nothing to say, is the great distinguish-ing feature of educated Englishmen, and is the one which always strikes foreigners with surprise."[12] Trollope objects to such simplistic formula-tions: "A composure of the eye, which has been studied, a reticence as to the little things of life, a certain slowness of speech unless the occasion call for passion, an indifference to small surroundings, these, – joined, of course, with personal bravery" do not, in his opinion, "constitute manliness" (*PR* ch. 68).

Some of the cultural references used to facilitate interpersonal relations obviously reinforce Englishness (or sometimes Britishness) in a quite direct fashion, such as quotations from Shakespeare, Milton, or Burns. Byron, one of Trollope's favorite poets, is less automatically supportive in this way, and we note Trollope's slight problematization of Englishness as shared practice. In Thackeray, Latin quotations bring with them a surge of nostal-gia for schooldays,[13] but in Trollope they refer resolutely to the adult world, while confirming a common educational background. The favorite quotations of many Victorians were from Horace, the Roman poet whose work had been central to public school education since 1700 because he was seen as a "man of the world," who would help to prepare the administrators of the British power structure, with all its trimming and compromises.[14] Because inclusion is negotiated, the boundaries are important, and in examining doubtful cases, involving the problematic balance between ends and means, Trollope may resort to quoting Horace's line *rem si possis recte, si non, quocunque modo*: "make money by right means if you can; if not, by any means whatever."[15]

A revealing example of the *private* use of a Latin reference occurs in *The Small House at Allington* when, over port after dinner, Lord De Guest "had asked Johnny to tell the name of the fair one, bringing up the remnants of his half-forgotten classicalities to bear out the joke. 'If I am to take more of the severe Falernian,' said he, laying his hand on the decanter of port, 'I must know the lady's name ... What! You refuse to tell! Then I'll drink no more'" (*SHA* ch. 22). (Falernum was reputedly the second-best wine of classical Italy.) The "half-forgotten classicality" in question is from Horace, *Odes* 1.27.9–10: *voltis severi me quoque sumere / partem Falerni?*: "You want me to take my part of the strong [*severum*] Falernian wine?" In fact the earl has summoned up a precisely apposite reference. In this ode Horace presents himself as arriving at a banquet just as the drinkers, now well under the influence, are about to quarrel. To defuse the situation, he says that he will not drink at all unless one of the company reveals confidences about his loves, just as the earl refuses to drink any more port unless Johnny reveals Lily's name. By this means, in the absence of a guiding father, he simultaneously teaches Johnny how to drink wine after dinner and how to use his "classicalities," as part of that young man's graduation from hobbledehoy-dom to masculine maturity. The incident, that is, acts out some of the mechanisms of inclusion.

Latin is just one of the social markers which make men readily acceptable in the prosperous middle-class masculine society, but there are other institutions, formal and informal, appropriate to other social classes and groupings, such as the fellowship of the commercial rooms in English inns, which are important as part of the total vision of *Orley Farm*, and which exclude the lawyer, Dockwrath. The characters grouped around Mr Moulder in the novel are, the narrator tells us, "pigs out of the sty of Epicurus," but, like the group of London characters around Johnny Eames in *The Small House*, form a locus in which an appropriate manliness is established and tested (*OF* ch. 24). In London, Johnny Eames must learn to resist vulgar blandishments in the person of Amelia Roper. The pattern is almost as old as English prose fiction: the middle classes, in whom virtue resides, must resist the traps of fashion on the one hand and vulgarity on the other. Certain masculine institutions permit mixing across class boundaries, though individuals are still socially labeled with some care. (The story "The Turkish Bath" of 1869 turns on the fact that class markers are absent among naked bathers.)[16] Among these more mixed masculine societies we find Trollope extolling the hunt and using enough Masonic language to remind us that Freemasonry too crossed class boundaries. As with so many other

Victorian phenomena, the recognition of manliness is often expressed in terms of social appropriateness, but is striking when it crosses class divides, as in a famous moment in *The Last Chronicle* when an old brick-maker advises Crawley: "It's dogged as does it" (*LCB* ch. 61) – a lower-class utterance embodying a truth for Trollopian men of all social standings, and rapidly included in dictionaries of quotations. Phineas Finn's landlord says, "The only respectable man I know ... is the man as earns his bread" (*PF* ch. 7). Outside the fiction, his granddaughter, Muriel Trollope, recalled in her old age an occasion when "a working-man" who had asked to borrow a copy of *An Autobiography*, returned it with the words: "Every young man should read it! Your grandfather always made the best of everything."[17] The term "working-man" meant "a member of the working-class" to Muriel Trollope, but it clearly connects this "working-man" across barriers of time and social class with that other working man, Anthony Trollope.

Work and masculinity

These examples demonstrate the emphasis which Trollope and his contemporaries placed on work and effort, whether or not the work was gainful employment. Frank Houston in *Ayala's Angel* is not "man enough to earn [his] bread" – a condition akin to impotence, as, despite wishing to open the world like an oyster, "he does not carry a sword" (*AA* ch. 28). The choice of a profession is almost a Trollopian obsession, and he has no hesitation in regarding any calling as akin to a trade. Notoriously he often compared authorship to shoemaking,[18] while in *The Bertrams* (1859), he refers to George Bertrams's university degree and other social and literary qualifications as his "stock-in-trade," in the language used throughout *The Choice of a Profession*, published in 1857, and after which chapter 5 of the novel is named.[19] Sir Lionel Bertram on the other hand considers that the word "profession" "signified a calling by which a gentleman, not born to the inheritance of a gentleman's allowance of good things, might ingeniously obtain the same by some exercise of his abilities. The more of these good things that might be obtained, the better the profession; the easier the labour also, the better the profession ..."

But George Bertram "had an idea that in choosing a profession he should consider, not so much how he should get the means of spending his life, but how he should in fact spend it" (*B* ch. 5). However, he lacks the strength of character to carry a choice into effect and achieve satisfactory masculine standing. So his high academic achievements are wasted, while the less fêted Arthur Wilkinson has all the personal qualities to make a success of his chosen profession and reach full manhood – once he has had the courage to face up to his dominating mother. Representative of the best in his generation in the matter of application, Plantagenet Palliser works conscientiously at his chosen profession of politics, despite the immense wealth which would allow him to spend his time in pleasure like his uncle. The dangers of idleness are not just moral, as the insanity of Louis Trevelyan shows in *He Knew He Was Right* (1868–69). A good income, it seems, may be a blessing only if it has to be earned, either at a profession or by managing a landed estate.

Prosperous endings seem to favor practically minded men who make their way in the world by their own efforts, such as Will Belton in *The Belton Estate* (1865–66) or the young brewer, Luke Rowan, in *Rachel Ray* (1863). Rachel's widowed mother and sister seek out clergymen to their respective tastes to replace the guidance hitherto given as head of the household by Rachel's dead father. Mr. Ray's working life was devoted to Church business, and he is representative of the paternal model of an earlier period, when the father was thought to provide moral and religious authority within the home. By 1863, women dominated the domestic scene, while the paterfamilias was no longer held up as the representative of God in the home, and Mr. Kennedy in *Phineas Finn* is old-fashioned and un-Metropolitan in insisting on being his wife's "lord and master" (*PF* ch. 23). A nostalgic regard for the old model is seen in 1862, the year in which Trollope wrote *Rachel Ray*, when a father reading the Bible to his family was chosen for illustration in both *English Sacred Poetry* and *Favourite English Poems*, to accompany the line, "The Priest-like father reads the sacred page," from a poem to which Trollope alludes in *Rachel Ray* (and elsewhere), Burns's "The Cotter's Saturday Night" (1786).[20] What Mrs. Ray wants advice about, in the absence of Rachel's "priest-like father," is whether her younger daughter can be allowed to go to a ball. Luke notoriously enjoys dancing, and Rachel becomes aroused in his arms. He represents the new model of responsible and natural man, and will make a fine head of the family.

Orley Farm gives us a number of young and less young men to compare, and the advantage lies with those who learn to be practical. Effective engagement with the world is what makes a man, while theory can lead to delusion. Lucius Mason's experimental farming is a typical young man's error, while the German jurisprudent, Von Bauhr, shows the irrelevance of dreams of a theoretically pure system of law. Felix Graham, before he falls off a horse and falls in love with a judge's daughter, tries to carry out a Rousseauan scheme of bringing up a girl to make him a perfect wife. These are the errors appropriate to youth or foreignness, but many young men in

Trollope lack confidence in affairs of the heart, and Luke's self-assurance to excite young women with the irresistible force of their animal spirits. As Laurie Langbauer has suggested in chapter 9 of this volume, in extreme cases these are "hobbledehoys," a word the narrator explains in *The Small House*:

> [T]he hobbledehoy, though he blushes when women address him, and is uneasy even when he is near them, though he is not master of his limbs in a ball-room, and is hardly master of his tongue at any time, is the most eloquent of beings, and especially eloquent among beautiful women ... But this eloquence is heard only by his own inner ears ... and, therefore, he wanders about in solitude, taking long walks, in which he dreams of those successes which are so far removed from his powers of achievement ... And thus he feeds an imagination for which those who know him give him but scanty credit. *(SHA* ch. 4)

This has often been placed alongside Trollope's account of his own habit of extensive fantasizing as a youth: "There can, I imagine, hardly be a more dangerous mental practice; but I have often doubted whether, had it not been my practice, I should ever have written a novel" (*A* ch. 3). In our author as manly exemplar, the weakness of the hobbledehoy is transformed by work and force of character into a profession, and provides a place in the world and a good income with which to support a family. Johnny Eames of course is the hobbledehoy in *The Small House*, who, helplessly in love with Lily Dale, attacks Adolphus Crosbie, who has jilted her. The deed may be misjudged – it earns Lily's disapproval – but it improves his standing as a male by making him a sort of hero in the local community, for an action which echoes an earlier attack – "what Frank Gresham did to Mr Moffat when he behaved so badly to poor Augusta" (*SHA* ch. 26)[21]– another piece of Victorian violence on the way to manhood, which does not prevent Frank Gresham from becoming a very useful Member of Parliament in *The Prime Minister*. Standing up to the bully, Sir Raffle Buffle, in *The Last Chronicle*, is the next stage in Johnny's upward path to manhood. There is a touching moment when the hopeless Tom Tringle in *Ayala's Angel* tries to construct himself as a man when he says of his love for Ayala, "I can't give it up. I won't give it up. When a fellow means it as I do he never gives it up" (*AA* ch. 11). The hobbledehoy suffers from an extreme form of the verbal awkwardness which afflicts the Englishman.

Those who relate principally to a world of men have restricted vocabularies to deal with the emotions or the great events of Victorian life, such as courtship, marriage, parenthood, and death, and often turn to the language of activities they do understand as models for these more slippery matters.

An extreme example is those who conspire to capture the widowed Julia Brabazon in *The Claverings*, for whom the only experience they can bring to the process of courtship is derived from the maxims of horsemanship in mastering a mare: "Let her know that you're there" (*C* ch. 17). The violent Lord Chiltern would, a character believes, treat his wife as well "as he does his horses. But he expects every horse he has to do anything that any horse can do; and he would expect the same of his wife" (*PF* ch. 13). A sympathetic character can be at a loss to understand the emotional life, Earl De Guest construing it in terms of the transmission of characteristics in cattle-breeding when he ask Eames, "Have you got into trouble? ... Your poor father used to be in trouble" (*SHA* ch. 14). The male brutality in *The Claverings* is reinforced by Sir Hugh Clavering, one of Trollope's brutal husbands who carry this approach into the home and the bedroom.

Elsewhere men's inability to understand women can be comic, as when in *Phineas Finn* various fellow politicians discuss why Phineas is successful with women: "'I think it is because he listens so well,' said one man. 'But the women would not like him for that,' said another. 'He has studied when to listen and when to talk,' said a third. The truth, however, was, that Phineas Finn had made no study in the matter at all. It was simply his nature to be pleasant" (*PF* ch. 13). Strong mothers, such as Lady Lufton, often guide young men aright. Fathers, such as Lord Brentford in *Phineas Finn*, can engender long resentments or even battles, though in *Phineas Redux* his son, Lord Chiltern, is eventually domesticated by Violet Effingham. When Major Grantly, a military hero and a "new man" par excellence,[22] puts his house on the market in defiance of his father, in order to marry Grace Crawley, the Archdeacon comes across a bill advertising the sale, and is dealt a blow which echoes Oedipus's killing of his father, happening, as it does, at "a place where three roads met" (*LCB* ch. 57).

All these things are not only central to the fiction, but a key to the processes of Trollope's writing. Arguably, *An Autobiography* displays the author haunted by childhood anxieties, seeking security through writing, and the complexity of the oeuvre derives from the unresolved interlacing of belonging and exclusion, on the one hand of corporate acceptance as "One of Us," and on the other the isolation of the individual, "as solitary, as alien, as inassimilable as ever."[23] So, while many critics have followed Henry James in praising the way Trollope "took possession of [the English girl], and turned her inside out,"[24] the construction of men characters has been less discussed. It seems that young women (James's "girls") are a suitable subject for almost taxonomic study, but that men, being represented by the author, the characters and the male readership, are, like all ideological constructs, effectively invisible to those who subscribe to them, in this case the male critics. Since patriarchy defines women from outside, the values involved are more clearly visible than those used in the negotiation of masculinity, which have remained largely invisible to "man, vain man."

NOTES

1 Ruth apRoberts, *Trollope, Artist and Moralist* (London: Chatto and Windus, 1971).
2 E.g. Andrew Dowling, *Manliness and the Male Novelist in Victorian Literature* (Aldershot: Ashgate, 2001).
3 John Hervey, *Men in Black* (London: Reaktion, 1995).
4 See John Tosh, *A Man's Place: Masculinity and the Middle-Class Home in Victorian England* (New Haven: Yale University Press, 1998), pp. 172–78.
5 Richard Holt Hutton (anon), *Spectator* 55 (December 9, 1882), 1573–74.
6 David Skilton, "Anthony Trollope," *The Cambridge Companion to English Novelists*, ed. Adrian Poole (Cambridge: Cambridge University Press, 2009), p. 217.
7 See for example Amanda Anderson, "Trollope's Modernity," *ELH* 74 (2007), 509–34.
8 Robert Louis Stevenson, "On the Choice of a Profession," written 1887–88 and published posthumously. See *Essays Literary and Critical* (London: William Heinemann, 1923), p. 17.
9 Jane Austen, *Pride and Prejudice* (Oxford: Oxford University Press, 2004), p. 1.
10 See Dryden, "Alexander's Feast," lines 9–10.
11 Robarts senior is indicated in the title of chapter 1, in which a line from Terence's *Andria*, which the narrator translates as "all men began to say all good things to him, and to extol his fortune in that he had a son blessed with so excellent a disposition," hints that the son will risk going to the bad, before the comic resolution of the plot.
12 James Fitzjames Stephen, "Gentlemen," *Cornhill Magazine* 5 (1862), 327–42.
13 See David Skilton, "Schoolboy Latin and the Mid-Victorian novelist: A Study in Reader Competence," *Browning Institute Studies* 16 (1988), 39–55.
14 R. M. Ogilvie, *Latin and Greek: A History of the Influence of the Classics on English Life from 1600 to 1918* (London: Routledge, 1964), pp. 34–73.
15 Horace, *Epistles* 1.i.65–66; see for example *LCB* ch. 56.
16 See Mark W. Turner, *Trollope and the Magazines: Gendered Issues in Mid-Victorian Britain* (Basingstoke: Macmillan, 2000), pp. 201–7.
17 Muriel Trollope, "What I was told," *Trollopian* 2 (March 1948), 223–35.
18 E.g. *Autobiography*, ch. 7, ch. 17, and *Ayala's Angel*, ch. 4.
19 H. Byerley Thomson, *The Choice of a Profession* (London: Chapman & Hall, 1857).
20 Wood-engraved illustrations by Charles West Cope and John Dowson Watson in *Favourite English Poems* (London: Sampson Low, 1862), and *English Sacred Poetry* (London: Routledge & Co., 1862). See *A Database of Mid-Victorian Wood-Engraved Illustration* (www.dmvi.cf.ac.uk), items FE057 and ESP050, accessed 1 December 2008.

21 Frank horsewhips Moffat in chapter 21 of *Doctor Thorne*.
22 See Margaret Markwick, *New Men in Trollope's Novels: Rewriting the Victorian Male* (Aldershot, Ashgate, 2007), pp. 164–66.
23 See J. Hillis Miller, *The Ethics of Reading: Kant, de Man, Eliot, Trollope, James, and Benjamin* (New York: Columbia University Press, 1984), p. 95.
24 Henry James, "Anthony Trollope," *Century Magazine*, ns 4 (July 1883), 385–95.

I I

ELSIE B. MICHIE

Vulgarity and money

Anthony Trollope's novels reflect, with more nuance than almost any other works in the Victorian canon, the complex English reaction to the fact that, in the period when he was writing, "for the first time in history, non-landed incomes and wealth had begun to overtake land alone as the main source of economic power."[1] Associated with England's rise to world dominance as a financial power, these economic changes triggered a powerfully ambivalent response. The English were at one and the same time proud of their country's commercial achievements and fearful that those achievements meant they were living in a plutocracy, a nation ruled by wealth. Trollope's novels capture this ambivalence with peculiar intensity. They show all the good things that money allows individuals to do and acquire, while at the same time under-scoring the culture's propensity to both worship and misuse the forms of wealth that developed as England's financial power began to rest in banking and sales rather than land and production. Trollope's emphasis on the posi-tives and negatives of the new wealth led critics to perceive him as excessively concerned with money; "no other novelist ... has made the various worries connected with want of money so prominent a feature in most of his stories" (*Crit. Her.* 216). In a world that wanted to deny and rise above the power of wealth, Trollope insistently reminded readers of the material sources that fueled England's greatness. For Victorian critics, the word that most accur-ately conveyed the dangers of Trollope's materialist leanings was vulgarity.

The frequent critical assessment of Trollope as vulgar may have arisen because his novels were, from early in his career, linked to those of his mother, Frances Milton Trollope,[2] whose writing was also stigmatized for its vulgarity.[3] Like her son, Fanny Trollope seems to invite such responses by writing directly about the behaviors that arise from the admiration of money. In the book that made her famous, *Domestic Manners of the Americans* (1832), she critiqued American manners, arguing that their general coarseness derived from the fact that "every bee in the hive is actively employed in search of that honey of Hybla, vulgarly called money."[4] She presented this perception as not just her own but the general English view of America; "I heard an Englishman, who had long been resident in America, declare that ... he had never overheard Americans conversing without the word DOLLAR being pronounced between them. Such unity of purpose, such sympathy of feeling, can, I believe, be found nowhere else ... The result is exactly what might be anticipated. This sordid object, for ever before their eyes, must inevitably produce a sordid tone of mind."[5] When the book was first published, these descriptions were read as strategic responses to the imminent passage of the First Reform Bill, which changed England's political landscape by extending the franchise to new groups of voters. Fanny Trollope's writing described in America what the English feared would happen as their own country became more democratic. Yet, in her writings, as in those of her son, democracy is associated less with the rising power of the people than with the power of money.

This association is reflected in the changing meaning of the word vulgarity. Traditionally associated with the working classes or the masses, it came, over the course of the nineteenth century, to describe not just the new money but also the forms of behavior associated with it, loud dressing and manners, the tendency to be too direct or explicit, and even, as Ruskin famously argued, the excessive scrupulousness by which the *nouveau riche* attempted to avoid crassness.[6] Anthony Trollope's novels address all these issues. As his favorite reviewer, Richard Holt Hutton, commented in a posthumous assessment of Trollope's career, "Natural selection had brought speculating stockbrokers, American senators, and American heiresses into the foreground of Mr. Trollope's pictures before he left us, and the advance of both plutocratic and democratic ideas might have been steadily traced in the vivid social pictures with which he so liberally supplied us" (*Crit. Her.* 504). Though Hutton's comment, like *Domestic Manners*, links the intertwined dangers of plutocracy and democracy to America, writers in the middle of the 1860s, at the time of the passage of the Second Reform Bill, which further extended voting rights, increasingly feared England was becoming identical to America as Frances Trollope had described it in 1832. The economist Walter Bagehot, for example, writing in *The English Constitution* (1865), argued that only the aristocracy "prevents the rule of wealth – the religion of gold. This is the obvious and natural idol of the Anglo-Saxon. He is always trying to make money; he reckons everything in coin; he bows down before a great heap, and sneers as he passes a little heap."[7] In 1866 the radical art critic John Ruskin described his country as devoted to "this idol of riches; this idol of yours; this golden image, high by measureless cubits, set up where your green fields of England are furnace-burnt into the likeness of the plain of Dura."[8]

Though Trollope was partially sympathetic to such positions, he refused throughout his career to utterly condemn wealth. He criticized Ruskin in reviews of both *The Crown of Wild Olive* (1866) and *Sesame and Lilies* (1865), complaining that "the gist of Mr. Ruskin's teaching is simply a denunciation of all property."[9] Trollope insisted in non-fiction prose and novels that "'the greatest mistake any man ever made is to suppose that the good things of the world are not worth the winning'" (*BT* ch. 38). Linking religion and material acquisition he argued that "the reader,– even our most unthinking reader,– knows that mines and iron furnaces are essentially necessary, that they have been given by God as blessings, that the world without them could not be the world which God has intended."[10] From the earliest of his novels through to the posthumously published *An Autobiography* (1883), he insisted that, "all material progress has come from man's desire to do the best he can for himself and those about him, and civilization and Christianity itself have been made possible by such progress" (*A* ch. 6). But this was the position that made Trollope's Victorian readers uncomfortable with his work. His publisher, William Blackwood, tried to have the passage on material progress expunged from *An Autobiography* because of the damage he feared it would do Trollope's reputation.[11] Trollope's son insisted that the passage be included, and the autobiography is often cited as a sign of Trollope's crass attitude toward wealth. But the image of Trollope as vulgarly explicit about money had been formed long before his death. It emerged in the middle of his career as he moved from the Barsetshire novels about the clergy written in the 1840s and 50s to the Palliser novels about politics that stretch from the 1860s to the 1880s.

Reviews of the early novels praise him as able "to give characteristic touches, and yet escape vulgarity" (*Crit. Her.* 47); he is "a novelist who can paint vulgarity ... while he manages to inspire a constant conviction that he himself is not in the least vulgar" (*Crit. Her.* 186). But this critical assessment shifts with the publication of the first of the Palliser novels, *Can You Forgive Her?* (1864), and of *Miss Mackenzie* (1865). This was the period when both Ruskin and Bagehot were describing England as a plutocracy. It was also the moment when Trollope's writing began to be deemed explicitly vulgar. We have an extreme version of such an assessment in Thomas Carlyle's vitriolic reaction to Trollope's 1865 review of Ruskin's *Sesame and Lilies*. Carlyle wrote that Ruskin's book "must be a pretty little thing. Trollope, in reviewing it with considerable insolence, stupidity and vulgarity, produces little specimens far beyond any Trollope sphere of speculation. A dirtyish little pug, that Trollope; irredeemably imbedded in the commonplace, and grown fat upon it, and prosperous to an unwholesome degree."[12]

This, in exaggerated form, is a view of Trollope that continues to dog him to this day. Recent essayists, even defenders of Trollope, feel free to use terms like "stupid" and "unmannerly," to characterize him in a way they wouldn't with other Victorian authors.[13] In using such adjectives they follow up on the image of Trollope that Henry James crystallized in his reviews of *Miss Mackenzie* and *Can You Forgive Her?* There James insisted that Trollope's characters behave so *"stupidly"* he must have "deliberately selected vulgar illustrations" (*Crit. Her.* 235). In a passage that rings with the disgust we hear in Carlyle, James insists that reading Trollope "makes the reader's ear tingle and his cheeks redden with shame" (*Crit. Her.* 236).

The distasteful vulgarity of Trollope's writing was thought to have deepened as he moved through the Palliser series. The reviews became increasingly negative with the publication of *The Prime Minister* (1876) and the non-Palliser novel about the speculator Augustus Melmotte, *The Way We Live Now* (1875).[14] By that time Trollope was seen as having created a world exactly like the one his mother had painted in *Domestic Manners of the Americans*, where money is *the* driving social force. As the editor of the *Spectator*, Meredith White Townsend, argued, he has

> surrounded his characters with an atmosphere of sordid baseness which prevents enjoyment like an effluvium. The novel, which is unusually long, is choked with characters, all of whom, with perhaps two exceptions, are seeking in dirty ways mean ends, working, playing, intriguing, making love, with the single object of obtaining either cash or social position of the most vulgar and flaunting kind. (*Crit. Her.* 397)

But, as this review also acknowledges, Trollope had begun thinking about the issues raised in *The Way We Live Now*, with its portraits of everyone on the make, as early as 1857 and 1858, when he proposed to publishers a satirical volume on the role of advertising in commercial culture entitled *The Struggles of Brown, Jones, and Robinson* (Serialized in *Cornhill* 1861–62; first authorized edition 1870). This was the same period in which he was working on one of the early Barsetshire novels, *Doctor Thorne* (1858), which was praised for its lack of vulgarity.

Parallel passages from these two early works convey Trollope's vision of the deeply divided attitudes England had to its own commercial success at mid-century. *Doctor Thorne* contains a famous exhortation, typically cited to prove Trollope's dislike of commerce and endorsement of the Tory values associated with the possession of land. There the narrator exclaims:

> England a commercial country! Yes; as Venice was. She may excel other nations in commerce, but yet it is not that in which she most prides herself,

in which she most excels. Merchants as such are not the first men among us; though, it perhaps be open, barely open, to a merchant to become one of them. Buying and selling is good and necessary; it is very necessary, and may, possibly, be very good; but it cannot be the noblest work of man; and let us hope that it may not in your time be esteemed the noblest work of any Englishman.   (*DT* ch. 1)

But that passage looks somewhat different when juxtaposed to what I read as its sister passage, the satiric encomium from *The Struggles of Brown, Jones, and Robinson*:

O Commerce, how wonderful are thy ways, how vast thy power, how invisible thy dominion! Who can restrain thee and forbid thy further progress? Kings are but as infants in thy hands, and emperors, despotic in all else, are bound to obey thee! Thou civilizest, hast civilized, and wilt civilize. Civilization is thy mission, and man's welfare thine appointed charge. The nation that most warmly fosters thee shall ever be the greatest in the earth; and without thee no nation shall endure for a day.   (*SBJR* ch. 2)

This passage articulates in mocking form a set of precepts that the Victorians knew to be true, particularly the precept that commerce is what makes nations great. But it was precisely these precepts that, as the quotation from *Doctor Thorne* shows, the English were eager to deny. They sought to insist that their nation's greatness was not based in commerce but in nobler values. As the word "noble" suggests, those were the values Trollope's contemporaries would have associated with the landowning tradition. But in Trollope's period that sector of society was being systematically undermined, or at least transformed, by the increasing power of those who had access to money from sources other than land.

The 1860s and 70s marked the emergence of a class of commercial millionaires, individuals who derived their fortunes not from the production of steel and cotton and the development of railways, the primary sources of non-landed wealth in the 1830s and 40s, but from the sale of commodities. This was the era of "the new shopocracy," men like Sir Thomas Lipton, the tea magnate, the brewers Bass and Guinness, the soap manufacturer Lord Leverhulme, and others.[15] Trollope provides a fictional portrait of such commercial magnates in the ointment heiress Miss Dunstable,[16] who appears first in *Doctor Thorne* then in *Framley Parsonage* (1861) and *The Last Chronicle of Barset* (1867). By creating a character said to be worth "'half a dozen millions of money – as I believe some people think,'" Trollope evokes both the fears and the desires triggered by the new wealth (*FP* ch. 38). Miss Dunstable's money elicits the adulation deplored by Ruskin and Bagehot; she is described as Plutus and Croesus, and we hear that, "mammon in her person, was receiving worship from the temporalities and spiritualities of the land" (*DT* ch. 16). But she also exudes an energy that is pleasurable. Embodying what Bagehot calls, "the rough and vulgar structure of English commerce [that] is the secret of its life,"[17] she enters *Doctor Thorne* refusing to take a nap after her journey and telling others about how she travels all night when she has business to attend to. When she reappears in *Framley Parsonage* and *The Last Chronicle of Barset*, "we are made to feel the vitality and appeal of her fast-paced life."[18]

This vitality is associated with the possession of wealth that derives not from land – "she had no family property,– no place to keep up" – but from commerce (*LCB* ch. 52). The liquidity of her economic possessions enables her to be both extraordinarily free and generous; "they who came within the influence of her immediate sphere should be made to feel that the comforts and luxuries arising from her wealth belonged to a common stock, and were the joint property of them all" (*LCB* ch. 52). The wording of this passage, with its references to common stock and joint property, likens Miss Dunstable to the joint-stock banks that were funding England's financial expansion in the period. Trollope's novels are filled with references to the instruments associated with such banks: bills of exchange in which the lender promised to pay the borrower at some date in the future and bank checks whose use was becoming increasingly widespread in the 1860s and 70s.[19] Though Trollope often represents such instruments as dangerous, he shows, in the case of Miss Dunstable, that money that is not tied to land makes it possible to accomplish what he argues in his autobiography all individuals wish to achieve: "who does not desire to be hospitable to his friends, liberal to all, munificent to his children, and to be himself free from the carking fears which poverty creates?" (*A* ch. 6). This was the side of Trollope that was so troubling to his contemporaries, the side that affirmed their happiness was in part based on England's financial success and that critiqued those who denied the positive impact of wealth. In his autobiography he seems to be writing about the country as a whole when he argues that people who denounce commerce are "like clergymen who preach sermons against the love of money, but who know that the love of money is so distinctive a characteristic of humanity that such sermons are mere platitudes called for by customary but unintelligent piety" (*A* ch. 6).

He insisted not just that fictions should address the question of money but that writers should admit they work for money. Acknowledging that he is "well aware that there are many who think that an author in his authorship should not regard money,– nor a painter, or sculptor, or composer in his art" (*A* ch. 6), he presents himself as laboring at his novels like a cobbler, thereby reinforcing an image that persisted throughout his career. As a critic for the *North British Review* explained in 1864, "the whole tone and habit of mind implied in these novels is that of a man of activity and business, rather than a man of letters" (*Crit. Her.* 213).[20] But Trollope would have his contemporaries refuse the "rather than" distinction. One could be both an artist and a businessman. Such an attitude was characteristic of those who sought to defend England's commercial achievements. As Bagehot famously argued,

> Shakespeare was worldly, and the proof of it, that he succeeded in the world ... The reverential nature of Englishmen has carefully preserved what they thought the great excellence of their poet – that he made a fortune. It is certain that Shakespeare was proprietor of the Globe Theatre – that he made money there, and invested the same in land at Stratford-on-Avon, and probably no circumstance in his life ever gave him so much pleasure.[21]

The gesture made here, of linking economic concerns with England's most famous author, is the kind of outrageous gesture Miss Dunstable makes throughout Trollope's novels. She identifies the importance of money in a society that wants to pretend it is above mercenary motives.

From the moment of her first entry into Trollope's world, she is vulgar in the sense of being explicit. She bluntly identifies the culture's love of wealth, telling her admirers with a laugh that her unfashionable curls will always "pass muster ... when they are done up in bank-notes" (*DT* ch. 16). She points out others' desire to suppress their pecuniary needs, telling the vicar, Mark Robarts, "you clergymen are so proud – aristocratic would be a genteel word, I know – that you won't take the money of common, ordinary poor people. You must be paid from land and endowments, from tithe and Church property. You can't bring yourself to work for what you earn, as lawyers and doctors do" (*FP* ch. 3). Such acknowledgements are, from Trollope's point of view, crucial because it is those who seek, genteelly, to deny that their daily existence depends on money who are most vulnerable to the abuses of the financial instruments whose use was proliferating with the expansion of the commercial and credit economy. In *Framley Parsonage* it is the "aristocratic" Mark Robarts who gets into trouble when he signs his name to a bill of exchange, believing, as his acquaintance tells him, that it is only for convenience's sake. In *The Last Chronicle of Barset* it is an idealistic clergyman who refuses to have anything to do with money who is accused of stealing a bank check that, it turns out, another well-meaning character gave him, because, as she confesses, "I thought that cheques were like any other money; but I shall know better for the future" (*LCB* ch. 78). The bumbling difficulty characters have facing money matters in the Barsetshire novels is replaced in the Palliser novels with a parade of speculators calculating on using the financial system to obtain the wealth that no one will admit they want.

In the first of those novels, *Can You Forgive Her?*, George Vavasor uses bills of exchange his fiancée has signed to stave off his debts, selling them at less than their face value to buyers who are expecting to recoup the full value of the notes when they fall due. The possibility of speculating on future value is fully explored in *The Prime Minister,* which details the exploits of Ferdinand Lopez, who deals in commodities and knows that:

> in such a trade as this ... there was no need at all of real coffee and real guano ... "If I buy a ton of coffee and keep it six weeks, why do I buy it and keep it, and why does the seller sell it instead of keeping it? ... It is just the same as though we were to back our opinions. He backs the fall. I back the rise. You needn't have coffee and you needn't have guano to do this ... I needn't buy everything I see in order to make money by my labour and intelligence."   (*PM* ch. 43)

To be successful in these markets you put money not into the product but into advertising. As Lopez tells Lizzie Eustace when she asks him how they will get people to drink Bios, the health beverage he plans to import from Guatemala,

> Advertise it. It has become a certainty now that if you will only advertise sufficiently, you may make a fortune by selling anything. Only the interest on the money expended increases in so large a ratio in accordance with the magnitude of the operation! If you spend a few hundreds in advertising, you throw them away. A hundred thousand pounds well laid out make a certainty of anything.   (*PM* ch. 54)

This was a position Trollope had already advanced in *The Struggles of Brown, Jones, and Robinson,* where the advertiser Robinson is sure that the firm fails because his partner Brown put his money into buying items for the store rather than into purchasing advertising for products they do not actually possess.

The stance that Trollope offers as a counter to this world of speculative fluidity is the one represented by Miss Dunstable in the Barsetshire novels. If the enterprises of traders such as Lopez and Melmotte in *The Way We Live Now* are a tissue of lies, a juggling act that, when it collapses, reveals there was never any actual money involved, they can be resisted through the direct and honest acknowledgement of the presence and power of money. The character who articulates that position most consistently in the Palliser novels is their title character, Plantagenet Palliser, the son of the Duke of Omnium, who holds political positions first as Chancellor of the Exchequer then as Prime Minister. In his autobiography, Trollope describes Palliser as, "a very noble gentleman, – such a one as justifies to the nation the seeming anomaly of an hereditary peerage and of primogeniture" (*A* ch. 10). Trollope therefore places belief in the honorable pursuit and use of money in the mouth of a man whose wealth comes from the possession of land. Indeed, it is in addressing the person who will inherit his own land, his son, in the last of the Palliser novels, *The Duke's Children* (1880), that Palliser is most explicit about the importance of viewing money as pure. Using terms that might make a reader think of Karl Marx's theories of value, he argues that,

> Money is the reward of labour ... or rather, in the shape it reaches you, it is your representation of that reward. You may earn it yourself, or, as is, I am afraid, more likely to be the case with you, you may possess it honestly as prepared for you by the labour of others who have stored it up for you. But it is a commodity of which you are bound to see that the source is not only clean but noble. (*DC* ch. 65)

Here Plantagenet is reiterating the stance that he took in the first of the Palliser novels where he argues that,

> There is no vulgar error so vulgar – that is to say, common or erroneous, as that by which men have been taught to say that mercenary tendencies are bad. A desire for wealth is the source of all progress. Civilization comes from what men call greed. Let your mercenary tendencies by combined with honesty and they cannot take you astray. (*CYFH* ch. 25)

Though Palliser speaks eloquently in these passages about not regarding the pursuit of wealth as vulgar, Trollope also shows that, in practice, when Palliser's own wife, Lady Glencora, begins to spend her money in service of his political career, he cannot keep himself from finding her actions vulgar. Glencora, who appears in Trollope novels from 1864 (*The Small House at Allington*) to 1880 (*The Duke's Children*), resembles the great landowners of Trollope's period who were able to survive the agricultural depressions of the 1860s by deriving income from sources other than land, "from railways, canals, mines, and urban property";[22] Glencora "was the great heiress of the day," but her wealth comes not from entailed property, which descends through the male line. It comes from "the mines in Lanark, as well as the enormous estate within the city of Glasgow" (*SHA* ch. 55). In *The Prime Minister* her use of that money threatens to make her what Ruskin calls a "Britannia of the Market" or "Goddess of Getting-On,"[23] the person you go to when you desire power, position, or political advancement. Her enormous wealth makes itself felt in the "improvements" she makes to the Palliser family estate as she transforms it into a venue for political negotiating. In the confrontation between husband and wife over these changes Trollope provides an allegorical representation of the shifting relation between land and the new forms of wealth that were becoming both politically and socially dominant in the last third of the nineteenth century.

And, in a chapter aptly entitled "Vulgarity," he also shows the role the epithet "vulgar" played in such interactions.

Brought face to face with the "improvements" his wife's money has made to his family's estate, Palliser is horrified. He sees "some device for throwing away money everywhere"; "all was sheer display," "an assumed and pre-posterous grandeur that was as much within the reach of some rich swindler or of some prosperous haberdasher as of himself" (*PM* ch. 19). In these sentences, Trollope captures the fears of his era, that a set of values associated with non-landed wealth, like Glencora's mines and rental properties, was penetrating old establishments until the lifestyle of the landowners became indistinguishable from that of those who derived their wealth from commerce. As historian F. M. L. Thompson explains, "in the short run ... the old aristocracy might have absorbed and dominated the new wealthy elements and imposed the pattern of their standards of behaviour on the plutocrats, had it not been for the fact that these standards themselves were shifting towards a greater preoccupation with pleasure and money."[24] The term "vulgar" allowed upstart, non-landed wealth to be accepted into the culture but also to be defined as qualitatively different from its landed equivalent. That term captures the assumption that new wealth will always show its crassness in the objects it purchases, which will bear too visibly the marks of their non-landed origin. As the Duke of Omnium's agent explains when Miss Dunstable's wealth allows her to acquire an estate he sought, she is "a gallipot wench whose money still smells of bad drugs" (*FP* ch. 42).

In *The Prime Minister* Palliser reacts to Glencora's use of her money by exclaiming that, "There is a – a – a – I was almost going to say vulgarity about it which distresses me." The very difficulty he has pronouncing the word reflects its enormous social power, a power the narrator underscores by announcing in the following sentence, "Vulgarity! There was no other word in the language so hard to bear as that" (*PM* ch. 19). This comment creates sympathy for the character who is condemned as vulgar as much as for the one who does the condemning. Trollope understood that pain because he was condemned in terms of the same adjectives he has Palliser apply to Glencora. In the first of the Palliser novels, Plantagenet discovers in her "a tone of loudness, a touch of what he called to himself vulgarity" (*CYFH* ch. 49). This is how Anthony Trollope was described. Even a close friend characterized him as "bluff, loud, stormy, and contentious, neither a brilliant talker nor a good speaker."[25] Society hostesses "found him 'too loud'" and "'vulgar, like his books.'"[26] These were also the terms used to excoriate the commercial millionaires of the period, whom the socialist Beatrice Webb called "the new vulgarians, these loud, extremely rich men."[27] Trollope came to be seen as vulgar for much the same reason as these millionaires and the fictional Lady Glencora were thought vulgar; he made the monetary aspects of the culture visible, forcing Victorian audiences to see what they did not want to admit: their society's own increasing dependence on non-landed wealth.

Trollope's work was effective and unsettling because, as a review of *The Way We Live Now* put it, "for all its exactitude ... it is neither a caricature nor a photograph; it is a likeness of the face which society wears today" (*Crit. Her.* 407). Novels like *The Prime Minister* functioned as mirrors, presenting an image of a social world in which the Victorians could see the strategies they used to stigmatize the wealth that was permeating their culture. Trollope invokes both the traditional landholding values and their opposite, the values associated with the new money. But he does not simply elevate one set of values over the other: he shows the interaction between the two, the process by which one group deems another vulgar. W. H. Auden once argued that, "of all novelists in any country, Trollope best understands the role of money."[28] But one might say that Trollope is the novelist who speaks most clearly about society's ambivalent reactions to money. The explicitness with which he depicted these social interactions made Trollope successful but also necessitated his critical reception as vulgar. You are supposed to refer to money indirectly, in suppressed, refined, delicate, almost inaudible tones, the dignity of banks with their marble halls, of investment offices with their deep carpets, of haute couture with clothes so understated only the cognoscenti know how much they cost. Trollope stood in the midst of Victorian society, but, instead of speaking quietly, he talked about money as Miss Dunstable does, loudly, brashly, bluffly, and so could be perceived as unrefined. But, in fact, Trollope is anything but crude in his fictions. It is the precision with which he depicts what the Victorians already knew about the monied nature of their culture that made his writing so unsettlingly accurate. Like the author, the likenesses provided in these fictions were both successful and denigrated for depicting too explicitly the material underpinnings Victorian society wanted both to acknowledge and to disavow.

NOTES

1 Harold Perkin, *The Rise of Professional Society in England Since 1880* (London: Routledge, 1989), p. 64.

2 The *Spectator*, in reviewing *The Small House at Allington*, comments that Anthony "has more than his mother's power of comedy in painting broad vulgarities" (*Crit. Her.* 200).

3 In reviewing Fanny Trollope's *Tremordyn Cliff* in 1835, the *Spectator* complained that "in painting the vulgar, the half-bred, or better still, the underbred, she seems

to luxuriate with a congenial zest" (quoted in Helen Heineman, *Frances Trollope: The Triumphant Feminine in the Nineteenth Century* (Athens: Ohio University Press, 1979), p. 120.

4 Fanny Trollope, *Domestic Manners of the Americans* (London: Penguin, 1997), p. 38.

5 Trollope, *Domestic*, pp. 234–35.

6 See John Ruskin, "Of Vulgarity," *The Complete Works of John Ruskin*, vol. VI., *Modern Painters*, vol. V (New York: Thomas Y. Crowell & Co., 1900), pp. 261–76.

7 Walter Bagehot, *The English Constitution*, ed. Paul Smith (Cambridge: Cambridge University Press, 2001), p. 69. See also Asa Briggs, "Trollope, Bagehot and the English Constitution," *Cambridge Journal* (1951–2), 327–38.

8 John Ruskin, *Unto This Last and Other Writings* (London: Penguin, 1997), p. 249.

9 Anthony Trollope, "*The Crown of Wild Olive*," *Fortnightly Review* (June 15, 1866), 383.

10 Trollope, "*Crown*," p. 382.

11 See N. John Hall, *Trollope: A Biography* (Oxford: Oxford University Press, 1993), p. 146.

12 Quoted in Hall, *Trollope*, p. 274.

13 See Richard Dellamora, "Stupid Trollope," *Victorian Newsletter* 100 (2001), 22–26, and James R. Kincaid, "Anthony Trollope and the Unmannerly Novel," *Annoying the Victorians* (New York: Routledge, 1995), pp. 207–24.

14 For readings of *The Way We Live Now* and *The Prime Minister* and money see Paul Delany, *Literature, Money, and the Market: From Trollope to Amis* (London: Palgrave, 2002), pp. 19–31; Tara McGann, "Literary Realism in the Wake of Business Cycle Theory; *The Way We Live Now*," *Victorian Literature and Finance*, ed. Frances O'Gorman, (Oxford: Oxford University Press, 2007), pp. 133–56, and Audrey Jaffe, "Trollope in the Stock Market: Irrational Exuberance and *The Prime Minister*," *Victorian Studies* 45:1 (Autumn 2002), 43–64.

15 Martin J. Wiener, *English Culture and the Decline of the Industrial Spirit, 1850–1980* (Cambridge: Cambridge University Press, 1981), p. 64.

16 See W. D. Rubinstein, *Men of Property: The Very Wealthy in Britain Since the Industrial Revolution* (New Brunswick: Rutgers, 1981), pp. 79–80, for a list of nineteenth-century patent medicine millionaires.

17 Walter Bagehot, *Lombard Street: A Description of the Money Market* (New York: John Wiley & Sons, Inc., 1999), p. 11.

18 John Kucich, *The Power of Lies: Transgression in Victorian Fiction* (Ithaca, Cornell University Press, 1997), p. 72.

19 See Mary Poovey, *Genres of the Credit Economy: Mediating Value in Eighteenth- and Nineteenth-Century Britain* (Chicago: The University of Chicago Press, 2008) for a discussion of bills of exchange, pp. 36–42, of checks, pp. 51–55, and of the role of such instruments in Trollope's *The Last Chronicle of Barset*, pp. 384–413.

20 See Walter M. Kendrick, *The Novel-Machine: The Theory and Fiction of Anthony Trollope* (Baltimore: The Johns Hopkins University Press, 1980).

21 Walter Bagehot, *Literary Studies* (London: Longmans, Green, and Co., 1879), vol. I, pp. 170–71.

22 Weiner, *English Culture*, p. 12.

23 Ruskin, *Unto*, p. 244, p. 245.
24 F. M. L. Thompson, *English Landed Society in the Nineteenth Century* (London: Routledge, 1963), p. 300.
25 W. P. Frith, quoted in Hall, *Trollope*, p. 508.
26 Quoted in Barry A. Bartrum, "The Parliament Within: A Study of Anthony Trollope's Palliser Novels" (Ph.D. Dissertation, Princeton University, 1976), p. 96.
27 Webb, quoted in Thompson, *English Landed*, p. 302.
28 Quoted in Hall, *Trollope*, p. 55fn.

12

Trollope and the law

To talk of Anthony Trollope and the law might be to invoke the obvious. Like many of his Victorian counterparts, but even more so, his novels are famously (and infamously) populated with legal actors: solicitors, barristers, judges, and jurors, with the odd criminal and breacher of contract thrown in for good measure. The law also provides the novels with well-wrought plot lines, often involving social and communal regulation of property, and in particular, landed property and questions of inheritance. In addition, Trollope, whose novels exalt truthfulness, honor, and honesty, frequently mined the crimes of forgery and perjury for his plots and for the moral edification he sought to bestow on his readers. All of these have made him a perennial favorite in law-and-literature scholarship from the days of his contemporary reviewers (who so reveled in pointing out his legal errors, especially in *Orley Farm*, that he famously sought legal counsel for *The Eustace Diamonds*) to the present. It is perhaps a testament to Trollope's attempts at verisimilitude and his vivid realism that some of his novels have been treated as real-life legal cases, analyzed by lawyers and legal scholars for their insight into their legal questions.

Trollope's novels are also renowned for their social observation and their precise portrayal of interpersonal and group interactions. Arguably, no other Victorian author or critic was as aware of the community's ability to make meaning or portrayed these intricate processes as skillfully. But his texts are more than entertaining novels of manners and social mores; the social interactions portray a mode of communal self-regulation and a subtle if rigorous determination of norms. Combining the two commonplaces about Trollope's novels – that they are obsessed with the law and with the social power of a community – I argue that Trollope draws on the law not only to introduce moral themes and plots into his novels but also to show how the two obsessions are one and the same. The novels show that the jurisprudential upheavals and the legal reforms that characterized the British nineteenth century were in fact part of the ongoing cultural and social crisis facing Englishness itself. Reading Trollope in this way helps us understand the law as part of a larger turmoil in English culture.

Law and literature are two important ways by which people make sense of their lives and their changing national and/or communal culture. No one, it seems, understood that better than Trollope, who turned to the law both thematically and structurally. As R. D. McMaster has argued, law structures Trollope's understanding of English life: "The law is a sort of skeleton, underlying it, giving it shape, allowing for possibilities of action and setting limitations."[1] In other words, not only are the novels filled with legal events and actors, they also engage in Victorian legal culture even when there is no lawyer or forged document, disputed codicil, or question of entailment in the vicinity. As I show below, the novels engage with the law in the epistemological questions they raise, in their understanding of history and tradition, and above all in their obsession with understanding what it means, exactly, to be English.

"An English barrister and an English gentleman"

A closer look at Trollope's legal actors, events, and issues reveals that questions of Englishness and questions of law are inextricable, and that what appear as struggles over legal doctrine, ideology, or character, are in fact questions about the commonality which they serve and regulate. The plot of *Orley Farm*, the most discussed of Trollope's "legal" novels, revolves around the legal issues of inheritance, landed property, primogeniture, and forgery. But the novel has more than all these at its center. At one point, many of its legal actors travel to an international congress on law reform in Birmingham, where, as Kieran Dolin has noted, "the central issue is whether lawyers should be primarily concerned with finding the truth or with promoting the interests of their clients." But that which Dolin sees as a "discourse on the law as it should or should not be," where "'law' becomes a metaphor and metonym for society's normative project" also betrays an anxiety over what constitutes Englishness.[2] The two are not metaphors or metonyms for each other. Rather than reflecting each other, law and the culture of which it is part are mutually constitutive.

Indeed, questions about English commonality are often elaborated through lawyers and legal issues. One of the scenes in which questions of Englishness and the law are brought together most revealingly is the meeting between Lady Mason's lawyers in *Orley Farm*. Mr. Furnival, her solicitor, seeks the help of the Old Bailey barrister, Mr. Chaffanbrass, in assessing the case. In the exchange, Furnival describes Lady Mason's social status, affiliations, and connections: "She has done her duty admirably since her husband's death. You will find too that she has the sympathies of the best people in her neighbourhood. She is staying now at the house of Sir Peregrine Orme, who would do anything for her" (*OF* ch. 35). As Mr. Furnival sees it, Lady Mason's case hinges only on the quality and quantity of her affiliations. Even doing "her duty" does not entail answering to a higher authority, but rather doing what is expected by the community; instead of a specific, immutable set of behaviors, it is a performance of commonality.

Furnival continues to invoke her connections, "And the Staveleys know her. The judge is convinced of her innocence." Chaffanbrass, the vulgar ("dirty") yet brilliant barrister tries to make the separation between law and communal standing: "'His conviction expressed from the bench would be more useful to her. You can make Staveley believe everything in a drawing-room or over a glass of wine; but I'll be hanged if I ever get him to believe anything when he's on the bench'" (*OF* ch. 35).

Trollope here shows the full complexity of legal culture. Chaffanbrass insists that *who* Lady Mason is and who her friends are are immaterial and that only what can be *proved* against her counts in the law. But he is also described as a "dirty little man"; his very neutrality or impartiality is presented as opportunistic, even mercenary. At the same time, Mr. Furnival, who by this point is defending a woman whom he strongly suspects of criminal acts, is presented as an honorable Englishman. When Chaffanbrass suggests Solomon Aram as attorney for Lady Mason's defense, Furnival is aghast, "'Isn't he a Jew?'" Chaffanbrass's response reflects his lack of regard for social standing or other communal affiliations and his singular concern for what is posited by the law: "Upon my word I don't know. He's an attorney, and that's enough for me" (*OF* ch. 35).

Victorian jurisprudence: natural, common, and positive law

The lawyers Chaffanbrass and Furnival of *Orley Farm* are acting out one of the central jurisprudential debates of the nineteenth century, that between "natural law" and its immutable values of right and wrong as represented by William Blackstone's *Commentaries on the Laws of England* and the more relative approach in the skeptical tradition of Hume and his followers, Bentham, Mill, and Austin, proponents of "positive law." Natural law regards the law as a manifestation of universal principles of abstract justice, while positive law severs the essential connection between ethics or justice and the law; a law is a valid law if posited, in the proper manner, by a recognized authority, regardless of its moral implications.

Thus, one can read the discussion between Furnival and Chaffanbrass as underscoring the historical shift from law based on a known community and communal values to one based on impartiality. In the former, as exemplified by Furnival's pleas that Lady Mason should be judged by her character and social status, "the judgment of a person must be according to the laws or customs of that person's community; such judgment must be by those with knowledge of those customs or – what amounts to the same thing – by those who share in those customs and belong to the same community."[3] With the advent of positive law in the nineteenth century, the link between that claimant and the jurors became that of impartiality, as advocated by Chaffanbrass above. This creates a strange inversion: "Where once all were insiders of communities who knew their own law, all are now observers of a world that posits truth of fact."[4]

The tension between natural law, which puts a premium on content (whether the law is just or moral), and positive law, which values procedure (whether the law has been posited correctly), was mediated through the changing role of the *common law* in the late Victorian period. The "common law" is the unwritten law which is generally derived from cases decided by courts, and not from the express authority posited by a statute.[5] Its authority derives from usages and customs of immemorial antiquity, or from the judgments and decrees of the courts recognizing, affirming, and enforcing such usages and customs and particularly the ancient unwritten law of England. In general it is a body of law that develops and derives through judicial decisions, as distinguished from legislative enactments. While the common law (unlike natural or positive law) is a legal system rather than a school of jurisprudence, it is vital to understanding the legal culture of Victorian England. Because its authority is diffuse and stems from custom and tradition, it tends to consolidate its power by inclusion and accommodation of conflicting elements *over time*. The inherent flexibility of the common law – permitting continuity with change – had been regarded as a strength of the English legal system.

But social, economic, political, and jurisprudential changes in the late eighteenth century, and throughout the nineteenth, created a steady erosion of the prestige and authority of the common law. The exigencies of empire, of a rapidly expanding legal system, and of an ever-growing number of participants in the legal process, presented a major challenge to the common law. Once limited in scope, more or less known by its practitioners, it reached dimensions far too large to be comprehended or known by a single individual. The growing numbers and kinds of participants in the legal system challenged the very *commonality* of the common law, expanding its membership and purview. Partly in response to these challenges, proponents of positive law advocated the ascendancy of statute law and legislative codification over judge-made law. Common law, they argued, seemed less able to contend with a growing and increasingly heterogeneous population with increasingly complex legal needs.

And indeed, discussions of legal and political reform in the British nineteenth century are usually anchored in a series of well-known parliamentary acts and not in the courts. The First Reform Bill (1832), the Second (1867), and the Third (1884); the Corn Laws (1815) and their repeal (1846); the Factory Acts (1801, 1819, 1831, 1833) and the Married Women's Property Act (1882) are all invoked, among others, as the cornerstones of nineteenth-century legal transformation. Whether Victorian reform is seen as a story of failure or success, (or, increasingly, neither or both) parliamentary legislation is considered the backbone of the history of Whig reform.

Moreover, the process of reform through legislature has come to signify a turning point not only in English political history but also in its legal history and doctrine. Legal historians trace a shift in the primary mode of law-making: from judge-made common law to the legislative "reform" advocated by the proponents of positive law, most notably Jeremy Bentham and John Austin. As legal historian David Lieberman argues, "For later reformers and historians of English law, the first decades of the nineteenth century seemed to mark an important break in legal development, the opening chapter of an extended process of Victorian law reform through the vehicle of legislative enactment."[6] In other words, reliance on statutory reforms is perceived as a departure from the centrality of judge-made common law and the beginning of a new post-enlightenment focus on positive law and parliamentary codification.

The two sources of law were seen as not only separate but also competing: legislative success could undermine the authority of the common law. Judge-made common law was increasingly required to defend and fortify its position and authority as the primary source of British law. However, Lieberman shows how this perceived rivalry between statute law and common law was largely artificial. He not only problematizes the common law/codification binary, but shows how the reforms of the nineteenth century (many of them regarded as failures) can be viewed in terms of their continuities with earlier orthodoxies.

This problematization of the common law/positive law opposition emerges from a close reading of Trollope's novels, which also engage in the debates over what should be the dominant modes of legal formation in Victorian Britain. In the rivalry between judge-made common law, which had dominated English legal culture for hundreds of years, and the more recent positive law, which was thought to have replaced it, Trollope shows just how powerful and influential the common law culture and its communal modes of meaning-making still were.

With this in mind, we return to the two lawyers from *Orley Farm*. Notably, the novel does not take a stand for any side, common law, natural law, or positive law. The scene between Chaffanbrass and Furnival, like the novel as a whole, only complicates the problem. Justice (natural law) is aligned with the dirty Chaffanbrass and with positive law, whereas communal sentiment, Englishness, and time immemorial are aligned with the honorable Furnival and injustice. Moreover, the narrator and – by virtue of his narration – the readers are sympathetic to the side of injustice. This misalignment of honor and justice on the one hand, and the revulsion at positive law's apparent mercenary ideology on the other, leave the narrator and readers with no mooring for judgment, a confusion which is compounded by the strong and morally unambiguous tone of the narrator. Natural law values, which were considered universally just, are shown to have changed. A closer look reveals that the changes are not due to an external force or decision, but happen because the once-fixed community is rapidly changing, and its values follow. Natural law values are thus exposed as communal and variable, rather than universal and immutable.

The unbearable state of affairs by which the honorable lie and the guilty are acquitted is astounding to the narrator:

> And more than this, stranger than this, worse than this, – when the legal world knew – as the legal world soon did know – that all this had been so, the legal world found no fault with Mr. Furnival conceiving that he had done his duty by his client in a manner becoming an English barrister and an English gentleman. (*OF* ch. 72)

Note that his astonishment is less at the disparity between what the law is and what the law ought to be than at the fact that the "legal world" sees Furnival's behavior as proper and, even more so, properly English, a manner becoming an English barrister and an English gentleman. The narrator is not at odds with what is considered good law or justice, but with what it means to be an Englishman. The two – good law and Englishness – are equated.

Similarly, in his autobiography, Trollope expresses his unfashionable belief in the superiority inherent in the English gentleman (once again exemplified by a judge, underscoring the legal/communal connection). But in expressing the immutable value he ascribes to the gentleman he is at loss to describe what a gentleman is, and resorts to the implied communal understanding: A man who publicly claims exclusive rights (and commissions) to being a gentleman, writes Trollope, "would be defied to define the term [gentleman],– and would fail should he attempt to do so. But he would know what he meant, and so very probably would they who defied him" (*A* ch. 3).

The Greshams of Greshamsbury

Matters of inheritance and landed property in Trollope show most force-fully just how much the communal is ever present even in positive law and in legislative reform. Consider the opening chapter of *Doctor Thorne*, "The Greshams of Greshamsbury," whose title emphasizes the inseparability of the Englishman and his landed property. The title foreshadows one of the main plot lines, one of Trollope's favorites: because of the family's dwindling financial resources, the land must be sold unless the eldest son, Frank Gresham, forsakes love to marry money. The narrator presents this expectation as inherent in English custom and law: "It has become an institution, like primogeniture, and is almost as serviceable for maintaining the proper order of things. Rank squanders money; trade makes it; – and then trade purchases rank by re-guilding its splendour" (*WWLN* ch. 57). The chapter title not only describes the current state of affairs – the Greshams live on their hereditary land – but also implies – if not without a healthy dose of irony – that things are in their proper place and under rightful ownership. Moreover, the title evokes temporal continuity: the Greshams not only own their land and live on it, they are *of* their land. Unlike "Baker of Mill Hill" or "Bateson of Annesgrove" whose estates' names imply former ownership, the Greshams are intrinsic to Greshamsbury and it to them (*DT* ch. 1). Family and land name – *entitle* – each other and this connection is seemingly timeless, existing, much as the common law has, since time immemorial.

The Trollopian narrator is explicit about the Englishness inherent in entitlement through *longue dureé*. Speaking of the Gresham motto "Gardez Gresham" and its uncertain origin or meaning, he waxes eloquent about its symbolic value:

> But the old symbols remained, and may such symbols long remain among us; they are still lovely and fit to be loved. They tell us of the true and manly feelings of other times; and to him who can read aright, they explain more fully, more truly than any history can do, how Englishmen have become what they are.　　　　　　　　　　　　　　　　　　　　　　　　(*DT* ch. 1)

In other words, while the quotation implies ironic criticism of this value, it nevertheless provides an important observation: the Gresham motto is still powerful not *in spite of* its uncertain meaning and origin but *because of* them. The passage of time might have dulled the original meaning, but it has also consolidated the motto's strength and power as a symbol, and an English one at that. Note that the narrator does not advocate a return to times of yore, when the Greshams ruled through fear or violence. Rather, he suggests that the power of the symbol derives from its sedimentation *over time* and its wide recognition by a community. Even though the community no longer remembers its origin, it recognizes the motto as a symbol, and in so doing recognizes itself as a community. The residues of power – like them or not – still carry authority, even if the authority is communal and historic rather than stemming from existing physical and political power. Denying the symbolic power, the narrator tells us, is tantamount to denying the history of "how Englishmen have become what they are," leading to a gross misunderstanding of what it means to be English. This carries direct legal consequence and meaning: since the common-law relies on custom and on the passage of time to create its rules and consolidate its power, its symbolic aspect becomes authoritative.

Despite its erosion by the legislative reforms of the nineteenth century, the legal power inherent in land continued to have a strong hold over the English communal imagination. This hold, as Trollope shows, was not frivolous, or a simple nostalgia, but had real legal meaning. Because of common law's dependence on custom and the cumulative power of "time immemorial" the communal imagination was just as much a part of the legal culture *and of the law* of late Victorian England, as the legislative reforms which have made it famous. Landed property became a major site for the battle between older forms of ownership based on natural law, communal status and custom, and newer positive ones which gave greater freedom of contract and exercise of free will (see my discussion of Roger Carbury below). Moreover, these wars were culture wars just as much as they were property ones. The two – English communal culture and English law – exist inextricably, even when positive law sought to transcend this link.

Who "We" Are

Lawyers and landed property are obvious manifestations of a society's legal culture. But another of the important ways in which Trollope's work testifies to the persistency of commonality in the legal culture of late Victorian England is less obviously related to the law: his reliance on and his understanding of the elusive yet mighty power of "everyone." His novels perform repeated inquiries into the power of communal meaning, that which is taken for granted and naturalized by a common understanding or "common sense." Nowhere is this more prominent than in his 1875 *The Way We Live*

Now where "everybody" seems to be the main actor, motivator, and object of almost every aspect of the novel. In fact, the novel seems preoccupied with one central question, namely, "Who are 'we', when we live in this way?" Georgiana Longstaffe, on the verge of being cast out from the "set" to which she has belonged by virtue of her family's name, her money, and her value on the marriage market (the latter two rapidly diminishing), appeals anxiously to her friend Lady Julia Monogram, pleading to know why she has been "cut." Lady Monogram replies,

> Of course I shall be delighted to see you. I don't know what you mean by cutting. I never cut anybody. We happen to have got into different sets, but that is not my fault. Sir Damask wouldn't let me call on the Melmottes [with whom Georgiana has been staying]. I can't help that. You wouldn't have me go where he tells me not. I don't know anything about them myself except that I did go to their ball. But everybody knows that's different.   (*WWLN* ch. 32)

Lady Monogram, busy drawing social boundaries and rules, uses "everybody" as the rule of inclusion and exclusion. And indeed "everyone" or, as we might say today, everyone who is anyone, does go to Melmotte's party but does not call on him at home. In so doing Lady Monogram and her set not only act like everyone else, but affirm and confirm their place in the realm of "everybody." Of course, not everybody (in the world or even in the novel) is invited to Melmotte's party, and not everybody goes to it (Roger Carbury, for instance). Moreover, some people do call on him at home. Ironically, "everybody" does not denote inclusion but rather exclusion. Moreover, this exclusive group, defined not by external characteristics but by a certain performative vicious cycle (you are part of everyone if you do what everybody does) is inherently unstable. The rule of inclusion is not posited, or even articulated, but rather always already known and widely accepted. Georgiana Longstaffe's exclusion is yet another way for the community to reinforce its communal identity.

Similarly, later in the novel, London society is trying to decide whether the proper thing to do would be to go to Melmotte's dinner:

> It does sometime occur in life that an unambitious man, who is no degree given to enterprises, who would fain be safe, is driven by the cruelty of circumstances into a position in which he must choose a side, and in which, though he has no certain guide as to which side he should choose, he is aware that he will be disgraced if he should take the wrong side . . . The great thing was to ascertain whether the others were going.   (*WWLN* ch. 59)

Note that right and wrong here are used to describe not an action but a side. In other words, right and wrong are not absolute values (associated with natural law) or even formal or structural (one must follow a certain rule, because it is the rule) but rather a shifting allegiance. The men and women are not concerned with whether or not Melmotte is guilty of criminal acts, or even with how much money he really has. Their concern is how many others are going to be at the party. The right thing to do becomes a numbers game, ("If a hundred or more out of the two hundred were to be absent how dreadful would be the position of those who were present!" [*WWLN* ch. 59]) another speculation in the game of smoke and mirrors played by Melmotte.

The lament is clear if implicit: whereas "everybody" used to be a known, stable if exclusive group, defined by class, status, and wealth, Lady Monogram's "everybody" is just another speculation, on par with Melmotte's financial gambles and every bit as dubious. Lady Monogram's letter to Georgiana Longstaffe betrays her own social insecurity, her insistence that the exclusions she is carving out are, in her very words, in fact self-evident.

The reader, like the characters, eventually discovers that Melmotte has in fact forged the title deeds to his securities. However, forgery in *The Way We Live Now*, unlike that in *Orley Farm*, is not a question of character, or of moral failure. That Melmotte's character is bad – or "wrong" – is never in doubt by "everyone," from Roger Carbury to Dolly Longstaffe, from narrator to reader. But the question raised by the legal plot of this novel is not if he is immoral, or if he is guilty, or even if he can pull it off. The only question asked by the characters is "how does his behavior affect me?" Will I ultimately be aligned with the winning side or the losing one? Melmotte, too, understands that the facts relevant to his case are not whether or not he forged the documents but what public opinion will be: "It isn't what I've lost that will crush me, but what men will say that I've lost" (*WWLN* ch. 81). In a society which no longer shares common values, commonality itself becomes superficial and cannot be the basis of law. At the same time, since the question of Melmotte's guilt is immaterial – or rather, material only to the extent that it might make his supporters look bad – this passage also laments the ability of empiricism and positive law to replace the communal in any meaningful way.

In many of his novels, but most forcefully in *The Way We Live Now*, Trollope portrays a society that has lost its moral moorings and, with them, its social anchors. Like the capitalist speculation led by Melmotte, right and wrong are determined only in hindsight, by success or failure, which in turn depend on the quality and especially the quantity of people who adopt a certain view. It doesn't help that the same people – "everybody" – are at the same time trying to figure out what "everybody" thinks. In terms of the legal cultural debates laid out above, it initially appears that the (in)famously "conservative" Trollope is yearning for a lost natural law past – with immutable and universal values. Unlike the speculative, unstable, and valueless present – which, as its manifestation in positive law, prizes form over content – the past, here as in much of Trollope's more nostalgic prose, appears solid. But a closer look at one of his most conservative – and worthy – characters reveals a more complicated approach to natural law, and to the past.

Arguably, the most distinct representative of natural law in Trollope's novels is Roger Carbury of *The Way We Live Now*. Carbury's legal conservativeness is most prominently manifested in his severe adherence to the law of primogeniture: being bound to leave his estate to "a Carbury," even when this Carbury is his despicable and completely undeserving nephew, Sir Felix. The irony is that by law his ability to bequeath the land is "in no degree fettered." Nonetheless, Carbury describes this decision to adhere to the laws of natural descent in terms of restriction and external control: he feels himself "constrained, almost by divine law to see his land went by natural descent" (*WWLN* ch. 14). Carbury, almost masochistically, rejects the law – which allows him to bequeath his land freely – in favor of a higher authority, the coils of duty and custom, a long-standing implied commitment to the rest of his community, and to his place in that community.

The narrator presents this decision as admirable but also misguided. If Sir Felix does inherit the family property, not only would this be an unjust result (Sir Felix is one of the most despicable of Trollope's cads) but would also wrong the same customs and values Roger Carbury sacrifices himself to uphold. No one doubts that Sir Felix would lose the land soon after inheriting it (if not before) through his indolence, gambling, and general depravity. Ultimately, Roger Carbury decides to relinquish the custom of natural descent and leave the land to Sir Felix's deserving sister Hetta and her husband, Paul Montague. Interestingly, this decision is once again presented as a constraint; Roger Carbury needs to feel compelled to do so. "In such case Carbury *must be* the home of the married couple." He decides that "he *must* throw aside that law of primogeniture which to him was so *sacred*" (*WWLN* ch. 93, my italics).

Carbury's inheritance woes (like many other property inheritance cases in Trollope) reveal that "natural law" is no less communal and custom-based than common law. Trollope shows here that the immutability of natural law is immutable only as long as the communality and customs which it serves are stable and coherent. In fact, it is precisely the communal aspect of natural law that makes the two such a natural fit, as asserted by Blackstone. In other words, Roger Carbury's quandary is not primarily due to changing legal customs or practices but a deeper change in the community to which he is committed and of which he is a part.

Conclusion

Victorian legal culture, we are beginning to realize, did not consist of a declining communal system that was being replaced by a positive one, but rather a society and legal system that was ostensibly positivist but was at the same time also inherently communal. In focusing on legal procedures, systems, and ideologies, many nineteenth-century reformers did not realize that all sides of the debate – positive law, empiricism, common law, and natural law – are community-based. Expanding the scope of legal inquiry into the culture at large reveals what is missing from a more narrow focus on the history of doctrine and practice. It reveals that Trollope's obsession with the law and his obsession with social and communal formations are in fact one and the same. As I have shown briefly above, and elsewhere more at length, positive law and empiricism do not replace the lack of certainty and stability engendered by a rapidly changing society.[7]

While it is tempting to read in the novels a conservative Trollope yearning for the times of old, before the advent of a more relativist legal culture of positive law, a closer look reveals that his critique of natural law is just as strong. In different ways, his novels show just how much natural law – through the mediation of common law – was also just as dependent on communal, rather than absolute, values and customs. When Kieran Dolin writes that "the narrative desire for a just resolution of the plot depends finally on a legally conceived and culturally inherited sense of right,"[8] it is true of many of Trollope's novels, not only *Orley Farm*. However, my conception of legal culture shows that the "legally conceived" and "culturally inherited" are not separate elements that fuse together into a sense of right. Rather, as Trollope repeatedly shows, the basic tenets of the common-law legal conceptions are in themselves culturally inherited. Furthermore, it is precisely the cultural inheritedness of common-law practices and customs, by virtue of their commitment to time immemorial, and their symbolic power, that makes them authoritative legal conceptions.

Trollope's novels reveal a society and culture in flux, a flux that cannot be remedied either by a nostalgic appeal to older forms of the law *or* by an appeal to newer, ostensibly more appropriate ones. As becomes evident in these novels, the only thing left for Victorian law, culture, and society is to renegotiate a new commonality, one which is flexible enough to withstand rapid social change, yet strong enough to maintain ways for the making and maintaining of meaningful action and discourse.

NOTES

1 R. D. McMaster, *Trollope and the Law* (London: Macmillan, 1986), p. 11.

2 Kieran Dolin, *Fiction and the Law: Legal Discourse in Victorian and Modernist Literature* (Cambridge: Cambridge University Press, 1999), p. 99.

3 Marianne Constable, *The Law of the Other: The Mixed Jury and Changing Conceptions of Citizenship, Law and Knowledge* (Chicago: University of Chicago Press, 1994), p. 25.

4 Ibid., p. 147.

5 The common law includes both civil and criminal law; the former refers to the law of contract and tort, the latter refers to the law of crime. The common law may also refer to law administered by the common-law courts as distinct from equity, which was administered by the Court of Chancery, until its dispersal by the Judicature Acts of 1873–75.

6 David Lieberman, "Legislation in a Common Law Context," *Zeitschrift für Neuere Rechtsgeschichte* 271 (2005), 1.

7 See also Ayelet Ben-Yishai, "The Fact of a Rumor: Anthony Trollope's *The Eustace Diamonds*," *Nineteenth-Century Literature* 62:1 (2007), 88–120.

8 Dolin, *Fiction*, p. 117.

13

JAMES BUZARD

Trollope and travel

The first word which an Englishman learns in any language is that which signifies a determination to proceed.

Trollope, *WISM* ch. 19

Anthony Trollope earned renown as the inventor of the quintessentially English county of Barsetshire, and though just a few of his forty-seven novels leave England to venture into foreign lands for any sustained period, their author was "a robust, indefatigable, unstoppable traveler": a resident of Ireland for nearly twenty years; a man who made his first tour to the Continent in 1853 and thereafter "would go abroad almost every year of his life"[1]; a voyager to the Mediterranean and the Middle East, to the West Indies and Central America, to North America (twice), to Australia (twice) and New Zealand, to South Africa and Iceland. He circled the globe two times. Some of these journeys were made in Trollope's official capacity as a representative of the British Postal Service, others as a private citizen: both his trips to Australia were connected to the fortunes of his son, who had set up as a sheep-herder in New South Wales. Few Englishmen of the age not in the military or the diplomatic corps could rival Trollope in miles covered and countries seen. Out of his travels came the substantial non-fiction books *The West Indies and the Spanish Main* (1859), *North America* (2 vols., 1862), *Australia and New Zealand* (2 vols., 1873), and *South Africa* (2 vols., 1877), in addition to numerous periodical pieces later collected in *Travelling Sketches* (1866) and, posthumously, *The Tireless Traveller: Twenty Letters to the Liverpool Mercury, 1875* (1941), this last describing his second trip to Australia.

Travel experience also seeded much of his short fiction: when collected in book form his volumes of stories were all but one issued as series of *Tales of All Countries*. Trollope's first two novels, total flops on publication were set in Ireland among the locations the author knew well from his Post Office work; he would set three other novels in that country, including his last, unfinished one, *The Landleaguers*. His other novels set entirely in foreign places he had visited are, like most of the stories, very slight productions: two that were published anonymously, *Nina Balatka* (1866–67) and *Linda Tressel* (1867–68), take place in Prague and in

Nuremburg, respectively, while *The Golden Lion of Granpère* (1867) and *Harry Heathcote of Gangoil* (1873–74) are set in Alsace-Lorraine and in Australia. These are hardly the works that established Trollope's reputation, and they are read today only by the absolute devotee. The English domestic novels that made him famous might include a few chapters here and there involving English characters abroad. *Can You Forgive Her?* (1864–65), the first of the Palliser novels, involves scenes of touring in Switzerland; *He Knew He Was Right* (1868–69) includes several chapters set in Italy; *Phineas Redux* (1873–74) puts one scene in Dresden; *John Caldigate* (1878) places four chapters in the gold fields of Australia.

The most extended use of his travel experience in a major fictional work is in *The Bertrams* (1859), a novel Trollope came to consider among his worst, and of which one reviewer complained, "The narrator keeps apologizing for the travel commentary, but doing it all the same."[2] Toward the beginning and the end of this work, the hero, George Bertram, travels in Palestine and Egypt, occasionally touched by Oriental romance or spiritual insight, but mainly finding himself in situations that undermine such lofty sentiments. The filth in the streets, the torture of a Turkish saddle, the outrageous assaults by would-be guides, all these and more prove fatal to romanticized perception. Moreover, George's access to what is foreign in the places he visits is checked by the fact that he moves among his countrymen and stays in the hostelries recommended to the English, institutions that create an enveloping little England abroad. Stepping into the public room of his hotel in Jerusalem, George hears "a Babel of English voices, and ... a clatter of English spoons" (*B* ch. 6). In Cairo, "Mr Shepheard's hotel ... is to an Englishman the centre of Egypt ... And certainly our countrymen have made this spot more English than England itself" (*B* ch. 38). An unofficial embassy of sorts, the hotel seems to confer on its guests an extraterritorial status: within five hundred yards of it, the English tourist "is still in Great Britain" (*B* ch. 38). Tourists can also tend to regard the ongoing life in a foreign place as irrelevant or even an obstacle to their aims in being there. At one moment in *The Bertrams*, the narrator proposes,

> Let us go into some church on the Continent – in Italy, we will say – where the walls of the churches still boast of the great works of great masters. Look at that man standing on the very altar-step while the priest is saying his mass ... How he shuffles about to get the best point of sight, quite indifferent to clergy or laity! All that bell-ringing, incense-flinging, and breast-striking is nothing to him: he has paid dearly to be brought thither; he has paid the guide who is kneeling a little behind him; he is going to pay the sacristan who attends him; he is quite willing to pay the priest himself ... but he has come there to see that fresco, and see it he will. (*B* ch. 9)

If, in this work that reviewers and the author himself disparaged, there is a distracting amount of attention paid to travel experience, in the novel Trollope thought his best – *The Last Chronicle of Barset* (1866–67) – we find a form of traveling while hardly paying attention at all. The Barsetshire plot (did Mr. Crawley steal the twenty pound check?) comes to depend on information that can be supplied only by an Englishwoman sojourning, offstage, in Italy, and that information is successfully obtained when Johnny Eames makes a whirlwind trip to that country to seek the woman out. As if to account for the insular preoccupation of all his major fiction, Trollope points out that Eames's pursuit of Mrs. Arabin is so single-minded that the hero scarcely looks to the right or left of him, scarcely registers that he is in a foreign land at all. Johnny charges forward, not stopping to sleep, to Paris, Venice, and Florence, conceiving of his journey as romance quest and trial by ordeal. His thoughts are full, not of the sights he rushes past, but of Lily Dale back home, to the winning of whose favors his quest is devoted. Arriving at Venice only to learn that Mrs. Arabin has moved on to the Tuscan capital, our hero is

> vexed, but [he] became a little prouder than before as he felt it to be his duty to go on to Florence before he went to bed ... There was just time to have a tub and breakfast, to swim in a gondola, to look at the outside of the Doge's palace, and to walk up and down the piazza before he started again. It was hard work, but I think he would have been pleased had he heard that Mrs. Arabin had retreated from Florence to Rome. (*LCB* ch. 70)

If, like Eames, Trollope's major novels are so lovingly focused on English people and places that they have little attention to spare for foreign lands, his wide-ranging travel books might appear to be those novels' perfect complement. Yet for all that they cover lands far distant from England and involve confrontations with peoples as alien to the English as Trollope could possibly imagine, one finds in them their own insular preoccupation. The four travel books were mainly reports on former or current British colonies, and one of Trollope's leading interests was to determine how viable each region was as a site for large-scale settlement by British or Irish emigrants. His question was, are these suitable lands to which to send the United Kingdom's surplus laboring men? Generally speaking, two of the books say no (*The West Indies and the Spanish Main* and *South Africa*), two emphatically yes (*North America* and *Australia and New Zealand*). And everywhere Trollope went on the journeys that yielded these books, if he did not always move within the envelope of a little England abroad, he always remained within the portable boundaries of a racial identity he wanted to believe proof against alien influences.

One of the most familiar assertions about travel is that it broadens the mind, breaks down ethnocentrism, makes for world understanding and peace. The very first entry on a website listing "the fifty most inspiring travel quotes of all time" reads: "'Travel is fatal to prejudice, bigotry, and narrow-mindedness.' – *Mark Twain*."[3] But as to this truism the reader of Trollope's travel writing must demur. It is not that Trollope learned nothing on his various journeys; on the contrary, his books are stuffed with information. In reading them one learns the prices of meat, the going rates of workmen's wages, the amount of wool exported in a year, the organization of governments, the state of the hotels and the transportation system, the workings of farms and factories – and much, much more. Trollope's own description, from his *Travelling Sketches*, of the "Tourist in Search of Knowledge" applies well to the author himself. This figure

> will listen with wondrous patience to the details of guides, jotting down figures in a little book ... And he looks into municipal matters wherever he goes, learning all details as to mayors, aldermen, and councillors, as to customs, duties on provisions, as to import duties on manufactures, as to schools, convents, and gaols, to scholars, mendicants, and criminals. He does not often care much for scenery, but he will be careful to inquire how many passengers the steamboats carry on the lakes, and what average of souls is boarded and lodged at each large hotel that he passes. (ch. 6)

But for all of the diligent finding of facts, nowhere in Trollope's travel writings do we come across a substantial alteration of perspective; very nearly nowhere does prejudice falter; repeatedly we encounter expressions of bigotry and narrow-mindedness wholly conventional in Trollope's culture. It is not too much to say that, in spite of all the places he visited and people he encountered, Trollope hardly ever changed his mind.

One time he did was in Ireland, where the twenty-six-year-old postal employee took a position as clerk to a regional surveyor in the West of the country. At a time when many English Protestants looked askance at their Irish Catholic subjects as less-than-civilized slackers with a fondness for whiskey and violence, Trollope learned to love the Irish, emphasizing in his *Autobiography* and in one particular short tale, "Father Giles of Ballymoy," that for this time, at least, the expectations with which he had arrived in a country had been overturned. The short story's narrator informs us that "On this my first visit into Connaught, I own that I was somewhat scared lest I should be made a victim to the wild lawlessness and general savagery of the people" (Thompson 440). Ironically enough, it turns out to be the visiting Englishman who acts rather savagely toward a kindly priest; as for the Irish – to borrow language Trollope used of himself in the

Autobiography – they "did not murder me, nor did they even break my head" (*A* ch. 4). The revision of his initial outlook is noteworthy because so rare, and it probably owes much to Trollope's gratitude to Ireland for liberating him from the "wretched" condition of his earlier years, spent in England (*A* ch. 4).

Then again, Trollope's affection for the Irish could sometimes savor of condescension, as in the concluding scene of his *North America*, set in the Irish port of Queenstown, where Trollope's transatlantic ship has made port. The traveler suddenly finds himself surrounded by beggars, a phenomenon he has not encountered in the United States. "I myself," he writes, "am fond of Irish beggars. It is an acquired taste ... But I certainly did wish that there were not so many of them at Queenstown." That wish leads to the reflection that "The Irishman when he expatriates himself to one of those American States loses much of that affectionate, confiding, master-worshipping nature which makes him so good a fellow when at home. But he becomes more of a man" (*NA* ch. 36). Trollope's Celtophilia did not prevent him, either, from concluding that Ireland *deserved* the awful famines of the 1840s: they had been "ordained by Providence" as "the punishment of her imprudence and idleness," and, by thinning the population, they had turned out to be Ireland's "greatest blessing."[4]

A mark of the respect Trollope was gaining from his superiors came in January 1858, when he was commissioned to negotiate a new postal treaty with Egypt. His trip there and to Palestine, Malta, and Gibraltar furnished material not only for *The Bertrams* but for short stories such as "An Unprotected Female at the Pyramids," "The Banks of the Jordan," "John Bull at Guadalquivir," and "George Walker at Suez." By November of the same year Trollope had departed on another sensitive Post Office mission, to the West Indies; by the beginning of 1859 he was under contract to write his first travel book.

Trollope considered *The West Indies and the Spanish Main* "the best book that has come from my pen" (*A* ch. 7) – a statement that strains credulity. He visited Jamaica about a generation after the abolition of slavery, and one of his chief interests was to determine how the sugar plantations were faring under the dispensation of paid labor. Though he favored emancipation, his sympathies were stirred on behalf of the plantation owners, whom he recognized as fellow countrymen: the Jamaican planter, he wrote, "has so many of the characteristics of an English country gentleman that he does not strike an Englishman as a strange being" (*WISM* ch. 6). Trollope saw the planters as manfully attempting to carry on their businesses without benefit either of slaves or of the tariffs that were supposed to help them stay competitive with sugar-producing colonies of other nations, which still used slave labor (such as Cuba, which Trollope visited). The planter's biggest problem, Trollope believed, was that his available supply of labor – the freed slaves, "fitted by nature for the hardest physical work" (*WISM* ch. 4) – would not labor. "The negro's idea of emancipation was and is emancipation not from slavery but from work. To lie in the sun and eat breadfruit and yams is his idea of being free" (*WISM* ch. 6). (In both the travel book and the short story "Miss Sarah Jack, of Spanish Town, Jamaica" Trollope sympathetically projects himself into the viewpoint of the planter; not once does it occur to him to attempt a similar exercise on behalf of the ex-slave.) Trollope's recommended solution is the importation of cheap labor. "Place the Coolie or the Chinaman alongside of [the negro], and he must work in his own defence. If he do not, he will gradually cease to have an existence" (*WISM* ch. 14).

Trollope commonly expressed his opinions on racial and colonial questions as if they were those of a rock-solid consensus back home: in the passages dealing with these matters one frequently encounters such phrases as "all of us feel" or "we all believe." But he also practiced the rhetorical strategy of presenting his unoriginal bigotries as if they were oppositional, a radical challenge to what he characterized as the view "lately become prevalent in England" – that of the sentimental Philanthropist who, writing from a distance, vastly overestimates the negro's capabilities and accomplishments (*WISM* ch. 4). Believing that much harm came from such overestimation, Trollope took up the rhetorical stance of the blunt-speaking enemy of cant. In British Guiana, where the unexploited fertility of the land seemed to cry out for field hands, he found a village of black men attempting to set up as freeholders to be an illustrative failure (*WISM* ch. 12). In New Granada (Colombia), "Civilization . . . is retrograding" "under the influence of unlimited liberty and universal suffrage": the black population, emancipated in 1851, had been given the franchise (*WISM* ch. 16). When Trollope wrote of the "negro" he hewed to the notion that race conferred fixed qualities designed to serve an everlasting objective: "God, for his own purposes . . . has created men of inferior and superior race" – the former to serve, the latter to lead (*WISM* ch. 4). When he turned to the mixed-race "coloured" population, though, he developed a different theory – that "Providence has sent white men and black men to these regions in order that from them may spring a race fitted by intellect for civilization; and fitted also by physical organization for tropical labour" (*WISM* ch. 5). On this view, race appeared a far more malleable category, and blacks and whites were destined to interbreed so as to produce a new race "fitted by nature for the burning sun, in whose blood shall be mixed some portion of northern energy, and which shall owe its physical powers to the African progenitors" (*WISM* ch. 4). When, on that far distant day by which "sufficient of our blood shall have been infused into the veins of those children of the sun; then . . . we may be ready, without stain to our patriotism, to take off our hats and bid farewell to the West Indies" (*WISM* ch. 5). In view of this divine blueprint, miscegenation becomes righteous begetting.

On the first page of Trollope's next travel book, *North America*, the author declared, "It has been the ambition of my literary life to write a book about the United States" (*NA* ch. 1). (In spite of its title and its inclusion of some chapters on Canada, the book's focus was clearly on the United States.) This was so for two reasons. First, Trollope's mother had written a notorious text on the subject, *The Domestic Manners of the Americans* (1832), which had "created laughter on one side of the Atlantic, and soreness on the other" by its exposure of the "social defects and absurdities" of the young republic (*NA* ch. 1). A great admirer of the progress made by his American cousins, her son intended to produce a more judicious account that would attempt to "add to the good feeling which should exist between two nations which ought to love each other . . ." (*NA* ch. 1). The reason why they ought to love each other is the second reason Trollope had longed to write the book – because of the Anglo-Saxon brotherhood uniting England and its former colony. The political independence of the United States Trollope tended to regard as both appropriate and, where race was concerned, irrelevant: all of Britain's white settler colonies should achieve statehood of their own when they were ready for it, and their doing so would in no way efface the super-political unity of what Charles Dilke would call the "Greater Britain" that spanned the globe.[5] Trollope's experiences of the United States in the early stages of its Civil War, however, made for a set of responses more complicated than his wholly benevolent intentions might have prepared him for. (Amanda Claybaugh's chapter, "Trollope and America," in this volume provides further information on this topic.)

In his third major work on travel, *Australia and New Zealand*, Trollope faced two indigenous populations, which he ranked differently: the Australian Aboriginal, "infinitely lower in his gifts than the African negro" (*ANZ* vol. 1, ch. 4), and the Maoris of New Zealand, "the most civilized" of "all the people whom we have been accustomed to call savages . . ." (vol. 11, ch. 19). But he consigned them – as he thought God had done – to the same fate. "Of the Australian black man," he writes, "we may certainly say that he has to go" (*ANZ* vol. 1, ch. 4). The Maoris earn an anticipatory elegy: "It is with pain that I write as I do about a gallant people, whose early feelings towards us were those of kindness and hospitality, and as to whom

I acknowledge that they have nearly had all the gifts which would have enabled us to mix with them on equal terms ... But the Maoris are going" (*ANZ* vol. ii, ch. 25). Even for them, much more for the Australian Aborigine, the attempt to lift them to higher levels of civilization seemed to Trollope a "game ... not worth the candle": there was no point in "prepar[ing] for them a prospective course of civilized life, which can only be of real use to them on the condition that they are to remain among us as a permanent people" (*ANZ* vol. i, ch. 32).

Trollope distinguished between "true" colonies, such as Australia and New Zealand, which, upon the "going" of native populations, would be fit for "the occupation of our multiplying race," and other imperial holdings such as India and Ceylon (*ANZ* vol. i, ch. 1). He found the progress of white settlement in Australia satisfactory but uneven. Of Victoria he concluded that "No single British colony has ever enjoyed prosperity so great and so rapid" (*ANZ* vol. i, ch. 24). That prosperity had come in part from gold, first struck in the colony in 1851: Trollope dutifully visited the diggings at Ballarat and Sandhurst, but he remained skeptical of the speculative nature of gold mining, believing that the metal extracted probably did not exceed in value the expense of extracting it, and feeling that the pursuit tended to degrade those who engaged in it. At the other end of the spectrum from Victoria was Western Australia, a huge region populated by only 25,000 – of whom 10,000 were convicts: the colony might have failed completely had it not turned to receiving transported criminals, at so late a date that "the system of transportation had already become odious to the other colonies" (*ANZ* vol. ii, ch. 5). Salvation came at the cost of bearing the deepest convict taint on the continent: when Trollope left the colony, he needed to present a certificate at its border attesting that he "[was] not and never has been a prisoner of the Crown" there (*ANZ* vol. ii, ch. 6). In Queensland, he was heartened to see the sugar fields being worked by imported South Sea islanders who seemed to "know the comforts conferred and the power given by accumulated possessions – and who are therefore capable of receiving the blessings of civilization" (*ANZ* vol. i, ch. 8). Tasmania he found lovely but a little contemptible for its continuing dependency on the mother country and lack of the proper go-ahead spirit. Of Adelaide, South Australia, he wrote, "no city ... gives one more fixedly the idea that Australian colonization has been a success," although he felt the ratio of city to country residents in the colony imbalanced toward the former (*ANZ* vol. ii, ch. 10). In New South Wales, Trollope was enchanted by Sydney but devoted most of his attention to the strife in the countryside between "squatters" and "free selecters" – a major subject of the book as a whole. The former were the sheep-herders who had come first to the country and leased huge tracts of grazing land from the government; the latter were the more recently arrived agriculturalists who purchased properties sometimes carved out from the squatters' leaseholds. Trollope acknowledged that "all the early success of Australia was due to the squatters of New South Wales" (*ANZ* vol. I, ch. 17), but he felt that "the encouragement ... of the genuine free selecter who intends to reside upon the land ... is and should be the first aim of colonial government" (*ANZ* vol. I, ch. 2). His one great objection was to the defensive insularity he found in the separate Australian colonies. He noted that "in no instance does a railway run from the capital of one colony to that of another," there being "a feeling that were this done the intimacy would be too great" (*ANZ* vol. I, ch. 11). More problematic still was the colonies' practice of charging customs duties upon each others' goods, which stymied the development of a unified Australian spirit and negated much economic opportunity. In passage after passage Trollope urged the creation of a pan-Australian customs union. Free intercolony trade would be the crucial first step toward the creation of an Australian national spirit.

As self-styled teller of hard truths, Trollope repeatedly confronted his readers with colonization's unsavory realities where indigenous peoples were concerned: "No one, I think," he writes in one such passage, "will say that the English should have abstained from taking possession of Australia because such possession could not be secured without injury to the blacks" (*ANZ* vol. I, ch. 32). When writing in this vein he was not incapable of imagining how the people on the receiving end of British colonialism might regard it. He goes farthest in this direction when treating of New Zealand and the comparatively admirable Maoris – as when he declares that, in New Zealand, "it is impossible not to feel that whereas the strangers had no moral right to attack the natives, the natives cannot have been morally wrong in attempting to destroy their invaders" (*ANZ* vol. II, ch. 19). In this context, the tension between Trollope's sympathy for the conquered and his legitimation of conquest also increases. It is "absurd," he claims, to accuse the Maori fighters against the British of "treachery and rebellion" when they were only defending themselves against unprovoked aggression (*ANZ* vol. II, ch. 25); yet Trollope himself speaks of their "rebellion" in a passage of unstable attitude that occurs only two pages later: "Without punishment rebellion could not be put down – and [yet] there seemed to be cruelty in hanging men who felt that they were fighting for the preservation of their own property" (*ANZ* vol. II, ch. 25). At the time Trollope was writing, open conflict had subsided without a conclusive victory for the settlers, and the best course seemed to be to let things "drift" and to wait out the natives' inevitable "melting [away]" (*ANZ* vol. II, ch. 25). As if to vouch for that outcome's inevitability, even in the case of this almost-civilized people, Trollope strikes the "little England abroad" theme with particular frequency in the New Zealand portion of the book. Indeed, "the great drawback to New Zealand," we learn, "comes from the feeling that after crossing the world and journeying over so many thousand miles, you have not at all succeeded in getting away from England. When you have arrived there you are, as it were, next door to your own house, and yet you have a two months' barrier between yourself and your home" (*ANZ* vol. II, ch. 20). So English is the country already – in landscape, wildlife, manners, and institutions – that it will be realizing its full potential only when it is populated exclusively with English men and women.

The series of letters Trollope supplied to the *Liverpool Mercury* about his second trip to Australia, in 1875, includes much repetition of *Australia and New Zealand*, though there is new material, some of it from the journeys out and back. The first letter deals with the challenges faced by Italy in the early years of unification; the second with the newly opened Suez Canal and the British outpost at Aden. Several deal with the Crown Colony of Ceylon, in the early days of which "some things were done by us of which we can hardly boast," though more recently, the British had learned to administer benevolent government to an increasingly prosperous "coloured population."[6] A stop in Hawaii, at that time still a monarchy, elicited the judgment that Honolulu was far superior to "any other town on the world's surface which at the present moment is nominally under the dominion of savages" (Letter 19). This visit to Australia coincided with the setting out from Sydney of an expedition to New Guinea, and with the news that Fiji had just been proclaimed the newest British colony; Trollope felt that expansion had gone far enough. "There is ... at home," he reckoned, "a general opinion that Great Britain possesses enough of the world – as much as she can well manage – and that new territorial possessions must be regarded rather as increased burdens than increased strength" (Letter 17).

In South Africa, which he visited in 1877, Trollope confronted a new set of complications – not merely the presence of a vast and diverse black population "by no means inclined to go" to make room for whites, but also the presence of the earlier white settlers, the Dutch Boers (*SA* vol. I, ch. 2). Each leg of the triangle of English, Boer, and African featured conflicts particular to it. The Boers resented the interference of the dominant English, and they repeatedly trekked away to interior regions in an attempt to put themselves beyond the reach of English law. The enforcers of that law,

Trollope believed, had shown themselves "not quite [able to] make up their minds whether it was or was not their duty to go after the wanderers" and to exert sovereignty over them (*SA* vol. II, ch. 2). Just before Trollope's visit, they had "gone after" them in the Transvaal, summarily annexing the district and putting an end to its short-lived Dutch republic. Trollope wondered "whether there is a precedent for so high-handed a deed in British history," but he also called it a "great deed" and considered it justified by its results (*SA* vol. II, ch. 3; vol. I, ch. 1). The more successful Boer republic of the Orange Free State presented a significant obstacle to the consolidation of British overlordship in the region, – for British traffic passing from the Cape Colony in the south to the Transvaal and the Diamond Fields had to pass through it, "and there would necessarily arise questions of transit and of Customs duties which would make it expedient that the districts should be united under one flag" – but Trollope could not "foresee any pretext" by which the British could annex the Free State (*SA* vol. I, ch. 4). The Boers' preference for living in isolation, on huge farms which they lacked the labor power to develop fully, was deeply troubling to Trollope, for "the consequences are that there is not room for fresh comers and that nevertheless the land is not a quarter occupied" (*SA* vol. II, ch. 5). In this book, the Boers occupy the position held by the "squatters" in *Australia and New Zealand*: they opened up the land but are now an impediment to its continued development.

As a "true" colony (or set of colonies), South Africa was not very successful: the total British population of 120,000 amounted to less than half that of the city of Melbourne; and the British had been in South Africa since 1795. White immigration was discouraged not only by the uncooperative Boers but also by persistent conflict with some of the African tribes and by the existence, and the apparent capacity for industriousness, of a significant African labor force. It was forcefully impressed upon Trollope that "an Englishman in South Africa will not work along side of a coloured man on equal terms" (*SA* vol. I, ch. 9). Africans outnumbered Boers and English together by 5 to 1 and were "a strong and increasing people ... Such as they are we have got ... to rule them and teach them to earn their bread – a duty which has not fallen upon us in any other Colony" (*SA* vol. I, ch. 4). The Basutos, terrible foes of the Boers, were showing signs of settling down as productive agriculturalists. The most promising group seemed to be the Zulus, of whom Trollope entertained the "fair hope that they will become a laborious and educated people," although at present, the independent-minded Zulu "is a gentleman and will only work as it suits him" (*SA* vol. I, ch. 17, ch. 15). Trollope had a lower opinion of the "Kafirs" of the Cape Colony, although the spectacle of thousands of them working the Kimberley diamond mines inspired optimism. Kimberley, in fact, though a rough and ugly town, struck him as "one of the most interesting places on the face of the earth," because he knew of "no other spot on which the work of civilizing a Savage is being carried on with so signal a success" (*SA* vol. II, ch. 9). He foresaw it eventually becoming "a large town with a settled Kafir population which will fall gradually into civilized ways of life" (*SA* vol. II, ch. 9). It would be long, however, before Britain's African subjects would be ready to participate in their own government: Trollope was convinced that colonization was steadily improving them but that "were there to be a vote tomorrow among the Kafirs whether the white man should be driven into the sea, or retained in the country, the entire race would certainly vote for the white man's extermination" (*SA* vol. I, ch. 6). He opposed explicitly restricting the franchise by race – as the Boers of the Orange Free State did – but, given the population ratio, could foresee it being asked, "why should we not have a Kafir Prime Minister at Capetown, and Kafir Parliament refusing to pay salary to any but a Kafir Governor?" Trollope conceded that "in coming ages a Kafir may make as good a Prime Minister as Lord Beaconsfield. But he cannot do so now – nor in this age – nor in many ages to come" (*SA* vol. I, ch. 4). The compliment paid to this future African Premier is undermined by the fact that Trollope actually detested Benjamin Disraeli (Beaconsfield).

With the exception of a privately printed volume about an excursion to Iceland made in 1878, *South Africa* was Trollope's last travel book, and in it Trollope returns yet again – and again – to the question of the legitimacy of the colonial project, this time pressing even harder on the claim he otherwise so vigorously upheld, that England's seizure of land from indigenous peoples is justified by the "necessity" of finding homes for its surplus population. Here he asks, "But what is necessity? A man must die. A man, generally, must work or go to the wall. But need a man establish himself as a farmer on another man's land?" The skeptical energy of the question is considerable, but it is immediately recircuited, as Trollope adds, "The reader will understand that I do not deny the necessity – but that I feel myself to be arrested when I hear it asserted as a sufficient excuse" (*SA* vol. I, ch. 2). Trollope's travel writings do not contain nearly as many unstable passages, like this one, as they do facts about cost of living, governmental structures, tariff rates and the like; but they do contain a sizable number of such passages, reverting to the subject and reworking the same arguments frequently enough to suggest that Trollope never stopped searching for a finally satisfying articulation of England's wishful belief that it was working the Creator's will in the colonies.

NOTES

1 N. John Hall, *Trollope: A Biography* (Oxford: Oxford University Press, 1991), p. 130.
2 Quoted in Hall, *Trollope*, p. 161.
3 www.bravenewtraveler.com/2008/03/07/50-most-inspiring-travel-quotes-of-all-time/. Last accessed July 3, 2010.
4 Quoted in Hall, *Trollope*, pp. 113, 129.
5 See Charles Wentworth Dilke, *Greater Britain: A Record of Travel in English-Speaking Countries during 1866 and 1867* (1869; rpt. New York: Cosimo Classics: 2005).
6 Anthony Trollope, *The Tireless Traveller: Twenty Letters to the Liverpool Mercury* (1875; rpt. Berkeley: University of California Press, 1941), pp. 53, 54.

14

NICHOLAS BIRNS

Trollope and the Antipodes

On both voyages Anthony Trollope made to Australia, in 1871 and 1875, he passed through the Suez Canal.[1] Suez was not originally British in inspiration, and was not, in origin, the arterial capstone of empire it later became.[2] This is visible in Trollope's short story, "George Walker at Suez" (1861), where an Englishman's unglamorous participation in the canal construction hardly bespeaks the later pivotal role that Suez played in visions of empire. In this story, the squalor of Suez is contrasted with the comforts of Friday Street in London. Yet Suez was to be the channel by which British comforts were able to reproduce themselves many times over in lands beneath the equator.

On his trips to "the Antipodes" (a term covering both Australia and New Zealand and signifying their being nearly at the opposite end of the world from Britain), Trollope had to make long-term plans: wrapping up novels before he left, conducting whirls of socializing on the advent of his departure, making complicated logistical arrangements.[3] Yet before Suez the voyages would have been so long as to be virtually implausible. After Suez they became so routine as to be prosaic, as Trollope observed after his second journey in 1875.

James Belich has spoken of the "recolonial" effect Suez had on New Zealand.[4] Suez, and the relatively short fifty-day voyage it enabled, connected the Antipodes more closely, in terms of economy and communication, to the mother country and thus retarded national self-assertion. This effect was medium-term, not long-term, and astute observers such as Trollope saw the conceivability and indeed the necessity of self-rule for Australia and New Zealand. But Suez nonetheless meant that the drift of Australia away from Britain would be arrested.

The post-Suez idea of space changed the way Australia was represented in fiction. Previously, the assumption was that when characters went to Australia – as prisoners, exiles, or simply, like the Micawbers, Peggotty, and Little Emily in Dickens's *David Copperfield* (1850), to make a new start, they would not be likely to come back, or at least come back often – the voyage was simply too difficult. An assumption like this undergirds the ending of the novel Trollope wrote on board, ironically enough (and Trollope himself was to delight in giving ships in his Antipodean novels ironic names), the *Great Britain*, on his first voyage to Australia. This was *Lady Anna*, which can perhaps be considered the first of Trollope's Antipodean novels. The novel's denouement, the highly controversial marriage of Lady Anna Lovel, whose legitimacy and aristocratic parentage had been revealed in the course of the novel, to the tailor Daniel Thwaite, entailed an Antipodean aspect to the marriage plot. Australia is the place where the couple can be happy together and yet not outrage class norms, outside as well as within the novel. But no explicit mention is made of the couple returning to England.

The action of *Lady Anna* mirrors the course of its composition: both author and characters end up in Australia.[5] Intriguingly, Trollope seems to promise his readers an Australian sequel specifically to *Lady Anna* in its closing pages – somewhat like Thackeray's *The Virginians* (1857–59) was to *Henry Esmond* (1852). Trollope wrote no such book. This suggests that once he got to Australia he saw different possibilities. The crucial difference is between a pre-Suez Australia, from which it is difficult to return, and a post-Suez Australia, from which one can return – with complications! Such complications are amply aired in Trollope's most substantive Antipodean novel, *John Caldigate* (1879).

Before he wrote any fiction set in Australia, Trollope composed his series of travel essays about his journey, eventually published as *Australia and New Zealand* (1873). These essays were not just a record of his own journey but a comprehensive account of the lands visited. Trollope visited every part of Australia, something demanding on the stamina of a traveler in even later times. The essays appeared in the *Daily Telegraph* – a rising newspaper especially famed for its foreign correspondents – signed by "An Antipodean." Though it was well known that this was Trollope, the sobriquet implied at least a temporary adoption of that identity.

Trollope came to Australia and New Zealand later, more personally, and more prophetically than he came to any other places outside the British Isles that he wrote about. Yet Trollope first came to the subject fifteen years before he ventured south of the Equator – in his treatise *The New Zealander* of 1855, not published in Trollope's lifetime and seeing print only in 1972. N. John Hall calls the text "curiously entitled."[6] In truth there is nothing in it of New Zealand other than the premise (taken most immediately from Thomas Babington Macaulay) that a future New Zealander will visit the ruins of London just as a Victorian Englishman might visit the ruins of

Rome, wondering about the nature of a past, now bygone civilization. New Zealand is thus at once the future of Britain and the index of Britain's diminution. New Zealand was probably chosen as it was the newest settler colony, with the Maori still contesting white settlement at the time Macaulay and later Trollope employed the trope.

The Antipodes thus persistently related to futurity in Trollope. Yet that Trollope first visited Australia at the comparatively ripe age of fifty-six meant that his particular sounding of the idea of the Antipodes being countries of the future was tinged with the author's own sense of aging and increasing bodily vulnerability. Furthermore, that his son Fred settled in Australia, and indeed sired a line of Trollopes that became baronets and continue in Australia to this day, meant that Trollope had a personal stake in Australia, and in literal terms left something behind there. The prophetic aspect also has to do with his age, suitable for the clairvoyant dignity of a prophet, but has more to do with the politically unformed nature of Antipodean civil society. Whether Australia would be united or a collection of several states, a republic or part of the British imperium, was yet to be determined. Much of *Australia and New Zealand* is concerned not just with these territories' economic prospects but with their political future.

All these circumstances combined to make the Australian contexts more determinative of Trollope's identity as author than the other lands he visited. Trollope comes close to writing temporarily as "an Australian." Trollope's letters show how seamlessly he functioned in Australia, how undisrupted was his logistical routine. He tried to set up business opportunities for his son Fred with Henry Parkes, later one of the principal movers of Australian federation. He established a friendship with the Melbourne historian G. W. Rusden. Rusden's translations of Gérard de Nerval, commended by Trollope, not only show literary cosmopolitanism in Australia, but disclose that Trollope, in his temporary Australian identity, could still be in a literary milieu (*Letters* II:555). The friendship with Rusden shows Trollope continuing to lead a vigorous literary social life while abroad, and also reveals the cosmopolitan, Bohemian aspects of Melbourne in the 1870s, showing its aspirations to sophistication and urbanity.[7]

Trollope heard of Charles Reade's illicit adaptation of *Ralph The Heir* for the London stage and gently reprimanded him. He mourned the death of the Irish novelist Charles Lever. He complained to George Eliot and George Henry Lewes about Forster's biography of Dickens (*Letters* II:557–58). He operated both globally and locally while in Australia.

As Trollope was still British while in Australia, an Australian tinge colored the works he produced upon his return. On his return to England, Trollope composed *The Way We Live Now* and *The Prime Minister*, arguably the most comprehensively "social" and "political" novels he ever wrote, suggesting the Antipodean sojourn not only gave him perspective on England but, more crucially, extended his idea of what a social body could be. J. H. Davidson even described *The Way We Live Now* as a "sequel" to Trollope's "glowing" portrait of the Antipodean colonies.[8] Thus the idea of an "Australian Trollope" can be stretched even beyond *Lady Anna*.

A Trollope who, as Laurie Langbauer puts it, conjectured "an indefinite series of differences" but also generally exemplified what Hall terms "conservative liberalism" would have found something particularly congenial in the juxtaposition of identity and displacement Australia provided to the British.[9] Australia was the most exclusively Anglophone of the English settler colonies. Furthermore, Australia was basically already self-governing, and there was not much Britain could do to compel it.[10] Trollope privileges "that Englishmen may be happy" over the alternate goal "that England may be great," and says that "justice and philanthropy" call for gradual, orderly decolonization (*ANZ* 12). It is proliferation of Englishness, not hegemony of Britain, which concerns Trollope. This sense of Australian proliferation is made textual by the fact that *Australia and New Zealand* is not Trollope's only Australian travelogue. In twenty letters sent to the *Liverpool Mercury* on the occasion of his second voyage in 1875, Trollope has occasion to reflect on his first book, to reaffirm his conclusions, but also to accommodate critiques of his book made by Australians and to provide a metatextual supplement which adds to the sense of both literary and geographic proliferation in Trollope's approach to the Antipodes. Australian textuality discloses Australia's potential as a site of good government. There is no Arnoldian "force till right is ready."[11] In the Antipodes, right is already ready.[12]

This emphasis on the democratic normality of Australia helps explain the business-forecast element in *Australia and New Zealand*, which presents a mundane image of Australia:

> The merchant is of course bound to see that the security on which his money has been advanced is not impaired. Consequently the whole produce of the run goes into the merchant's hands. When the wool is sent off,– say direct to London – an estimated sum of its value is placed to the squatter's credit. When the wool has been sold the balance is also placed to his credit. But the money does not come into his hands. This rule prevails very generally with regard to sheep sold. (*ANZ* 95)

Even allowing for the thorough style of Victorian journalism, this reads like a government White Paper. Far from being a locale for adventure and derring-do, Australia is positioned as the civil servant's ideal, an orderly society new enough for rational procedures to be put into place as normative. In the few chapters concerned with New Zealand, Trollope is less economically concerned and seems to enjoy himself more, perhaps because these more utilitarian analyses had already been made for the larger country. This latter conclusion is fortified by the more casual tone of the letters from the second Australian journey. Trollope refers several times to the Englishness of New Zealand, which he seems to have found comforting as contrasted to the Australian landscape. But it is also clearly the disjunction endemic to the *redeployment* of Englishness to New Zealand that gives him pleasure. Trollope notices, and is unenthusiastic about, the greater influence of Evangelical Protestantism on New Zealand culture, in a vein not unlike his portraiture of Samuel Prong in *Rachel Ray* (1863) and Obadiah Slope in *Barchester Towers* (1857).

Trollope is also concerned with the internal government of Australia. Here he launches a trope relating to capital cities that will resonate throughout his Antipodean oeuvre. In writing about the town of Gladstone, in central Queensland, he speaks of it as "the future capital of Queensland" – in other words, as an artificial capital, like Ottawa in Canada, Gladstone would be the compromise between Rockhampton and Brisbane (*ANZ* 42). That Trollope got this profoundly wrong has not to do just with the demographic fact that the population of Rockhampton never got large enough to rival Brisbane's and so mandate a compromise. It has to do with the fact that, in all cases, the largest city of each Australian colony is its political capital. The difference here is not with Britain, where the same is true, but with the United States – Trollope refers to "Albany or Harrisburgh (sic)" as being capital cities of their states, not New York or Philadelphia (*ANZ* 43). Australia from Trollope's time onward has been an emphatically urban nation, with its intellectual and cultural life strikingly (as compared to the United States) headquartered in its five large cities. Trollope understood this. But he guesses wrongly on a related matter: that there will be "further separation" within the Australian colonies, that they will subdivide into smaller political units (94). This did not happen. But the genesis of this expectation was Trollope's sense that, compared with the United States, Australia was likely to have too few states.

Trollope's theorization of the present and future in Australia is continued in *Harry Heathcote of Gangoil*. Here, the reader is first told it is Christmas, and prepared for all the generic conventions of the Christmas story, and then abruptly told that this is Christmas in Australia, with expectations of a wintry Christmas upended to a summer one. The physical and social background is Australian. But the novel is a Trollope novel with a Trollopian conflict and a Trollopian resolution. The motto adopted two decades earlier by the University of Sydney – *Sidere mens, eadem mutato* (the stars change, but the mind remains the same) could well be applied to *Harry Heathcote*. The "squatter" Harry Heathcote opposes the marriage of his sister to the "free selector" Giles Medlicot. The squatter is a sheep-farmer who has come earlier before land sales were regulated and amassed a huge estate; the free-selector is a small farmer who purchased a specific plot of land under an agreement with the government, or, as Heathcote pejoratively puts it, "A man who would take advantage of the law to buy a bit of another man's land" (*HHG* ch. 2). Squatters have land and privilege, but not legal sanction; free-selectors are more prosaic and limited in their ambition, but have paid for their land through a governmentally supervised process. The distinction, though, is made less for its own sake than for the sake of the plot overcoming it. Medlicot *does* marry Heathcote's sister – and for the sake of showing that Trollopian plots can overcome class distinctions in a world quite unlike England. The need for resolution is paramount. Australia is a land where distinctions, in general, can be overturned, where the future will be more malleable than the past. It is a winning but also slightly bland ending. Any sense of what Marcus Clarke famously termed the "weird melancholy" of the Australian landscape is absent.[13]

Absent also from *Harry Heathcote* is the larger reality that *both* Medlicot and Heathcote were claiming "a bit of another man's land" – the land in which the indigenous people of Australia had dwelled for many millennia. Trollope gives more space to Aboriginals in his travelogue, but negatively so. The fourth chapter of *Australia and New Zealand* is full of unadulterated racism, with an Aboriginal man described as "a sapient monkey imitating the gait and manners of a do-nothing white dandy" (*ANZ* 60). This saddles him with the liabilities of both backwardness *and* decadence. Trollope denounces Aborigines for not working for their bread in the service of the white man, without asking why they would want to do this work. Trollope even finds the corroboree, the ritual dance that fascinated many European observers, tedious.

Jill Durey argues that when Trollope gets to Western Australia he becomes more tolerant of and empathetic towards Aboriginals, lambasting a white-run judicial system inherently unfair to indigenous peoples.[14] Even here, though, Trollope sees this as partially because Aboriginals are insufficiently mentally fit to comprehend the charges against them. Durey's advocacy of Trollope's fundamental anti-racism, though, receives support in the 1875 letters. There, he is apologetic about the way the opening of the colonies to "British enterprise and British life" has been accompanied by "the terrible injustice" of the dispossession, and, Trollope envisioned, the extirpation of the indigenous peoples, although Trollope's assumptions throughout are that whites are a higher race.[15] Even more pointedly,

Trollope criticizes the already accomplished annexation of Fiji and warns against annexing New Guinea. Trollope's motives for opposing "an extended dominion over black subjects" (*ANZ* 200) were not ideal, He felt the annexation of New Guinea would "hamper ourselves" by bringing Asian migrants too close to Australian shores (*ANZ* 127). These comments illustrate Trollope's participation in hegemonic discourses of racism, but also demonstrate that he made anti-imperialist if not anti-racist gestures. Trollope indeed makes sagacious observations about the South Pacific. Though he did not actually visit Fiji, he even gives a more phonetically correct spelling for the Fijian king, "Thakombau" than the "Cakobau" that became accepted (*ANZ* 187).

Whatever his perspective, Trollope's non-fiction *can* accommodate indigenous peoples. But they are fundamentally absent from his fiction, although H. E. Blythe's contention that the euthanasia in *The Fixed Period* draws upon Trollope's descriptions of Maori cannibalism is suggestive.[16] As a genre the English novel – popular, robust, capacious – is yet fragile enough for the question of whether it can be stretched to include other geographies and traditions to be an open one. Britain had no trouble establishing a global empire in the nineteenth century. There were debates about the wisdom of such a course, debates in which Trollope stands out as a partial skeptic. Yet that it was feasible was undisputed. The novel was not so easily globalized.

Trollope prefers the Maori in New Zealand to the Australian Aborigines. He sees them as (correctly) of Polynesian and (incorrectly) of Malay background, but does not go so far as others to give them an ancestry cognate with Europeans. *The Aryan Maori*, written a decade after Trollope's visit to New Zealand by a man with the Trollopian name of (Edward) Tregear, makes similar conjectures.[17] The Maori were successful barbarian invaders perceived as coming from somewhere else. The greater antiquity of the Australian Aborigines in the land counted against them. They had not triumphed through an alleged "historical process," and, conversely, they had an indisputable claim to the land, whereas it could be argued the Maori were but the first in a wave of invaders. Trollope writes about the Maori Wars with such empathy one would think he was a longtime resident of New Zealand or at least halfway a native informant. Strikingly (given the title of Trollope's 1855 book) he refers to Maoris as New Zealanders, in a way he certainly did not refer to Aborigines as Australians. Perhaps the future visitor to London was a Maori?

Just as Trollope did not totally dismiss the claims of indigenous people, he could readily rebuke what he saw as the wrong sort of white settler. "Catherine Carmichael: Or Three Years Running" is another "disjunctive

Christmas" story, this time taking place over successive summer Christmases. It features a rare indigenous fictional character, a Maori servant who is one of Catherine's few succors in her loveless marriage to her distant cousin Peter Carmichael: "a hard, dry, middle-aged man," a marriage forced on her by the loss of her father and consequent impoverishment.[18] The allegorical implications of Catherine being oppressed by a brute wielder of power, are multiplied even more by the benign younger rival of the husband's also being surnamed "Carmichael." Not only are imperial relations a question kept within the family, but it must be made sure that the mild-mannered, administratively assured relative prevails over the rough-hewn, domineering one, "meaner than a crawling worm."[19] In fact, the title of the story, which at first seems obvious – simply the name of the main character – becomes an aspect of suspense: by virtue of which of the two men will Catherine bear the name "Carmichael" at the end? Trollope's clear preference for the younger Carmichael is grounded in compassion and a championship of women's right to make affective choices. He also makes John's courtship of Catherine so moving in its restraint and even passivity that his humility precludes any sense of incipient swagger. But it also has the effect of castigating the older Carmichael on class grounds. He is too much part of what F. E. Maning called "Old New Zealand" for Trollope: the coarse man who had helped build the colony but who was now to make way for smoother, more presentable men, who could lead New Zealand into competent self-rule.[20] The one story where a non-white is positively portrayed in the Antipodean Trollope is the one that comes near to demonizing working-class whites.

There are two spouses in *John Caldigate* as well. But here they are women, and, at least potentially and in the eyes of the law, they are not successive. There is a long association with bigamy and the sensation novel with an Australian component: seen famously in Mary Elizabeth Braddon's *Lady Audley's Secret* (1862) but also in Captain Sir Frederick Lascelles Wraxall's *Only A Woman* (1860).[21] One factor connecting Australia and bigamy is sheer distance: "when the cat's away, the mice will play," and what Geoffrey Blainey termed "the tyranny of distance" offers characters ample possibilities for marital hanky-panky.[22] Bigamy images the ways in which Australia is both something uncanny and yet also a copy whose mores are reassuring in their familiarity. Australia's status as a "second England" parallels the sense of duplication inherent in bigamy, its combination of the difference of a new person with the sameness of a reproduced legal status, which Monica Young-Zook, in the context of Wilkie Collins's *Armadale* (1866), calls "colonial metonymy through presence."[23] That the statement of Caldigate's which is read as marriage is his telling Euphemia "I would marry you" – a declaration of sentiment, but also a statement of intent that does not totally perform its meaning – sounds the themes of futurity and undetermined legal status that are always in Trollope's mind with respect to the Australian colonies.

That Trollope flirted with calling the novel *Mrs. John Caldigate* presents the same specter as "Catherine Carmichael"; the suspense lies in just what relation the name denotes. Euphemia Smith, the "Australian" Mrs. Caldigate, is an amoral conniver, reminiscent of Lydia Gwilt in *Armadale* or Lady Audley in Braddon's novel. The "English" Mrs. Caldigate, Hester Bolton, is virtuous and kind, patiently enduring her humiliation when her husband is tried for bigamy and jailed. The sensation-novel villainess and the novel's abundance of plot bring it very near to the sensation genre, or at least to what Jennifer Phegley has called "domesticated sensationalism" – indicated perhaps by the very prosaic nature of Mrs. Smith's surname as opposed to "Lydia Gwilt."[24]

Euphemia Smith is entrepreneurial, using femininity to muck up the workings of legality and transparency and to point to the operative limitations of these concepts in their Victorian enunciation. She not only attempts to foil a conventional domestic resolution but renders *John Caldigate* formally unsalvageable as a domestic novel even after the marriage-plot outcome is ostensibly sealed. And both Euphemia's allure and her taint are linked to Australia. Yet Australia is not simply a land of peril and degradation for John Caldigate. He is unhappy in his origins, in the Cambridgeshire town of Folking, which name signifies an almost oppressively organic hominess, and also alludes to the two nearby shires, Norfolk and Suffolk, which, according to Victoria Glendinning, "did not appeal to" Trollope.[25] In Australia, Caldigate makes his fortune, proves his character, and, although waylaid by the wiles of Mrs. Smith, nonetheless develops an enriched sense of self that makes him, in Hester's eyes, represent broader possibilities than the repressive Evangelical religion of her mother. Daniel Caldigate, John's father, is in fact described in terms reminiscent of Peter Carmichael as "a stout, self-constraining man," and John Caldigate at the end of his narrative is as personally enlarged as is Catherine Carmichael upon her husband's demise (*JC* ch. 1). Caldigate has diversified himself in Australia. Though, in a post-Suez world of easy access, his mistakes come home to haunt him in England, his personal growth Down Under also redounds to his benefit.[26]

Trollope's willingness to invent faux-Australian place names like Nobble or Ahalala, both coming near the nonsensical-sounding, testifies to the high spirits with which he roared through the fictional goldfields. Trollope's greatest delight though is in his portrayal of Bagwax, the postal inspector who finds that the postage stamp alleged by Euphemia to prove the circumstances of her case against Caldigate is a forgery. Bagwax is acknowledged by Trollope to be self-referential – Trollope worked for the Post Office, and Bagwax operates as Trollope as "author" sometimes does to externally resolve the narrative action. Bagwax stages the overturn in the plot that in fact is ultimately staged by the author. He is the authorial surrogate in viewpoint more than action. Trollope is engaging in self-deflation in his depiction of Bagwax. But Trollope is also making an important point about the nature of the governmental relationship between Britain and Australia. The colonies and the metropolis communicate not through imperial government, but through routine bureaucracy. Bagwax's role as what Robert Tracy calls "one of society's official agents" is civil, but not political.[27] Like Trollope in both his vocations, he deals with information and its dissemination. The ratiocinative, workmanlike elucidation of truth by Bagwax suggests that, in the Antipodes, right is ready, eventually to be exercised by the descendants of Harry Heathcote and of Daniel and Anna Thwaite.

Like Trollope, Bagwax, at the end of the novel, goes to Sydney, does well, and comes back. This mirrors the back-and-forth, the informational exchange, of the Post Office. Trollope's depiction of postal communication is not without play. Bagwax indicates the stamp "could not have served to pay the postage on a letter from Sydney to Nobble in May 1873," and one of the extra-narrative reasons for this is that there was no such town as Nobble in the "real" world (*JC* ch. 54). But Trollope emphasizes the post office as unobtrusively efficient and honest, not, as the sensation novel might, as an exemplar of informational insufficiency. Any irony is supplied not by any self-referentiality, but by the self-deflation of Bagwax, representing the author knowing his own pomposity and whimsically tolerating that aspect as long as it is in the service of good. Bagwax is a detective. He uses ratiocinative processes. The need for the postmark to nail down the truth of an event also brings *John Caldigate* closest to the sensation genre in that genre's curious foregrounding of fact: Robert Audley's hunt through old newspaper clippings in Braddon's novel, or, in Wilkie Collins's *No Name* (1862), Captain Wragge's outfoxing of Mrs. Lecount by having letters posted falsely saying her brother was ill. In Collins, the factual validity of the letter does not at all confirm the ontological truth of the event – a correlation not questioned in Trollope.[28]

The forged stamp bears the Queen's image, and the Queen is noticeably present as referent in *John Caldigate*, in two capacities where she has enormous symbolic but little actual power – the law courts and the colonies. It is mentioned that the Queen acts exclusively on the advice of her own ministers, but also at one point it is asserted that the Queen would do what is right if she knew the truth. That the Queen's sovereignty is at once normative and, in its practical powerlessness, a symbolic tautology, says much about the nature of colonial regulation in *John Caldigate* – the colonies are an extension of sovereignty that also foreground the fictive side of that sovereignty. That the stamps used in Australia are made in Britain and sent out – that their effectuality is belated, deferred – shows the curious braid of seamless Englishness and political separation Trollope envisages for Australia and New Zealand. Indeed, Trollope makes some local references that he must have known would mean more to eventual readers in the Antipodean countries than those in Britain. Naming a ship the *Julius Vogel* after the railroad-building New Zealand Prime Minister of the 1870s is a joke then and now far more likely to be understood by a New Zealand reader. Trollope ensures that in the midst of New Zealand literature there will be something forever Trollope. But he also stipulates eventual self-rule.

The climactic event in Trollope's last Antipodean fiction, *The Fixed Period* – published in book form in the year of his death, 1882 – is the temporary suspension of self-rule and the resumption of British control in fictional Britannula, a Pacific island nation to the north and east of New Zealand. In this science-fiction novel set a century in the future, a British mission, under the leadership of Sir Ferdinando Brown, is undertaken as what would later be called humanitarian intervention – to prevent the execution of the long-established plan of Britannula's elected President, John Neverbend, to institute a "Fixed Period" by which people would be euthanized before their sixty-eighth birthday. Trollope does not present this monstrous proposal with Swiftian irony; he makes Neverbend's plan seem reasonable, something that will eliminate a class of people too old to be socially useful, and thus save the state revenue and maximize the efficiency of resources. As a new country, Britannula has no population problem, and so the killing of old people by the state is not done for demographic reasons, but for economic-utilitarian ones, and, it is implied, as a kind of statement of independence,

There is also something of "the global South" in the book's mode of narration. The story is told in the first person by Neverbend, thus manifesting an orality which is not out of place in a South Pacific setting. Neverbend as narrator, not just as subject, also brings the novel close to the Latin American genre of *novela del dictador*, pioneered by Domingo Sarmiento's *Facundo*.[29] These subaltern aspects offset the many ways in which Britannula is a future Britain, and that its story gives a glimpse of what Britain itself will be in the "1980" of its setting. Trollope is aware he is writing about a date that will somehow be a "real" year, and thus he gives specific but not general details about the world of *The Fixed Period* – stating that the Duke of Hatfield, a member of the Cecil/Salisbury family, will be Colonial Secretary, but, wisely, refraining from giving the gender of the current British sovereign, although he indicates there is still a Royal Family. Notably, the House of Lords is "now" elected, and Englishness survives England: the news of the Britannulan experiment is brought to Britain by means of a touring cricket team.

Trollope is, on the one hand, relinquishing authorial control by postulating a future he knows will not be predictive, in a novel set in a land that not only had not but never will have existed. On the other hand he is prolonging authorial control well beyond his lifetime by hypothesizing a future that readers reading after the occurrence of the "actual" date will have to incorporate as part of their archive of what the referent of the "actual" date signifies. (Did Trollope, for instance, suspect that when *The New Zealander* finally saw the light of publication, it would be just a few years short of 1980?)[30]

The Fixed Period, the idea of euthanizing the old, is not just a megalomaniac idea fixed in the mind of Neverbend. It is the general policy of Britannula, although, since those who settled Britannula at first were young, the issue did not come up practically for many years.

That the first victim of the Fixed Period is Neverbend's closest friend, Gabriel Crasweller, provides the domestic plot of the novel, complicated by Neverbend's son, Jack, falling in love with Crasweller's daughter, Eva. Jack does not share his father's Fixed Period convictions and, like John Carmichael in Trollope's New Zealand story, represents a younger, post-pioneer generation. The tenderness of the young couple's relationship is more than notional in the novel, and leavens the antagonism between their two parents. It also demonstrates a realm in which love, not tendentious law, ultimately prevails. But its functioning in the book is much like the customary marriage plot, resolving disputes and allowing generational succession. Younger people must marry and nudge older people out of the spotlight. Even if Britannula had room for many generations, the novel as a genre does not. Does the novel, as a genre, kill off old people so that the young can marry? Does the marriage plot ordain a Fixed Period for the old beyond what nature already demands? Was Trollope's own genre calling extra attention to the brevity of his years? Much as in *John Caldigate*, there is self-reflexivity generated by Trollope's extension of the novel into the new, post-Suez global space. Once again in Trollope's Antipodean oeuvre, the future of the South Pacific colonies, the flexibility of the novel as a genre, and Trollope's own aging are intimately braided.

Another link between fictive Britannula and "real" Australia is in the capital of Britannula being "Gladstonopolis" – named, we are told, after the great-grandson of the Victorian Gladstone, but also recalling Trollope's interest in Gladstone, Queensland, being a possible state capital, one named after "our own statesman" (*ANZ* 42). Once again, the question is not will the colonies become independent – this is inevitable – but will their cities ever overshadow London? As much as Trollope admired Gladstone, the parodic tinge of "Gladstonopolis" suggests he was still wondering if Englishness could survive England – and hoping it would. Yet Britannula does not love Britain. When Neverbend is taken off to exile to Britain at the end, it is clearly a form of death (for instance, his wife will not accompany him) and he is being politically interfered with as he aspired to interfere with others.

There is certainly something resistant to any idea of the "recolonial" about Britannula at first being proud of its social experiment and then wishing Washington and London would pay no attention to it. Furthermore, for all the appalling nature of his central policy tenet, Neverbend is not a monster, just a rational man with a terrible blind spot. He is also a democrat who has represented popular will and has been democratically elected. Britain's resumption of authority is only temporary. The mother country can serve as a normative reserve power, but after an interval Britannula will once again be on its own. That the ship that brings Sir Ferdinando and dispatches Neverbend (and no doubt passes through Suez both times) is called the *John Bright* – a man universally known in Trollope's day as a prominent free-trader – means that Trollope is still upholding the general principle of self-rule, even if it has gone awry in Britannula. *The Fixed Period* is perhaps Trollope's most unusual book, full of political and social speculation but also laden with unusual affect for the often wooden genre of the South Sea parable. We are far away from the displaced but mechanically ratified formulas of *Harry Heathcote*. But in both novels and beyond, Trollope's message with respect to the Antipodes is consistent: they are a faraway physical place that can also provide vistas of the future. In deploying himself to a land not his own, Trollope widened the reach of his oeuvre in both space and time.

NOTES

1 N. John Hall, *Trollope: A Biography* (Oxford: Oxford University Press, 1993), pp. 363 and 402.
2 Cara Murray, *Victorian Narrative Technologies in the Middle East* (London: Routledge, 2008).
3 For more on the concept of "the Antipodes," see Paul Giles, "Antipodean American Literature: Franklin, Twain, and the Sphere of Subalternity," *American Literary History* 20 (Spring/Summer 2008), 22–50.
4 James Belich, *Paradise Reforged: A History of the New Zealanders Since 1880* (Honolulu: University of Hawai'i Press, 2001).

5 Trollope wrote the latter chapters of *Is He Popenjoy?* on his second voyage to Australia in 1875 but that novel contains no Australian action.

6 Anthony Trollope, *The New Zealander*, ed. and intro. N. John Hall (Oxford: Clarendon Press, 1972), p. 214.

7 Andrew McCann, *Marcus Clarke's Bohemia: Literature and Modernity in Colonial Melbourne* (Melbourne: Melbourne University Press, 2004).

8 J. H. Davidson, "Anthony Trollope and the Colonies," *Victorian Studies* 12 (March 1969), 305–37.

9 See Laurie Langbauer, *Novels In Everday Life: The Series in English Fiction, 1850–1930* (Ithaca: Cornell University Press, 1999), p. 87, and Hall, *The New Zealander*, p. xvii.

10 Anthony Trollope, *Australia and New Zealand* (Chapman & Hall, 1873), p. 344. All subsequent references in this chapter are from this edition and are cited as *ANZ* with page number.

11 Matthew Arnold, "The Function of Criticism at the Present Time," *The Complete Prose Works of Matthew Arnold, Volume III*, ed. R. H. Super (Ann Arbor: University of Michigan Press, 1964), p. 265.

12 As Lauren Goodlad puts it, Trollope is "defining settler colonialism against territorial expansion as a form of non-imperialism." Lauren Goodlad, "Can the Antipodean Speak? A Response to Paul Giles," *American Literary History* 20 (Spring/Summer 2008), 51–56.

13 Marcus Clarke, "Australian Scenery," in *Australian Tales* (Melbourne: A. and W. Bruce, 1896), p. 1.

14 Jill Felicity Durey, "Modern Issues: Anthony Trollope and Australia," *Antipodes: A North American Journal of Australian Literature* 21(December 2007), 174.

15 Anthony Trollope, *The Tireless Traveller: Twenty Letters to the Liverpool Mercury* (1875; rpt. Berkeley: University of California Press, 1941), p. 124.

16 H. E. Blythe, "*The Fixed Period* (1882): Euthanasia, Cannibalism, and Colonial Extraction in Anthony Trollope's Antipodes," *Nineteenth Century Contexts* 25 (2003), 61–81.

17 Edward Tregear, *The Aryan Maori* (1885; rpt. Christchurch: Kiwi, 1995).

18 "Catherine Carmichael: Or Three Years Running," *Anthony Trollope: Later Short Stories*, ed. John Sutherland (Oxford: Oxford University Press, 1995), p. 496.

19 Ibid., p. 496.

20 F. E. Maning, *Old New Zealand* (London: Richard Bentley, 1884).

21 Jeanne Fahnestock, "Bigamy: The Rise and Fall of a Convention," *Nineteenth-Century Fiction* 36 (June 1981), 47–71.

22 Geoffrey Blainey, *The Tyranny of Distance: How Distance Shaped Australia's History* (Melbourne: Macmillan, 1975).

23 Monica Young-Zook, "Wilkie Collins Gwilt-y Conscience: Gender and Colonialism in *Armadale*," *Victorian Sensations: Essays on a Scandalous Genre*, ed. Richard Fantina and Kimberly Harrison (Columbus: The Ohio State University Press, 2006), p. 239.

24 Jennifer Phegley, "Domesticating the Sensation Novelist: Ellen Price Wood as Author and Editor of the *Argosy* Magazine," *Victorian Periodicals Review* 38 (2005), 180–81.

25 Victoria Glendinning, *Anthony Trollope* (New York: Random House, 1993), p. 360.

26 Interestingly, this expansion both enables and excludes Dick Shand, the man who provides his friend Caldigate with crucial exonerating evidence. Shand returns to Australia, but because his wearing the wrong sort of trousers symptomatically excludes him from English society, he ends up going to Queensland where he is to boss "Canakers" (Kanakas=Melanesian migrant workers) with the hint that he is no more assimilable into the dominant society than they are, and that only his color makes him superior.

27 Robert Tracy, *Trollope's Later Novels* (Berkeley: University of California Press, 1978), p. 236.

28 Trollope does not vouch for the factual truth outside fiction, and, like the Nobble referent, the truth of the postage stamp's date of issuance is something that *is true within the fiction*. For the realities of the particular mark Trollope highlights in the novel, see R. H. Super, *The Chronicler of Barsetshire* (Ann Arbor: University of Michigan Press, 1990), p. 363.

29 Domingo Faustino Sarmiento, *Facundo: Civilization and Barbarism* (Berkeley: University of California Press, 2004).

30 For more on "1980" as referent, see Nicholas Birns, "The Empire Turned Upside Down: The Colonial Fictions of Anthony Trollope," *Ariel* 27 (Spring 1996), 7–23.

15

GORDON BIGELOW

Trollope and Ireland

Ireland was the beginning of Trollope, and in many ways it was the end of him. When he accepted a station in Ireland with the postal service in 1841, he was just twenty-six and still certainly what he would later call a "hobbledehoy": a young man of abstract dreams and unsteady purpose. In Ireland he was recognized for his work and given increasingly wide responsibility. In Ireland he discovered what were to be the abiding fixations of his personal life: writing and hunting. While he had vague thoughts of novel-writing as a young man, Ireland provided both the means and the motive of his first two books, written and set in Ireland and in many ways following in the traditions of Irish fiction. And while he may have thought before of hunting – certainly would have been aware of hunters at Harrow school, as they talked of the sport's elaborate schedules and expensive kits – his Irish assignment provided the extra income to keep a horse, while the isolation of the Anglo-Irish gentry, resulting from Ireland's bizarre colonial demographics, seems to have made the social circumstances favorable to him. He made friends hunting, was welcomed in great houses, and thus reversed the agonizing arrangement of his school days, as a local "village boy" who was always made to feel his exclusion.

After the commercial failure of his first two novels, Trollope moved away from Irish matters in his fiction, returning to the subject only much later. At the end of his life, however, he plunged into the rising controversy over Irish land reform and the popular protests that came to be called the Land War. He traveled to Ireland twice to research what would be his last book, *The Landleaguers*. It would be his most overtly political novel, one that rejects the bemused irony of the Palliser novels and instead speaks of the Irish situation with a blinding sincerity. In November of 1882, after finishing more than three-quarters of the book, he suffered a stroke and died. It may be true that Trollope is "perhaps the only nineteenth-century Englishman ... to have benefited from an involvement" with Ireland.[1]

It seems equally true to say that he caught an interest in Ireland at a young age and that he eventually succumbed to it.

The Ireland that Trollope found in 1841 was the hothouse product of a colonial experiment begun during the religious wars of the seventeenth century, when virtually the entire island was regarded as confiscated land by conquering English troops. The land was awarded in huge swaths to loyal generals and political allies, setting up a system wherein a small number of foreign Protestant landlords received rent for land occupied largely by Catholics. By 1703 Catholic land ownership dropped below 15 percent. Most of the native aristocracy and gentry, those not killed in battle or deported as indentured servants to the sugar plantations of the Caribbean, fled to the Continent, leaving a country starkly divided by sect, language, class, and ethnic extraction.

For more than a century, this colonial experiment led to high agricultural output, producing bacon, butter, and beef that fed English sailors bound for the Americas as well as the mushrooming population of English towns during the industrial revolution. The clearest indication of this productivity is the growth of Ireland's own population in the period, which shot from roughly 2.5 million in 1767 to 8.2 million by the time Trollope arrived.[2] It owed much of this rapid growth to the potato, a remarkably nutritious crop which, if supplemented with small amounts of meat or dairy protein, could sustain life on its own. A laboriously cultivated potato garden could feed a large family, freeing up the rest of a tenant farmer's land for cash crops or grazing.

The pressure for agricultural profits, however, produced an economic and environmental monoculture, as potatoes became the sole food source for much of rural Ireland, and a once-diverse variety of potato species around the country was gradually lost in favor of a single very large and productive one, called the Lumper. Competition for land became intense, forcing tenant farmers to lease and sub-lease smaller and smaller plots of ground. When a fungal spore adapted to the Lumper potato infected the island, this odd and highly artificial socio-economic system crumbled. Rents went unpaid, and many estates became so mired in debt that a special act of Parliament in 1849 set up a commission to untangle them. Between 1845 and 1852 roughly a million people died of starvation; another million emigrated. For the next fifty years, the population of the island declined, decreasing by 1901 to 4.5 million.

The changes wrought by the Famine ensured the destruction of the Ireland Trollope first came to understand. While the Famine raged, Trollope seemed to take relatively little note of it; when he did come to write of it some years later, he tended to minimize its scale and exaggerate its potential long-term benefits. Thus in Ireland he seemed curiously blind to the most significant social and economic trends of his century, and this blind spot would come to define his later work.

In 1841, when Trollope was transferred to Ireland, he was sent to Banagher, in Kings County (now Offaly), a midlands town of about 1800 persons. When he arrived in mid-September, he would have been plunged into an utterly foreign cultural landscape. The town's annual fair was underway, a gathering which thronged its main street, leading uphill away from the river Shannon, with farmers and artisans from the surrounding districts. The crowd would have been largely Irish-speaking (roughly half the country had Irish as a first language); its games (like hurling) and its rituals of bargaining would all have been foreign to Trollope.[3]

At the head of the main street, on top of the hill, stood the town's beacon of Anglophone Protestantism, shining amongst this Catholic crowd. This was St. Paul's church, a dreary neo-gothic structure built in 1829. Further down the hill was a new Catholic church, St. Rynagh's, built on land donated by a local Protestant family. The gift indicates some sense of paternal obligation among the landowning families toward the needs of their tenants; such feeling, though often in evidence, was by no means universal or even widespread. Unlike in England, where a local squire was typically responsible for maintaining and improving the farms he let, in Ireland these expenses were left to tenants. When renters did invest in improvements, by draining a wet field or expanding a cottage, for example, their rents were often raised. Relations were thus in many regions strained and adversarial. When Toqueville toured Ireland in 1835, he was told, "We have all the evils of an aristocracy without any of its advantages. There is no moral tie between the poor and the rich."[4]

These social antagonisms form the subject of Trollope's first book, *The Macdermots of Ballycloran*, begun in 1843 and published in 1847. Trollope reports that the story was first suggested to him by the ruins of a large country house outside the village of Drumsna in county Roscommon (*MB* ch. 1; *A* ch. 4). Ruined structures are a common sight in the Irish countryside, from the dramatic ring-forts and dolmens of the second millennium BCE to the round towers of medieval monastic settlements. Antiquarian interest in all these structures was mounting just at the time that Trollope came to Ireland, with much literary and scholarly energy directed toward understanding the ancient societies that built them. Among the most famous of these sites is Clonmacnoise, less than ten miles from Banagher, built around a church established in 545 CE; still visible there are carved stone crosses from the ninth century, several Romanesque chapels, and a round tower. Thackeray sneered a bit at sites like this, "places where you may now see a round tower and a little old chapel, twelve feet square, where famous universities are once said to have stood."[5] But Trollope never displayed the least interest in such scenes; his attention was caught by a thoroughly modern ruin, a recent building of minor prowess, now crumbling. Trollope was attracted by the economic and social tensions that characterized modern Irish society, and out of the image of the ruined manor house, he told the story of its downfall.

The Macdermots of the title are one of the few remaining Catholic landholding families. Their small and ill-favored estate is encumbered by a mortgage on an outsized house, built by an ancestor determined to live like a lord, and the family continues to squander what capital remains in the land in effort to keep the soil from under their own fingernails. But the novel's central plot involves another crucial feature of Irish rural life, the secret societies formed among agrarian peasant communities. These groups seem to have emerged in the eighteenth century, becoming notorious for threats or acts of revenge to enforce the violation of community rule. Known in varying times and places as Whiteboys, Rockites, Ribbonmen, etc., the groups would act at night, often disguised or dressed in outlandish costume. In *Macdermots*, Trollope construes the Ribbonmen as a simple-minded group of bootleggers, distilling illegal whiskey and enforcing the secrecy of their operation by threat of midnight violence. A squadron of revenue police is stationed nearby to stop the moonshining, and the head of this force, Myles Ussher, seduces the daughter of the Macdermot house, Euphemia, called Feemy. Feemy's brother Thady, struggling to keep the family estate solvent and to prevent his sister from ruin, is drawn into contact with the Ribbonmen, who seem to offer him the promise of revenge both against Captain Ussher and against his estate's rapacious creditors.

The novel's tragic conclusion results when Thady stumbles on Myles and Feemy in the act of eloping. Thady, concluding that Feemy is being abducted, strikes Ussher and accidentally kills him. Since Thady has now been associated with the Ribbonmen, all assume that the killing was politically motivated, an act of open rebellion against one of His Majesty's officers. The plot thus condemns both the violence of the Ribbonmen – they hack off the foot of the lawyer Hyacinth Keegan in a notorious scene – and the stupidly inflamed imagination of Anglo-Irish landlords, who misconstrue Thady's act. This double representation of secret violence is especially suggestive given the importance of secret societies in the Irish countryside, but also given the nature of Trollope's own investment in other modes of secret agency. Trollope's membership in the Irish Freemasons, a fact only recently established, might account for his sympathetic understanding of the absurd theories of occult power that can arise in relation to groups that administer secret oaths. Trollope's name appears on the ledger of the Banagher Masons just after he arrives in the town. In this rural outpost, the Masons would have united Anglophone professionals and liberal gentry, providing a convenient means of entry for Trollope into the town's social life.[6]

But there is as well a much more powerful and pervasive code of secret organization cutting through his fiction, and that is the code of gentlemanliness. In the paranoid Protestant view, Irish secret societies arose spontaneously out of the landscape, revealing a high degree of organization and unity amongst the Catholic underclass. Gender systems function through a similar presumption of natural spontaneity, appearing to arise without discussion or premeditation but nonetheless to unite a society in a coherent pattern. Trollope makes no secret of his allegiance to the code of gentlemanly conduct. But when he does address it, it is often by affirming that the quality of gentlemanliness is impossible to define. It is a thing that the best men know instinctively; the worst are defined by their inability to master its ineffable canons. Violation of this typically unspoken code merits violent response, a response which is seen to be both fully justifiable and at the same time fully beyond the limits of the law. When Frank Gresham and his college friend act together to beat Mr. Moffat in *Doctor Thorne*, they invoke this conspiracy of violence. While technically on the wrong side of the law, they escape punishment because everyone seems to feel they are right, including poor Moffat, who fears to press charges lest in doing so he further spread the word of his perfidy toward Gresham's sister.

What is lacking in Irish society, as it is drawn in *Macdermots*, is this code of violence, a code that unites the society in condemning wrong. Had Thady been able to invoke this code, to gather his friends, beat Myles Ussher in the street, and receive the winking approbation of the community, moral order would be restored and the novel's tragic outcome averted. The novel suggests that Ireland's problem is not secret violence, but the *wrong kind* of secret violence. It is a violence, whether real or simply dreaded, perpetrated across the lines of class and religion, and it reinforces and widens these divisions. This fractured social whole produces distorted and inauthentic institutions, incapable of exercising a unifying moral authority.

Both in *Macdermots* and in his second novel, *The Kellys and the O'Kellys* (begun 1847 and published 1848), Trollope is concerned with the foreignness of Irish society, analyzing what made the island so distinctive and diagnosing its political and social ills. In each novel Trollope is both a shrewd and a sympathetic observer. "The difference of the English and Irish character," he writes in *The Kellys*, "is nowhere more plainly discerned than in their respective kitchens." In England the kitchen is "certainly the most orderly" room in the house. In Ireland it is "a temple dedicated to the goddess of disorder; and, too often joined with her, is the potent deity of dirt" (*KOK* ch. 4). This gentle mock-heroic mode, which Trollope is able more effectively to restrain in later work, often governs his depiction of the lower ranks of Irish society. It leads here to a portrait of the widow Kelly's dim kitchen in the Dunmore Inn:

> All you see is a grimy black ceiling, an uneven clay floor... a heap of potatoes in the corner, a pile of turf against the wall, two pigs and a dog under the single dresser... and a crowd of ragged garments, squatting, standing, kneeling, and crouching round the fire, from which issues a babble of strange tongues, not one word of which is at first intelligible to ears unaccustomed to such eloquence.
> (*KOK* ch. 4)

The passage rings all the bells typically sounded by the most disdainful English accounts of Irish life: the pigs in the house, the smoky darkness of the turf fire, the shock of hearing conversation in Irish. And yet Trollope goes on with measured praise for Mrs. Kelly's board: "a man need think it no misfortune to have to get his dinner, his punch, and his bed, at the widow's" (*KOK* ch. 4). When some chapters later he describes the comfortless manor of the Earl of Cashel, with its "excellent kitchen-range and patent boilers of every shape" (*KOK* ch. 11), his preference is clear.

Where *Macdermots* operates in tragic mode, *Kellys* is a comedy, with a bifurcated plot structure focusing on the two families named in the title, that of the widow Kelly, and that of her distant aristocratic relatives, led by the young Frank O'Kelly, Lord Ballandine. Both plots involve complicated plans of marriage, which are both nearly ruined by the mercenary designs of some related party. The crisis in each plot is resolved by the same extraordinary character, who by sheer force of will browbeats the villainous Barry Lynch into self-imposed exile and softens the heart of the self-regarding Earl of Cashel. This character is a Church of Ireland minister named Armstrong, rector of Ballandine Parish and thus, at least in name, Frank O'Kelly's spiritual guide.

The Church of Ireland is the name given to the Anglican church in that country, and it is another of Ireland's odd hothouse phenomena. Established in the sixteenth century, it functioned both as state church, levying tithes for its support, and as the spiritual center of Anglo-Irish life. In many communities this arrangement led to the absurd circumstance Trollope depicts in *Kellys*, where Mr. Armstrong, charged with the cure of souls in all of Ballandine Parish, typically finds himself preaching to a congregation of just one:

> The Reverend Joseph Armstrong was rector of Ballandine, and Mrs. O'Kelly
> was his parishioner, and the only Protestant one he had; and, as Mr. Armstrong did
> not like to see his church quite deserted, and as Mrs. O'Kelly, was, as she flattered
> herself, a very fervent Protestant, they were all in all to each other. (*KOK* ch. 21)

Protests against this circumstance, which required Catholics to maintain
minuscule Protestant flocks, mounted in the 1830s and came to be known
as the Tithe Wars. But it was not until 1869 that the church was disestab-
lished. Its parishioners at that point amounted to some 13 percent of the
population.

In settling both of the novel's major conflicts, Mr. Armstrong seems to
offer the gentlemanly authority so badly lacking in *Macdermots*. But this
authority is utterly unconnected with his spiritual leadership in the Church
of Ireland. Holder of the poor living at Ballandine, he is himself very much
guided by worldly concerns. "He never refused an invitation to dinner," the
narrator avers, and "was, in fact, a loose, slovenly man, somewhat too fond
of his tumbler of punch" (*KOK* ch. 21). Although we are told he is "very
staunch as to doctrine," he betrays no prejudice either in favor of his
embattled co-religionists or against his Catholic neighbors. When the mur-
derous Barry Lynch cries "Ain't I a Protestant, Mr. Armstrong, and you a
Protestant clergyman?" (*KOK* ch. 35), the rector ignores him. When
appealed to by the fulminating ultra-Protestant Mr. O'Joscelyn, a fellow
minister in the Church of Ireland, he goads the man terribly. O'Joscelyn
professes shock on hearing that Armstrong's congregation at Ballandine
boasts only one member. "If I wanted to fill my church," Reverend
Armstrong says, "the Roman Catholics think so well of me, that they'd
flock in crowds there if I asked them; and the priest would show them the
way – for any special occasion I mean; if the bishop came to see me, or
anything of that kind" (*KOK* ch. 38). O'Joscelyn is struck dumb.

In the Reverend Armstrong we can see clearly the sparks of comic energy
that would later ignite the raging popularity of the Barsetshire novels, with
their close observation of the Anglican Church's hierarchy and the often
shockingly mundane concerns of its officials. The struggles carried out on
the carpet of Bishop Proudie's study, between the Proudies' Evangelical
enthusiasms and the traditionary allegiances of Archdeacon Grantly, are
prefigured here, but with a crucial and telling difference. Satirizing the
doctrinal wars of Barsetshire works because it is clear that the doctrinal
differences matter very little and are often a transparent excuse for patronage and nepotism. No one could really say the same in the Irish case, for
there the Catholic question was no mere ghost lingering behind the Oxford
movement. It was a matter of millions of Roman Catholic believers who
even in the 1840s seemed increasingly determined and able to take over the

country. In short, Trollope's comic talent, so skillfully exercised here, sends up a squabble that to many readers was really not in the least amusing. Only in quieter English pastures, patrolled by English pastors, would his satire achieve its crucial proportions.

These two novels are thoroughly steeped in the traditions and conventions of nineteenth-century Irish fiction. They draw from and refer openly to tales of reckless landlords and half-ruined estates made famous by Maria Edgeworth's *Castle Rackrent* (1800) and Sidney Owenson's *The Wild Irish Girl* (1806). The name of Trollope's first protagonist, Thady Macdermot, recalls *Castle Rackrent's* mercurial narrator, Thady Quirk. Trollope's concern with peasant violence echoes that found in the work of John and Michael Banim and of William Carleton. The Irish provenance of Trollope's first two novels has been recognized by many readers, though still a subject of debate.[7] Soon after *Macdermots* was published, Sir William Gregory reportedly called it "the best Irish story that had appeared for something like half a century."[8] Gregory, whose Coole Park estate was to become W. B. Yeats's cherished retreat, had befriended Trollope soon after he arrived in Ireland, and it may have been through the library at Coole Park that Trollope studied the literature of his new country.

His novels were noticed by reviewers but not bought by readers. An *Athenaeum* review in 1847 suggested that "Twenty years ago *The Macdermots* would have made a reputation for its author" (*Crit. Her.* 548). But this book, bred out of the conflicts of pre-Famine Irish society and styled along the lines of the Irish national tale, could find no audience by the late 1840s, nor could *Kellys.* Trollope floundered for a subject. The society and the genre of fiction in which he had schooled himself would, he was told, have to be abandoned. "Readers do not like novels on Irish subjects," his publisher wrote to him (*A* ch. 4), but he persisted for a while. He determined in 1850 to write a traveler's guide to Ireland. Why English readers would wish to consider an Irish holiday after five years of newspaper reports of starvation is difficult to say; the publisher Trollope had in mind did not even bother reading the sample chapters he sent. In 1851 he wrote a series of letters about the Famine relief efforts devised by the British treasury, and these were published in the London *Examiner.* Here Trollope argues that the relief schemes were not just well-intended, but that they were largely well run and successful, a judgment generally denied by historians. After these letters, he writes nothing on Ireland for nearly a decade.

When he returns to Irish themes for *Castle Richmond* (1860), he attempts to represent the Famine directly, but what results is something oddly skewed. The novel contains important descriptions of Famine conditions: the stone hut of a starving family, where a mother sits with her child's corpse

(*CR* ch. 33); roads ruined by a Board of Works project undertaken to inject cash into the rural economy (*CR* ch. 25). It also contains what amounts to a series of essays explaining the relief efforts and repeating the argument of the *Examiner* pieces. All these moments are strewn rather thinly across a domestic narrative set in the great houses of the Anglo-Irish, a narrative involving a love triangle and a legal plot wherein the line of legitimate inheritance is threatened by a vulgar usurper. The novel is an odd hybrid, and this was noticed. One reviewer, complaining about the novel's fusing of love and politics, suggested that "the milk and the water really should be in separate pails" (*Crit. Her.* 113–14). It is not necessary to accept this nostrum in order to see that, in this case, the proportions of milk and water are completely outsized. The occasional visits to charitable works or descriptions of hungry workers are spread so thinly amongst the scenes in the great houses as to suggest that the devastation was not widespread. *Castle Richmond* is not a bad novel, but it is, in this way, a deeply shocking book to read, as scenes of love-making, hunting, and legal consultation proceed along conventional lines, with calamity forming the backdrop.

In *An Eye for an Eye*, a one-volume novel composed in 1870, Trollope chooses the Cliffs of Moher as his setting, and the well-designed narrative again features a sharp-eyed clergyman, this time a Catholic priest. However, the book is focused not on Irish society but rather on one of the most important themes of Trollope's later work, that is, the problem of subjectivity. Its protagonist, Fred Neville, is again and again surprised by himself, caught by powerful feelings and inclinations that arise afresh in some part of his being which only yesterday he foreswore. He is entangled in competing promises, made with his whole heart, but at different times, and the result is tragic. This is a story Trollope tells in many forms, the story also of *Phineas Finn* (1867–69), the book which launched Trollope's best-known Irish character. Both in love and in politics, Phineas, the young MP from the west of Ireland, is beset by fleeting and contradictory impulses, surprised by aspects of himself of which he was, only yesterday, unaware. The central interpretive question of this novel is whether these contradictory impulses are offered as a symptom of youth, curable by the process of time, or rather as a broader, and more corrosive, theory of the human subject.

However, Irishness does figure in at least one intriguing element of this book, and that is its oblique concern with race. *Phineas Finn* is much occupied with the operation of party politics in the House of Commons, and its recurring metaphor for the service of the party is chattel slavery. When Phineas is first elected, his mentor Mr. Low deprecates politics as a career choice: "You are to make your way up the ladder by pretending to agree whenever agreement is demanded from you, and by voting whether you agree or do not ... It is at the best slavery and degradation" (*PF* ch. 5). Later, when the liberal Lord Brentford is forced to vote the elimination of his own pocket borough at Loughton, one of his Tory rivals chuckles, "There's nobody on earth I pity so much as a radical peer who is obliged to work like a nigger with a spade to shovel away the ground from under his own feet" (*PF* ch. 50). Labor without self-interest is figured here as blackness, and at the same time offered as a blanket description for the dominant activity of the House. Ireland seems to be the vector that emerges from this conflicting energy of racial representation. Many nineteenth-century thinkers, confounded by the apparent savagery of the Irish, accounted them "white negroes." Here it is English MPs, in their "slavish" devotion to party, who live out a black whiteness; the question of Phineas's Irishness seems to stand for this problem of racial difference.

Aside from these somewhat indirect dealings, Trollope lets Ireland alone as a subject until his very last novel, and then he returns precisely to the questions of Irish land and politics which occupied him at the start of his career. In post-Famine Ireland, population had continually declined. Tenant farmers and farm laborers were reluctant to divide small farms for subletting – the practice that had led to such rapid population growth – and thus began a century-long pattern of late marriage, low birth rates, and emigration. Like many middle-class commentators, Trollope had argued that this population loss would, while painful, lead to economic and social improvement. In *Castle Richmond* he described famine as the "remedy" sent by "a merciful God" to solve the problem of Irish poverty. "All this will soon be known and acknowledged," he writes, "... as it is acknowledged that new cities rise up in splendour from the ashes into which old cities have been consumed by fire" (*CR* ch. 7). However, through the 1860s and 70s a series of increasingly tense stand-offs between landlords and tenants made it clear that no new equilibrium or social harmony would be emerging. This was a heightening of the social crisis Trollope had tried to analyze, not its end.

Gladstone's first Irish Land Act of 1870, debate over which figures in *Phineas Finn*, had mandated compensation for improvements carried out by tenants, an important grievance. But by the late 1870s, agitation was mounting for further reform, with many voices, including a number of English liberals, advocating a complete transfer of ownership from landlords to tenants. Agitation in the west of the country coalesced in 1879 into a national organization, the Land League. It organized a host of protests, among the most effective of which involved the withholding of rent from and total ostracism of opposing landowners. The most famous of these isolation campaigns took place at the large Galway estate at Lough Mask, overseen by an agent called Charles Boycott; his name attached itself to this new form of political action. A second Land Act in 1881 granted new regulation over rents and further limited the privileges of landlords, but by now the Land League was advocating a nationwide rent strike, and its language became increasingly violent. Though disclaimed by the League, acts of violence and intimidation increased. The period would come to be known as the Land War.

Trollope was absorbed by these political conflicts, conflicts which represented a tremendous amplification of the tensions he had witnessed first in the 1840s. He despaired over both the state of the country and the political solutions devised by Gladstone's liberal administration. Though in somewhat poor health, he traveled to Ireland in the summer of 1882, interviewing a number of landowners, commissioners, and political figures in preparation for a new novel. *The Landleaguers* was the result.

The title is a remarkable and telling choice. The book barely touches the lives of any Land League members, centering instead on the family of a Galway landlord, living on an estate which resembles the famous Lough Mask House.[9] Rents are withheld and crops are sabotaged, and the family struggle to keep the household running after their tenants and domestic servants have turned their backs on them. Threats of further sabotage and violence mount; a young son is killed, and other murders occur in the neighborhood. In short, then, the problem at the center of this book is the sheer and terrifying power of the kind of rural conspiracies which Trollope had addressed in *Macdermots*. The rather hapless Ribbonmen of that novel have here become a tightly organized and ruthless collective. The book tars the Land Leaguers with horrific crimes, but its entire narrative energy seems to grow from Trollope's dismay at their devastating effectiveness.

Perhaps the most astonishing and revealing aspect of the novel is to be found in one of Trollope's most familiar narrative gambits: the description of the hunt. Since his first arrival in Ireland some half century before, hunting had been a central preoccupation of both Trollope's life and his art. "Nothing," he wrote in *An Autobiography*, "has ever been allowed to stand in the way of hunting, – neither the writing of books, nor the work of the Post Office." He rarely completed a novel without some reference to his favorite diversion, and when he did he counted himself "deprived of a legitimate joy" (*A* ch. 4). As Trollope seems to be aware, readers sometimes complained of these ubiquitous and often extended scenes in his novels. But in Ireland during the Land War, there were much more vigorous protests against the practice on the land itself, protests which sternly denied the legitimacy of whatever joys it might offer.

While mounted pursuit of game animals had been a hobby of the Gaelic aristocracy before 1600, by the nineteenth century the sport was fixedly associated with the Protestant Anglo-Irish. It is an expensive sport, requiring not just horses and gear for individual hunters but the maintenance of hunting dogs by each regional club. In addition, as is scrupulously documented in the Palliser books, hunting requires a significant investment from all the landowners in a region, who must preserve the thickets or woods in which foxes could nest – called coverts – and fill in drains or holes elsewhere in which a fox might hide.

But it requires more than money to hunt; it requires the assent of those who occupy the land. Once a fox is driven from its den, the dogs may track it for many miles, following over the fences, hedges, and streams that mark farm boundaries. These long and impromptu steeplechase rides, with the course set by the escaping fox, lent the sport its chief attraction. A day's hunting might lead horses over a dozen farms, with considerable damage to crops or livestock as a result. The right of hunters to inflict this damage, and to pay for it when so inclined, accrued to the landlord. In Ireland, as Declan Kiberd puts it, "the hunt had always expressed the sovereignty of an upper class."[10] In an astonishing sequence in *The Landleaguers*, spreading over three chapters, a hunt is stopped by a good-humored and polite crowd of two hundred, which surrounds the covert appointed for that day's sport. The master of hounds, Mr. Daly, leads his dogs and fellow sportsmen to another covert some ten miles away, and thence to several others in a punishing afternoon's ride. "The conspiracy," however, "had been well arranged." Across the county, crowds form at every covert. "You'll not do much in the hunting way to-day, Muster Daly," says a man at one stop: "When we heard you were a-coming we had a little hunt of our own. There ain't a fox anywhere about the place now" (*L* ch. 11).

In the winter of 1881–82, hunts were stopped in just this fashion across the country, attracting considerable press attention on both sides of the Irish Sea. The *Illustrated London News* ran a print by Irish artist Aloysius O'Kelly depicting a hunt being blocked (see Fig. 1).[11] While in some locations hounds were poisoned, in most cases protesters simply assembled at coverts in large numbers, as in O'Kelly's scene. Increasingly, the crowds met at their own appointed times to take game themselves, in what came to be called "people's hunts" or "Land League hunts."[12] What Trollope described then was a widespread and highly politicized campaign, a deliberate refutation of the legitimacy of the colonial land system.

Landlords were quick to see the profound significance of the anti-hunting campaign. To them, the highly coordinated ritual of the hunt symbolized not their own sovereignty but the harmonious relations of all classes in Ireland. Trollope's depiction in *Landleaguers* of the hunting party and its reaction to the protest was closely observed and based in real events. One of

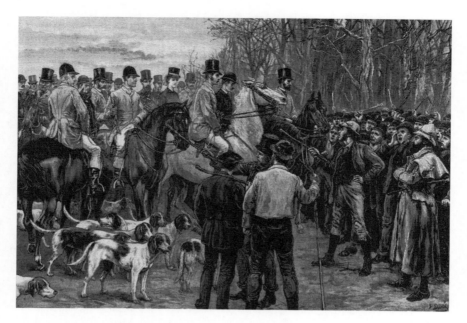

Figure 1. *The State of Ireland: Stopping a Hunt,* by Aloysius O'Kelly. Printed in the *Illustrated London News,* December 24, 1881. Image reprinted by permission of Niamh O'Sullivan.

the characters there is a Mr. Persse, presumably inspired by Burton R. Persse, a prominent Galway landowner and master of hounds. For avid hunters part of the sport involved observing the performance of different hounds in a pack, and to help keep track of the dogs an especially keen master might print up a list of hounds with each animal's name and age, sire and dam. The National Library of Ireland now preserves such a list of Mr. Persse's dogs; it was privately printed in 1881 and bound in red Morocco. However, by January 1882, with protests rising, members of the Galway hunt voted to cancel the rest of their season. A national sporting paper covered the meeting, where Mr. Persse declared that:

> He would rather never see a hound or a fox than hunt the country in opposition to the feelings of any class. He regretted very much that this unpleasantness had happened, because it should be a proud boast of his that he hunted the country for twenty-eight years with the good-will of all classes, and without an angry word being said to him [here Mr. Persse was much affected].[13]

Mr. Daly, Trollope's fictional master of the Galway hounds, is equally affected by his ruined day. As he takes to his bed that night, he is led for the first time to consider "by how weak a hold his right of hunting the country was held." Having seen this right once broken, he understands that "The occupation of his life was over" (*L* ch. 11).

It is impossible to conceive that Trollope himself would not have been much affected by the anti-hunting campaign. The stopping of the hunt in *The Landleaguers* reads very much like the end of his own "legitimate joy." Following his researches in Ireland, he returned to his house in Harting on August 1, 1882 and began to write. By August 11, however, he was convinced that he needed more material and set off for Ireland a second time, remaining until mid-September. On November 3, having completed forty-nine chapters out of a projected sixty, he suffered a stroke and would write no more. He lingered for another month and died on December 6, 1882. While in the 1840s Trollope provided a confident diagnosis of the ills that plagued Irish society, dismissing the peasant cause as something minor and misunderstood, in 1882 he could no longer maintain this view of Irish life. The quarrelsome and incompetent conspirators of *Macdermots* had become a highly controlled and undeniably powerful crowd. They would continue to carry out their own vision of a just society. They signal as a result that the occupation of Trollope's life was over.

NOTES

1 Robert Tracy, "'The Unnatural Ruin': Trollope and Nineteenth-Century Irish Fiction," *Nineteenth-Century Fiction* 37:3 (1982), 359.

2 Gearóid Ó Tuathaigh, *Ireland Before the Famine, 1798–1848* (Dublin: Gill and Macmillan, 1972), p. 5.

3 John Hynes, "Anthony Trollope's Creative 'Culture Shock': Banagher, 1841," *Eire-Ireland* 21:3 (Fall 1986), 125.

4 Alexis de Tocqueville, *Alexis de Tocqueville's Journey in Ireland: July–August, 1835*, trans. and ed. Emmet Larkin (Dublin: Wolfhound, 1990), p. 29.

5 William Makepeace Thackeray, *The Irish Sketch Book*, in *The Paris Sketch Book of Mr. M. A. Titmarsh; The Irish Sketchbook; and Notes of a Journey from Cornhill to Grand Cairo* (Chicago: Dunahoe, 1900), p. 7.

6 Derek Hawes, "Is he Worshipful Brother? Anthony Trollope's Links to the Freemasons," *Times Literary Supplement* (October 22, 1999), 16.

7 Tracy, "Unnatural Ruin," 362–65.

8 T. H. S. Escott, *Anthony Trollope: His Public Services, Private Friends, and Literary Originals* [1913] (Port Washington, NY: Kennikat, 1967), p. 61.

9 Robert Tracy, "Instant Replay: Trollope's *The Landleaguers*, 1883," *Eire-Ireland* 15:2 (Summer 1980), 36.

10 Declan Kiberd, *Irish Classics* (London: Granta, 2001), p. 374.

11 My thanks to Niamh O'Sullivan for assistance with this image and permission to use it.

12 Heather Laird, *Subversive Law in Ireland, 1879–1920: From "Unwritten Law" to the Dáil Courts* (Dublin: Four Courts, 2005), p. 93.

13 *Sport* (Dublin), January 7, 1882. Brackets appear in the original.

16

AMANDA CLAYBAUGH

Trollope and America

The Trollope family made something of an industry of visiting America and writing about it. In the late 1820s, Frances Trollope had gone to America in the hope of reviving the Trollope family fortunes. After trying and failing to establish a business on the western frontier, she decided to become an author instead. She first published a book about her American travels, *The Domestic Manners of the Americans* (1832), and then a novel, *The Refugee in America* (1832), and the success of these launched her on a prolific career. A generation later, Anthony Trollope would visit America four times. He stopped off briefly in the late 1850s after touring the West Indies, and he paid a more substantial visit in 1861, in order to write an American travel book of his own, *North America* (1862). He subsequently gave a public lecture in London about his experiences. In 1868, he returned to America in an official capacity, negotiating a new treaty for postal rates, and in 1875 he visited America a final time, crossing the continent from west to east at the end of his tour of the Pacific and publishing an essay about California in the process. America and Americans are also a frequent topic in his fiction. In addition to several short stories from the early 1860s, three of Trollope's later novels focus on America. The most memorable of these, perhaps, is *The Way We Live Now* (1874–75), which is set in a London entirely upended by two visitors from the American West, the speculator Hamilton K. Fisker and Mrs. Hurtle, an adventuress. Another novel, *The American Senator* (1876–77), follows the adventures of one Elias Gotobed, senator from the fictional state of Mikewa, as he makes his way through the English countryside, commenting on all that he sees. And the final chapters of a late novel, *Dr. Wortle's School* (1881), are set in America, as a young Englishman travels to California in search of a desperado who is threatening him and his wife.

The Trollopes were far from alone in writing about America. After the War of 1812 (which lasted from 1812 to 1815) confirmed that America was no longer under British control, authors on both sides of the Atlantic attempted to make sense of the relations between the two nations. For the most part, these authors presented America and Britain as different from – and opposed to – one another, and their writings established the terms in which this difference would be described. American openness and British reserve, American energy and British leisure, American merchants and British gentlemen: these oppositions are familiar even in our own day. Each of these nations thus represented what the other was not, but each also represented what the other might yet choose to become. In the eyes of the British, as the critic Paul Giles has shown, America embodied the full flowering of a dissenting tradition that had begun with the English reformation and then migrated across the sea. As a consequence, America was frequently invoked, as both exemplar and as cautionary example, in British debates about religion and politics.[1] In the eyes of the Americans, as the critic Lawrence Buell has shown, Britain set a cultural standard against which American achievements inevitably seemed inferior or, at best, belated. For this reason, the most ambitious American authors, including the ones belonging to the American Renaissance, explicitly rebelled against the British and European authors whom they secretly feared they could not equal.[2] In these ways, each nation defined itself both with and against the other, and claims about national difference seldom expressed simple opposition, but rather a more complicated mix of admiration and rebellion, envy and regret.

Of the many nineteenth-century writers who explored the British–American relation, Anthony Trollope was among the most discerning. He offers, I will show, an unusually nuanced account of national difference, establishing some of the national types that are still with us today but also subjecting this emphasis on difference to a searching critique. Moreover, he offers an unusually rich account of the relations between the two nations, emphasizing that the former colony stood poised to become a partner in imperialism. In the process, he describes an Anglo-American alliance held together by the ties of business, politics, and love.

National difference

At the beginning of *North America*, Anthony Trollope attempts to distinguish his own travel book from the one his mother had published thirty years before. Hers, he says, was "essentially a woman's book," while his will be the work of a man (*NA* ch. 1). By this, Trollope is referring in part to a difference of approach. Where his mother had recorded her rather haphazard experiences, he attempts a more systematic survey. Prevented by the outbreak of the Civil War from visiting the southern states, he nonetheless manages to visit all the states that remained in the Union, with the single exception of California. (When he did visit California, in 1875, he would decide that no city in the whole world was "less interesting to the normal tourist" than San Francisco.)[3] Where his mother had described vivid scenes and recounted telling anecdotes, he gives statistical tables of population and wheat production, along with charts of army expenditures. Trollope's own book is, however, less systematic and scientific than he claims it to be. Following the loose conventions of nineteenth-century travel writing no less than his mother had done, he describes places in the order he visits them and records his more general observations as they occur. He is particularly digressive when it comes to the postal service, the details of which he carefully notes as he learns them, even as he admits, quite charmingly, that they will interest no one but himself.

In Trollope's view, his mother's travel book was womanly in its focus, as well. She concentrated on describing the social arrangements of America, while he will concentrate on political matters instead. In drawing this distinction between their two books, however, Trollope fails to do justice to what his mother had achieved. For while it is true that she did concentrate on social arrangements and also true that she did identify such arrangements as a subject well-suited to the capacities of a woman writer, she nonetheless understood social arrangements to be a crucial index to a nation's political life. This is most clearly the case when judging the question of equality. All too often, she observes, equality is considered only in the abstract, either by British travelers who describe the structure of the American government without ever observing the kind of society it creates or by British radicals who stay at home and advocate equality only after their servants have brought in the port and respectfully shut the door. Equality is far more appealing as an abstract ideal than as a concrete reality, for it tends to manifest itself "in the shape of a hard, greasy paw, and [to be] claimed in accents that breathe less of freedom then of onions and whisky."[4] Indeed, so disillusioning is the reality of equality, Frances Trollope concludes, that the British government should not imprison radicals, but rather send them on an American tour in order to cure them of their views. For those who cannot take such a tour, her travel book must suffice. And so she devotes herself to describing equality as it is lived in practice, from the insistence on communal living in hotels to the impossibility of keeping decent servants in the home. Only in Canada are the poor still willing to bow and curtsy as the Trollopes pass.

More direct in his attention to political arrangements than his mother had been, Trollope reprints portions of the American Constitution and the constitution of the state of New York, as well as discussing the workings of American government more generally. But he also shares his mother's interest in the social manifestations of political equality. He, too, recoils instinctively from these manifestations, and his travel book records his shock at being addressed impudently by a railway porter or by a working-class woman on an omnibus. But he then tries to transcend his instinctive response and to view the world as these porters and women must see it. He is quick to recognize that the lack of servility in those who serve is their attempt to assert a claim to political equality in the face of real economic inequality. "Have you ever realized to yourself as a fact," Trollope asks his readers, "that the porter who carries your box has not made himself inferior to you by the very act of carrying that box? If not, that is the very lesson which the man wishes to teach you" (*NA* ch. 19).

Trollope has more difficulty coming to terms with the women on the bus. He prefaces his description of them with several paragraphs apologizing for daring to say anything at all critical of the female sex, and when the description actually comes, we can see why he would think an apology was necessary. For Trollope depicts the women on the bus not merely as coarse, but as actually revolting. He compares them to "unclean animal[s]," and he describes the dragging trains of their filthy dresses as giving "blows from a harpy's fins" as "loathsome as snake's slime" (*NA* ch. 14). But he recollects himself and tries to move beyond this revulsion when he visits one of the schools that produces women like these. Acknowledging that British women of this class are "humble" and therefore not offensive to the "squeamish," he nonetheless reminds himself that American self-assurance, no matter how impudent, is better than English humility – at least for the women themselves, if not for their middle-class observers (*NA* ch. 14). In passages like these, we can see Trollope divided between his immediate response to American equality and his subsequent willingness to reason beyond that response and accept, at least intellectually, different, more radical, conclusions.

But the most important divergence between Frances and Anthony Trollope is one that Trollope does not name: they differ in their accounts of British–American relations, and so, I will show, they differ in their accounts of national difference itself. For Frances Trollope, the history of British–American relations is a history of rupture, with the American Revolution (1775–83) creating an absolute break between the two nations. In her account, the Americans rejected everything they had inherited from the British, while creating almost nothing to put in its place. They rejected, for instance, British culture, but they have no real culture of their own. That is, they have no popular culture, "no fetes, no fairs, no merry makings, no music in the streets, no Punch, no puppet-shows" (*Domestic Manners* 164). Nor do they have a high culture. Their feeble attempts to imitate British literature and art are merely laughable to her, although she does approve of the few artists who confine themselves to distinctively American themes, such as the sculptors who carve sheaves of corn in their columns' capitals and the authors who write about the Native Americans.

Even worse, in Frances Trollope's view, is the fact that the Americans have rejected the customs of British social life, but not replaced them with any of their own. The result is a world that she finds entirely lacking in manners, and her travel book is a catalogue of revolting scenes. The Americans grab at their food and gulp it down, picking their teeth with their knives when they are done. Husbands do not speak to their wives, nor do tablemates speak to one another, and on the rare occasion where a conversation does occur, it focuses on "the DOLLAR" with all the single-mindedness of ants in an ant hill (*Domestic Manners* 235). And worst of all, the men constantly spit. In describing Americans as lacking in manners and lacking in culture as well, Frances Trollope is describing a nation that is not only fundamentally different from Britain, but fundamentally abhorrent to all. "I do not like them," she concludes, "I do not like their principles, I do not like their manners, I do not like their opinions" (*Domestic Manners*, 315). Nor is she alone in this. Several times, she pauses to emphasize that her shock at a particular incident is shared by the German or French observers nearby. All of Europe is united, it seems, in disgust at the Americans.

Anthony Trollope, by contrast, views the American Revolution as a painful but necessary stage in the history of British colonialism. Once the British established a settler colony in North America, it was inevitable, in his account, that the colonists would one day rise up against them, inevitable that the British would try to put them down, and inevitable that the Americans would ultimately succeed in winning their independence. Viewing the American Revolution in this way, Trollope does not see it as a rupture. On the contrary, he emphasizes that the Americans are still eager for British approval, that is, for "English admiration, English appreciation of [their] energy, and English encouragement" (*NA* ch. 3), and the British, for their part, are now willing to approve. They have ceased to resent the Americans for seeking independence and are now willing to acknowledge that the Americans have done well for themselves and "deserve well of all coming ages of mankind" (*NA* ch. 1). Indeed, Trollope wonders why the Canadians have not done the same. To go from America to Canada, as he describes it, is to go from "a richer country into one that is poorer, and from a greater country into one that is less" (*NA* ch. 4), and he attributes the difference to their failure to seek their independence. At the same time, Trollope is also quick to emphasize that the Americans, in their Revolution, did not reject nearly as much of their British inheritance as his mother had suggested. When the Americans achieved their independence, they could have done anything; but what they chose to do, Trollope observes with great satisfaction, was to retain their British ways. This point was so crucial that Trollope would emphasize it in italics: there is *"nothing in the history of the United States so wonderful as the closeness with which our laws and habits of rule have been adopted."*[5]

So close have the two nations remained, despite the frequent conflicts between them, that they now stand poised to share the work of imperialism, a project that Trollope sees as worthy of all praise. He acknowledges that the two countries may think of themselves as competing for world influence, with the British wanting to Anglicize the world and the Americans wanting to Americanize it. But these, he insists, amount to the same thing in the end: both words are merely synonyms for "civilize" (*PC* 55). Two of Trollope's short stories from the early 1860s reflect this view. They take as their subject neither Britain nor America, but rather a shared Anglo-American world of colonies and former colonies. In "An Unprotected Female at the Pyramids" (1860), English and American travelers are united by their shared language in a Cairo that is filled with Egyptians babbling an incomprehensible Arabic and Frenchmen speaking an accented and imperfect English. And "A Journey to Panama" (1861) describes an even more cosmopolitan world. This story is set onboard ship, among a community of passengers who are not so much tied to specific nations as in circuit among them. Some are going to North America and some to South America; some, to the West Indies or to Canada; some are Unionists and some are Confederates, but all are part of the project of colonizing the western hemisphere.

Given his views of British–American relations, it is hardly surprising that Trollope would offer a complicated account of national difference. On the one hand, he identifies fundamental differences between the people of Britain and the people of America, as we can see from this passage from *North America*:

> The American . . . is not like an Englishman in his mind, in his aspirations, in his tastes, or in his politics. In his mind he is quicker, more universally intelligent, more ambitious of general knowledge, less indulgent of stupidity and ignorance in others, harder, sharper, brighter with the surface brightness of steel, than is an Englishman; but he is more brittle, less enduring, less malleable, and, I think, less capable of impressions. The mind of the Englishman has more imagination, but that of the American more incision . . . In his aspirations the American is more constant than an Englishman – or I should rather say he is more constant in aspiring . . . But in his aspirations he is more limited than an Englishman. (*NA* ch. 14)

Unlike Frances Trollope, who had seen in America the absence of anything she valued, Anthony Trollope understands the Americans to be both different from the British and, as the balanced syntax of the passage implies, equal to them at the same time.

And yet, even as Trollope sets the terms of national difference in his travel book, he sometimes questions, in his fictional works, whether such differences really exist. We can see this in *The Way We Live Now*, which is filled with characters eager to generalize about national difference. The American adventuress Mrs. Hurtle, for instance, is continually deriding Britain as "a safe-going country," "an effete civilization," a "soft civilization," and a place structured by inequality, where everyone is either "too humble or too overbearing" (*WWLN* chs. 47, 42, 71). But while Mrs. Hurtle's experiences while visiting Britain might suggest that these views are correct, the novel elsewhere undermines claims of national difference. Some claims are mocked for being too exaggerated. Mrs. Hurtle's chief adversary, the very English Roger Carbury, is shown to be naive in thinking of America as a nation of rebels, like "Jack Cade or Wat Tyler" (*WWLN* ch. 87). And even more naive is the dim, but good-hearted, lord who confuses another American with a "heathen Chinee" (*WWLN* ch. 10). But the novel also mocks claims that are too trivial, as when the members of a gentleman's club find that they dislike a visiting American because "his manners were not as their manners; his waistcoat was not as their waistcoat" (*WWLN* ch. 10).

Trollope would expand on this latter idea in another novel, *The American Senator*, attempting to explain why such minor differences had come to seem so significant. The problem can be traced to the closeness between the Americans and the British. If a British man were to visit Japan, or a Japanese man to visit Britain, he would expect to be struck by all the differences and actually be surprised by the many similarities. But with the British and the Americans, the matter is reversed. Everyone expects to find similarities, and so the differences are more vivid – and more galling:

> When an American comes to us, or a Briton goes to the States, each speaking the same language, using the same cookery, governed by the same laws, and wearing the same costume, the differences which present themselves are so striking that neither can live six months in the country of the other without a holding up of hands and a torrent of exclamations. (*AS* ch. 77)

In this way, Trollope subjects to scrutiny the manners of the Americans, but also the insistence on national difference. And in his novels more generally, he would pay much less attention to the putative differences between Britain and America than to the many forms of interaction that connected them.

Anglo-American interactions

It was through business that the Trollope family first interacted with America. Frances Trollope came to the United States in the hope of establishing a shopping bazaar that would include, in a Moorish building complete with dome, a picture gallery, a refreshment room, a ballroom, and a concert hall. In this way, she intended to supply the needs of what Anthony Trollope would later describe as "the still unfurnished States" (*A* ch. 1). The plan proved to be an ignominious failure: the Trollope family ran out of money while the emporium was still being built, and when the goods finally arrived to supply the store, they were so poorly made that not even the Americans would buy them. Anthony Trollope, too, would have disappointing financial dealings with the United States. Writing at a time when there was not yet an international copyright law, he made from the American sale of his books only what the American publishers chose to pay. In his meticulous financial records, he would calculate the lost profits from each of his books and write "cheated" alongside them. These losses were made vivid to him when he visited America at last. Like other British authors, he was struck by the sheer size of the American market and newly conscious of all the money he was losing from it. We can see this in *North America*, when he marvels at how cheap books are in America and at how eager people are, as a result, to read. For both Trollope and his mother then, America stood as a vast market insufficiently supplied with local goods and so needing to import them, whether legally or illegally, from Britain.

These economic relations, and much else, would be changed by the American Civil War (1861–65). When the war broke out, Trollope had already arranged his trip to America and he was not willing to postpone it. And so the war became, against his intentions, the central subject of *North America*. When he arrived in America, he found that what he had understood as a war between the Union and the Confederacy was understood by the Unionists all around him as a conflict between the Union and Britain as well. Britain's economic interests lay with the cotton-producing southern states, but the British government nonetheless declared its neutrality in the war. But this was not enough for the Unionists, who felt that the British should explicitly take their side. Trollope therefore found himself questioned and challenged by all the Unionists he met. Matters grew even more tense while he was visiting Washington, DC. A British ship was boarded by the Union Navy, who seized the two Confederate diplomats it was carrying on an embassy to London. The British were outraged by this violation of their naval rights and diplomatic relations, and for a while it seemed as if the British might take sides in the war after all – if not directly, then certainly by challenging the Union blockade of the Confederate coast. And it also seemed possible, at least to Trollope, that all British subjects would soon be expelled from the Union. His letters show him to be "anxious to get out and see the people before war is declared," but he was forced to stay in his hotel room while a doctor tended to an infected cyst on his forehead (*Letters* 1:165). Soon, the matter was resolved through diplomacy, and Britain maintained its policy of neutrality until the war's end, thereby making a Confederate victory much less likely.

Upon his return to Britain, Trollope involved himself in the war more directly. He gave a speech in London about his American travels, in which he attempted to persuade his listeners to take the Union's side. He acknow- ledges from the beginning that English sympathies tend to be with the Confederacy – in part because its cause seems the more chivalric, and in part because it is attempting to break up a nation that sometimes presents itself as a rival to Britain. But he urges his listeners to remember that their sympathies more properly belong to the Union. He reminds them that the Confederacy supports slavery and that they themselves would not permit the Irish to secede. More importantly, he reminds them that the Union deserves their sympathy because it is, like Britain itself, a nation destined for greatness. The Union soldiers have displayed, if not military genius, then certainly "pluck," and have shown themselves to be "Anglo-Saxons to the backbone" (*PC* 54).

Trollope was hardly alone in urging his country to side with the Union – a number of other British authors would do so as well – but he was quite idiosyncratic in his understanding of the war more generally. He viewed it through the same lens as he had viewed the American Revolution. Just as it was inevitable for the American colonists to rebel against Britain and for Britain to try and fail to put them down, so it is equally inevitable for the Confederate states to try to secede from the Union and for the Union to try – and fail – to retain them. America has simply grown too large to maintain itself as a nation, and the western states, in Trollope's view, will be the next to secede. Viewing the Civil War through this lens, Trollope sees Confeder- ate secession as ultimately inevitable. The Union may achieve a military victory, but there is no clear way for them to force the Confederate states to participate again in the nation. (Here, Trollope proves to be prescient about the difficulties of Reconstruction.) And yet, Trollope advocates for the British to support the Union anyway because a military victory, while not preventing the secession of all the Confederate states, might retain the border states: Maryland, Virginia, Kentucky, and Washington, DC. And with these border states, the Union is certain to continue on its path to national greatness, for it is the Union that is dredging the canals, establishing the schools, building the cities, increasing the trade, and multi-plying the industries that a great nation needs. The southern states, as is typical of southern nations in Trollope's view, have no impulse for greatness, and so their destiny, after they secede, will be to provide a staple crop to British cotton mills.

Thus, Trollope's views on the Civil War. In his fictional works from the time, he is much less partisan. His "The Two Generals" (1863) is carefully balanced, as its title suggests, between the war's two sides. The story dramatizes the divisions that the war has caused through a pairing of protagonists: two brothers, one who has become a general in the Union Army and one who has become a general for the Confederates. But even as the story emplots division, its setting suggests the terms of reconciliation. Set in Kentucky, a slave state that nonetheless refused to secede with the rest, the story is careful to condemn both slavery and radical abolition, approving instead a gradual freeing of the slaves. Another story foregrounds the economic dimensions of the war, and the extent to which these involve Britain. The purpose of the Union naval blockade, notoriously violated by the Confederate diplomats, was to prevent the transport of southern cotton and so to disrupt the Confederate economy. It disrupted the British economy as well, as Trollope acknowledged in *North America* and explores more fully in "The Widow's Mite." Set in Britain, this story takes up the subject of the so-called "cotton famine," which was caused when southern cotton was no longer available for British mills. The story does not unfold among the workers, but rather among the members of a clergyman's family, who debate among themselves how best to aid the workers suffering around them. One of the young women in the family, who is engaged to an American man, decides that she will be married in her old clothes in order to show her sympathy for the suffering workers. The other characters mock this decision as both eccentric and pointless, and the story leaves undecided the wisdom of her actions, as it leaves undecided the more general question of how best to aid the poor. But the story does make one thing clear: for Trollope, the Civil War is as much a British experience as an American one. Indeed, the American textile workers suffer much less, he had noted in *North America*, than their counterparts in Britain.

If the Civil War threatened the existing trade relations between Britain and America, it would also create new ones, as the historian Eric Rauchway has shown.[6] In the course of fighting the war, the American government would take on a debt financed largely by British bankers. As a consequence, where antebellum America had been seen as a vast market undersupplied with goods, postbellum America came to be seen, much like the developing world today, as a place for the global speculations of international capitalists. These speculations are the subject of Trollope's most important novel, *The Way We Live Now*. America stands as the place where the British can make their fortunes, and the more naive characters believe that this is because the land is so fertile and full of resources. But the money to be made in America is to be made through speculation, and soon even the novel's hero has fallen in, somewhat against his will, with Hamilton K. Fisker, a smartly dressed westerner with a distinctive twang. Fisker associates the United States with speculation because he associates it with imagination: "we're a bigger people than any of you and have more room" (*WWLN* ch. 9). And what he imagines, implausibly enough, is a railroad running from Salt Lake City to Vera Cruz, one whose cost has not yet been computed, but whose distances are vast. And indeed, the work of selling the shares is only a work of the imagination. All that Mr. Fisker has done is make an elaborate prospectus filled with pictures of trains running through mountains and emerging beside beautiful lakes. Any resistance to this new mode of doing business is seen as a "John Bull scruple" (*WWLN* ch. 9), but it soon becomes clear that the British have few scruples at all.

In the same year that Trollope published *The Way We Live Now*, he also published his final piece of travel writing about the United States, his essay about San Francisco. In this essay, he identifies the city as the epicenter of all that *The Way We Live Now* had described. Everyone is buying and selling stocks, even chamber maids, and those who have overextended themselves are protected by others from bankruptcy so that the game can go on. Trollope condemns this, reminding his readers that the shame of bankruptcy is all that prevents men from gambling with other men's money, but he acknowledges that "such doctrines are altogether out of date in California" (*TT* 215). This, in Trollope's eyes, is the city of the future, but as his own writings have shown there is no way of separating this city from the Britain with which it is everywhere entwined.

In these ways, Trollope's fiction depicts the many business and political ties that connect Britain and America. But it is only with respect to a third form of connection, family feeling and love, that Trollope does not merely depict a trans-Atlantic phenomenon, but actually responds to it by altering his fictional form. Family metaphors were often used to describe the ties between America and Britain, even when those ties were most frayed. Trollope calls the Americans his "near relatives" (*NA* ch. 1) and speaks of the "old family quarrel" between them (*NA* ch. 6); Frances Trollope had done so as well, although she had been quick to note that family quarrels are often the most difficult to resolve. The making of these family relations is given narrative form by courtship plots, and these courtship plots most commonly involve a figure then known as the "American Girl," who personifies the self-assertion that was seen as typical of American women. Trollope himself had described this self-assertion, observing that American women are "much given to talking ... generally free from all *mauvaise honte* ... collected in manner, well instructed, and resolved to have their share of the social advantages of the world" (*NA* ch. 11). And on the American Girl was conferred an autonomy in courtship that was seen as distinctive of America as well: the American Girl, free to marry or not as she liked, was an appealing complement to masculine forms of political freedom. The most famous American Girl is, of course, Henry James's Daisy Miller, who horrifies and attracts James's narrator by her frankness, her freedom, and her unwillingness to follow convention. But an earlier version of this story is Trollope's own "Miss Ophelia Gledd" (1863). Trollope's story begins much as James's novella would end, with the narrator trying to classify the woman who has so beguiled him. Here, the question is whether a woman who does all that Ophelia Gledd has done can be considered a lady. Trollope knew such a woman himself, the Bostonian Kate Field, and his letters to her show him trying to persuade her to conform to more conventional models of female behavior: he refuses to lend her money to travel on her own to St. Louis, for instance, and he portentously advises her to marry.

Elsewhere in Trollope, however, the Anglo-American courtship plot does not follow this paradigm. In *The American Senator*, for instance, the novel's British heroine associates freedom in courtship as a British, rather than an American, trait: she reminds herself that it is only in other, presumably continental countries that girls must marry as their parents like. An earlier short story, "An Unprotected Female," offers a more complicated revision of the American Girl plot. Here, the eponymous female is a British woman traveling on her own in Egypt, looking for companions for a journey down the Nile or across the Sahara. But unlike the American Girl, who may well choose not to marry, this unprotected female is quite desperate to do so, and the story sets her stratagems against the more conventional courtship of a young American woman by a British suitor, who must submit to talking politics with the girl's father in order to win her hand.

But the most interesting revisions of the American Girl come in Trollope's late novels, *The Way We Live Now* and *Dr. Wortle's School*. Here, the American Girl is not a girl at all, but rather a mature woman. Mrs. Peacock, in *Dr. Wortle's School*, does not reveal her nationality in her accent or speech, much less in her manners; indeed, she is more freezingly correct than the British ladies around her. Far more familiar is the appropriately named Mrs. Hurtle from *The Way We Live Now*, who has not only a nasal twang in her speech, but also a "bit of the wild cat in her breeding"

(*WWLN* ch. 38) and is rumored to have shot a man in Oregon. What unites these two otherwise disparate women is the fact that each has been married before – and each turns out to be married still. Mrs. Peacock had been abandoned by her husband in Missouri and later told that he had subsequently died in Mexico; she then marries again, the man she truly loves, only to learn that her first husband is still alive after all. Mrs. Hurtle's situation is a bit more ambiguous. She had presented herself as widowed when being courted by a young British man and only much later admits that she is actually divorced; still later, there is some suggestion that she did not divorce her husband at all, but rather fought a duel with him, and that he might still be alive, albeit safely imprisoned in Leavenworth. The British characters dismiss this confusion as typical of American moral laxity. Mrs. Peacock's British neighbors speculate that the Americans do not get married at all, while Mrs. Hurtle's British rival suggests that "they get themselves divorced just when they like" (*WWLN* ch. 76). But Trollope mocks this view for its provincial ignorance, and both Mrs. Peacock and Mrs. Hurtle are much more compelling than the young British women they are set against, even though, in the case of Mrs. Hurtle, there is something alarming about a woman "so handy with pistols" (*WWLN* ch. 47). "You are a girl," Mrs. Hurtle says to her young British rival, "and I am a woman" (*WWLN* ch. 91).

Elsewhere in his American writings, Trollope had been quick to undermine claims of national difference. He emphasized that it was only the closeness between the two nations that threw the small differences between them into too-stark relief, and he also took care to depict the many ways in which the two nations were entangled. But here, with respect to courtship, one of Trollope's most serious and persistent concerns, he projects onto America differences of quite a different kind. For these compelling American women, with their shadowed American pasts, bring maturity and sexual experience into the courtship plot, even as this history is cordoned off from the present and confined to another country.

NOTES

1 Paul Giles, *The Atlantic Republic: The American Tradition in English Literature* (Oxford: Oxford University Press, 2006).
2 Lawrence Buell, "American Literary Emergence as Postcolonial Phenomenon," *American Literary History* 4:3 (Autumn 1992), 411–42.
3 Anthony Trollope, *The Tireless Traveller* (1875; Berkeley: University of California Press, 1941), p. 212. All further references to this edition will be cited in the text as "*TT*."
4 Frances Trollope, *Domestic Manners of the Americans* (1832; Stroud, Gloucestershire: Nonsuch Publishing, 2006) 102–3. All further references are to this edition and will be cited in the text as *Domestic Manners*.

5 Anthony Trollope, "The Present Condition of the Northern States of the American Union (1862 or 1863)," *Anthony Trollope: Four Lectures*, ed. Morris L. Parrish (Folcroft, PA: Folcroft Press, 1969), p. 40. All further references to this edition will be cited in the text as "*PC.*"

6 Eric Rauchway, *Blessed Among Nations: How the World Made America* (New York: Hill and Wang, 2006).

FURTHER READING

Since the reinvigoration of Trollope studies in the 1970s, there has been a steadily growing body of critical work on Anthony Trollope. What follows is a necessarily abbreviated list of primary sources, reference materials, and critical studies. For a full bibliography of recent criticism, see Mark W. Turner, "Trollope Studies: 1987–2004," *Dickens Studies Annual: Essays on Victorian Fiction* 37 (2006), 217–49.

Anderson, Amanda, "Trollope's Modernity," *ELH* 74 (2007), 509–34

apRoberts, Ruth, *The Moral Trollope* (Athens, Ohio: Ohio University Press, 1971)

Arkin, Mark, "Trollope and the Law," *The New Criterion* 26 (2007), 23–30

Birns, Nicholas, "The Empire Turned Upside Down: The Colonial Fictions of Anthony Trollope," *Ariel* 27 (1996), 7–23

Blythe, H. E., "*The Fixed Period* (1882): Euthanasia, Cannibalism, and Colonial Extraction in Anthony Trollope's Antipodes," *Nineteenth Century Contexts* 25 (2006), 61–81

Booth, Bradford (ed.), *The Tireless Traveller: Twenty Letters to the Liverpool Mercury, 1875* (Berkeley: University of California Press, 1941)

Bridgham, Elizabeth A., *Spaces of the Sacred and Profane: Dickens, Trollope, and the Victorian Cathedral Town* (New York: Routledge, 2008)

Clark, John W., *The Language and Style of Anthony Trollope* (London: Andre Deutsch, 1975)

Clark, Samuel, and James S. Donnelly, Jr. (eds.), *Irish Peasants: Violence and Political Unrest, 1780–1914* (Manchester: Manchester University Press, 1983)

Cohen, William A., "Skin: Surface and Sensation in Trollope's 'The Banks of the Jordan,'" in *Embodied: Victorian Literature and the Senses* (Minneapolis: University of Minnesota Press, 2009), pp. 65–85

Colella, Silvana, "Sweet Money: Cultural and Economic Value in Trollope's *Autobiography*," *Nineteenth-Century Contexts* 28 (2006), 5–20

Colón, Susan E., *The Professional Ideal in the Victorian Novel: The Works of Disraeli, Trollope, Gaskell, and Eliot* (New York: Palgrave Macmillan, 2007)

Corbett, Mary Jean, "Plotting Colonial Authority: Trollope's Ireland, 1845–1860," in *Allegories of Union in Irish and English Writing, 1790–1870: Politics, History, and the Family from Edgeworth to Arnold* (Cambridge: Cambridge University Press, 2000) pp. 114–47

Craig, Randall, "Rhetoric and Courtship in *Can You Forgive Her?*," *ELH* 62 (1995), 217–35

Curtis, Lewis P., *Anglo-Saxons and Celts: A Study of Anti-Irish Prejudice in Victorian England* (New York: New York University Press, 1968)

Dames, Nicholas, "Trollope and the Career: Vocational Trajectories and the Management of Ambition," *Victorian Studies* 45 (2003), 247–78

Davidson, J. H., "Anthony Trollope and the Colonies," *Victorian Studies* 12 (March 1969), 305–37

Dolin, Kieran, *Fiction and the Law: Legal Discourse in Victorian and Modernist Literature* (Cambridge: Cambridge University Press, 1999)

Durey, Jill Felicity, "Modern Issues: Anthony Trollope and Australia," *Antipodes: A North American Journal of Australian Literature* 21 (December 2007), 270–74.

Trollope and the Church of England (New York: Palgrave Macmillan, 2002)

Edwards P. D., *Anthony Trollope's Son in Australia* (Brisbane: University of Queensland Press, 1982)

Fisichelli, Glynn-Ellen Maria, "The Language of Law and Love: Anthony Trollope's *Orley Farm*," *ELH* 61 (1994), 635–53

Flanagan, Thomas, *The Irish Novelists, 1800–1850* (New York: Columbia University Press, 1959)

Flint, Kate, *Introduction* to *Can You Forgive Her?* (New York: Oxford University Press, 1991)

Frank, Cathrine O., "Fictions of Justice: Testamentary Intention and the (Il)legitimate Heir in Trollope's *Ralph the Heir* and Forster's *Howard's End*," *English Literature in Transition, 1880–1920* 47 (2004), 311–30

Gibbons, L., "Race against Time: Racial Discourse and Irish History," *Oxford Literary Review* 12.1–2 (1991), 95–117

Glendinning, Victoria, *Anthony Trollope* (New York: Random House, 1993)

Gray, Peter, *Famine, Land, and Politics: British Government and Irish Society, 1843–1850* (Dublin, Irish Academic Press, 1999)

Trollope: A Biography (Oxford: Oxford University Press, 1993)

Trollope and His Illustrators (London: Macmillan, 1980)

Hall, N. John (ed.), *The Letters of Anthony Trollope*, 2 vols. (Stanford: Stanford University Press, 1983)

The Trollope Critics (London: Macmillan, 1981)

Hall, N. John, James R. Kincaid, Ruth apRoberts, Juliet McMaster, Robert Tracy, Robert M. Polhemus, and John Halperin, "Trollopians Reduces," *LIT* 3 (1992), 175–87

Halperin, John, *Trollope and Politics* (London: Macmillan, 1977)

Halperin John, (ed.), *Trollope Centenary Essays* (New York: St. Martin's Press, 1982)

Hamer, Mary, *Writing by Numbers: Trollope's Serial Fiction* (Cambridge: Cambridge University Press, 1987)

Herbert, Christopher, *Trollope and Comic Pleasure* (Chicago: University of Chicago Press, 1987)

Jaffe, Audrey, "Trollope in the Stock Market: Irrational Exuberance and *The Prime Minister*," *Victorian Studies* 45:1 (Autumn 2002), 43–64

Jones, Wendy, "Feminism, Fiction and Contract Theory: Trollope's *He Knew He Was Right*" *Criticism* 36 (1994), 401–14

Kelleher, Margaret, *The Feminization of Famine: Expressions of the Inexpressible?* (Durham, NC: Duke University Press, 1997)

"Prose and Drama in English, 1830–1890," *The Cambridge History of Irish Literature*, vol. 1 (Cambridge: Cambridge University Press, 2006), pp. 449–99

Kendrick, Walter M., *The Novel-Machine: The Theory and Fiction of Anthony Trollope* (Baltimore and London: Johns Hopkins University Press, 1980)

Kincaid, James R., *The Novels of Anthony Trollope* (Oxford: Clarendon Press, 1977)

Kucich, John, "Trollope and the Antibourgeois Elite," *The Power of Lies: Transgression in Victorian Fiction* (Ithaca: Cornell University Press, 1994), pp. 41–74

Lansbury, Coral, *The Reasonable Man: Trollope's Legal Fiction* (Princeton: Princeton University Press, 1981)

Lloyd, David, "Violence and the Constitution of the Novel," *Anomalous States: Irish Writing and the Post-Colonial Moment* (Durham, NC: Duke University Press, 1993), pp. 125–162

Markwick, Margaret, *New Men in Trollope's Novels: Rewriting the Victorian Male* (Aldershot: Ashgate, 2007)

Trollope and Women (London: the Trollope Society with Hambleton Press, 1997)

Markwick, Margaret, Deborah Denenholz Morse, and Regenia Gagnier (eds.), *The Politics of Gender in Anthony Trollope's Novels* (Aldershot: Ashgate, 2009)

McMaster, Juliet, *Trollope's Palliser Novels: Theme and Pattern* (Oxford: Oxford University Press, 1978)

McMaster, R. D., *Trollope and the Law* (London: Macmillan, 1986)

Michie, Elsie B., "Buying Brains: Trollope, Oliphant, and Vulgar Victorian Commerce," *Victorian Studies* 44 (2001), 77–97

Miller, D. A., "The Novel as Usual: *Barchester Towers*," *The Novel and the Police* (Berkeley: University of California Press, 1988)

Morash, Chris, *Writing the Irish Famine* (Oxford, Clarendon Press, 1995)

Morse, Deborah Denenholz, *Women in Trollope's Palliser Novels* (Ann Arbour: UMI Research, 1987)

Nardin, Jane, *He Knew She Was Right: The Independent Woman in the Novels of Anthony Trollope* (Carbondale: Southern Illinois University Press, 1989)

Trollope and Victorian Moral Philosophy (Athens: Ohio University Press, 1996)

Newlin, George, (ed.), *Everyone and Everything in Trollope* (Armonk, NY: M. E. Sharpe, 2005)

Psomiades, Kathy Alexis, "Heterosexual Exchange and Other Victorian Fictions: *The Eustace Diamonds* and Victorian Anthropology," *Novel* 33 (1999), 93–118

Schramm, Jan-Melissa, *Testimony and Advocacy in Victorian Law, Literature, and Theology* (Cambridge: Cambridge University Press, 2000)

Skilton, David, *Anthony Trollope and His Contemporaries: A Study in the Theory and Conventions of Mid-Victorian Fiction*, rev. edn (Basingstoke: Macmillan, 1996)

Snow, C. P., *Trollope: His Life and Art* (New York: Scribner, 1975)

Speare, Morris Edmund, *The Political Novel: Its Development in England and in America* (Oxford: Oxford University Press, 1924)

Super, R. H., *Trollope in the Post Office* (Ann Arbor: University of Michigan Press, 1981)

Terry R. C., (ed.), *Oxford Reader's Companion to Anthony Trollope* (Oxford: Oxford University Press, 1999)

Tracy, Robert, *Trollope's Later Novels* (Berkeley: University of California Press, 1978)

"'The Unnatural Ruin': Trollope and Nineteenth-Century Irish Fiction," *Nineteenth-Century Fiction* 37 (1982), 358–82

Tuathaigh, Gearóid Ó, *Ireland Before the Famine, 1798–1848* (Dublin: Gill and Macmillan, 1972)

Turner, Mark W., *Trollope and the Magazines: Gendered Issues in Mid-Victorian Britain* (Basingstoke: Macmillan, 2000)

Victorian Literature and Culture Vol. 32, no. 1 (2004). Special issue on Trollope and Ireland. Includes articles by Laura M. Berol, Jane Elizabeth Dougherty, Patrick Lonergan, and Bridget Matthews-Kane

INDEX

Note: Works by Trollope appear under title; works by others under author's name.

Cambridge Companions to . . .

AUTHORS

TOPICS

4733261R00142

Printed in Great Britain
by Amazon.co.uk, Ltd.,
Marston Gate.